Practical Rhythmic Chinese

实用节奏汉语

印京华（John Jing-hua Yin）
孙怡清（Diana Yiqing Sun）　　著

外语教学与研究出版社
FOREIGN LANGUAGE TEACHING AND RESEARCH PRESS
北京　BEIJING

图书在版编目(CIP)数据

实用节奏汉语=Practical Rhythmic Chinese / 印京华，孙怡清著． — 北京：外语
教学与研究出版社，2008.12
ISBN 978－7－5600－8022－2

I．实… II．①印…②孙… III.汉语—对外汉语教学—自学参考资料 IV. H195.4

中国版本图书馆CIP数据核字（2008）第196640号

出　版　人：于春迟
责任编辑：陈　轩
装帧设计：孙莉明
出版发行：外语教学与研究出版社
社　　　址：北京市西三环北路19号（100089）
网　　　址：http://www.fltrp.com
印　　　刷：北京华联印刷有限公司
开　　　本：787×1092　1/16
印　　　张：30
版　　　次：2008年12月第1版　2008年12月第1次印刷
书　　　号：ISBN 978－7－5600－8022－2
定　　　价：140.00元（含1张MP3光盘）
＊　　＊　　＊

目 录
Table of Contents

编写说明

对外汉语教学，只有按照汉语的规律和特点来实施，才能提高效率。初学汉语者，首先要学习汉语语音。汉语的语音系统，究竟有什么规律和特点呢？首先，每个音节都带有声调，声调具有区别不同意义的功能。其次，每个音节都以元音或鼻辅音结尾，因此十分响亮。另外，汉语中一个字一个音节。英语就不同了：句子有句调，但音节并不具有区别意义的声调；其次，音节常常以辅音结尾，音节的音量因此受到影响，使音节不可能都那么响亮。另外，英语只有语素的概念而没有字的概念，而语素常常又不是一个音节。不把握住汉语区别于英语的这些规律和特点，我们的教学就难以改变国外学生中流传的"汉语难学"的观念。

汉语就其语音系统的特点而言，是一种具有很强节奏性、音乐性的语言。汉语的这个特点，使汉语朗朗上口，易于诵读。这个特点造就了中国历代的文人骚客，使他们得以洋洋洒洒地吟诗作词，使中国成了世界上诗歌数量最多的国家。不少美仑美奂的诗篇，至今人们还在吟诵。汉语节奏性、音乐性强的特点也成全了中国历代的民间艺人，使他们得以绘声绘色地通过评书、词话、相声、快板、小品等艺术形式向人们讲述过去，正视现在，指点未来。不少脍炙人口的段子，至今人们还津津乐道。汉语节奏性、音乐性强的特点也激发了中国历代教育家的灵感，使他们得以淋漓尽致地撰文著书，编制出一部部启蒙育人的蒙学课本。《三字经》、《百家姓》、《千字文》、《弟子规》等至今仍是国学启蒙的经典。我们教外国人汉语为什么不能继承传统充分利用汉语本身节奏性、音乐性强的特点呢？

充分发挥汉语节奏性、音乐性强的特点，并不是说我们要让初学汉语的外国学生背唐诗、宋词、元曲，也不是让他们来学说评书、词话、相声、快板，更不是让他们去念《三字经》、《百家姓》、《千字文》或《弟子规》。因为那样，我们就违反了外语教学应该遵循的循序渐进原则和交际性原则。如果初学汉语的学生未学说话先背诗，不仅难以知其所云，而且也难以帮助他们用简单汉语进行日常交流。我们在过去多年的教学中，根据初学学生要学的汉语日常用语和基础汉语语法概念，编写出了《实用节奏汉语》，全书共有56课，涉及的汉字有400多个。它的特色在于用有节奏的段子帮助学生在学习、理解和掌握日常用语和基础语法概念的同时，练习并掌握汉语声调。

　　《实用节奏汉语》可以用于辅助使用任何汉语教材的初级汉语教学。教师和学生既可以从头至尾、按部就班地使用书中的内容，也可以根据需要，从书中提取适当的内容使用。每一个段子都有学生在日常用语中会用到的基本词汇和句式，这既是学生用汉语进行日常交际的素材，也是学生提高汉语语言能力的基础。如果没有其他汉语课本可以利用，那么本书也可以作为主要教材。

　　使用书中每个段子的基本步骤是：一、听；二、边听边说；三、边听边看；四、边听边看边说；五、边看边说；六、说；七、边说边写。先让学生听几遍，就是先"输入"，刺激他们模仿的欲望。我们在教学实践中发现，学生听着听着，就跟着说起来。往往听了几遍后，就能跟着说了。这时再让学生边听边看汉字文本，帮助学生建立字音和字形的联系。接下来可以让学生边听录音边说。最后在不听录音的情况下能够说出来。学生听得越多，就会说得越好。汉字文本往往只起一个提示作用。如果学生说得流利自如了，还可以要求学生边说边学习写下来。

　　此外，为每个节奏汉语的段子都配有节奏鲜明的背景音乐，可以让学生以"独唱"、"二重唱"、"小合唱"、"大合唱"、"二部轮唱"等方法练习，并在期末时表演和比赛，增加学生的学习热情，达到学好汉语的目的。

　　我们在教学的实践中发现，使用"节奏汉语"有如下优势与成效：

一、　易于加大汉语"输入"重复量，学生模仿及"输出"的欲望随之增强。

二、　汉语教学富有娱乐性，学生学习的兴趣和积极性随之高涨。

三、　富有节奏韵律的汉语易于模仿和记忆，声调掌握比较好的学生人数随之增加。

　　《实用节奏汉语》使用的方法是我们在美国大学长期的汉语教学实践中探索和总结出来的。在编辑出版此书的过程中，外语教学与研究出版社的编辑给予了多方面的协助和宝贵支持，在此向他们表示衷心的感谢。谨以此书献给在对外汉语教学第一线辛勤工作的老师们和不怕困难、热心学习汉语的同学们。愿《实用节奏汉语》能在对外汉语教学的过程中，让汉语显现其音乐性强的本色，并使汉语教与学的经历令人愉悦和欢畅。

印京华　孙怡清

Foreword

Teaching Chinese as a foreign language can be improved for its efficiency only when it is carried out in compliance with the regularity and peculiarity of the Chinese language. For Chinese language beginners, the first thing they will have to learn is the Chinese sound system. However, what regularity and peculiarity does the Chinese sound system has? First, every Chinese syllable has tones, and the different tones of the same syllable can represent different meanings. Second, every Chinese syllable is ended with a vowel sound or a combination of a vowel sound and a nasal sound; therefore, it sounds quite loud. Third, one Chinese written character is pronounced with only one syllable. In other words, one syllable, one Chinese character. English is quite different in that it has sentence tones but no syllable tones. Secondly, a lot of syllables in English are ended with consonant sounds. Thirdly, English has morphemes, which are the smallest units that represent meaning, but unlike Chinese characters, many English morphemes contain more than one syllable. Only if we are keenly aware of these differences and are able to handle them tactfully in teaching, will it be possible to improve our teaching effectiveness and efficiency, and also will the opinion that "Chinese is a difficult language to learn" be changed.

Judging from the characteristics of the Chinese sound system, Chinese is a very rhythmical and melodious language. The rhythmicity and melodiousness of Chinese has made the language orotund and easy to chant, thus nurturing and bringing up in the past several thousand years in China many prolific poets and literati, who virtually made China the country that possesses the largest number of poems in the world. Many beautifully composed poems are still recited and chanted by Chinese people nowadays. The rhythmicity and melodiousness of Chinese have also helped folk actors and actresses of the past dynasties and of the present times in China to fulfill their wishes, enabling them to narrate history, react to the present, and provide a prospect of the future insightfully and vividly through such artistic forms as storytelling, comic dialogues, clapper talks, and sketches. Many pieces have remained appealing and popular among Chinese people. The rhythmical and melodious Chinese language has also inspired educators in the past dynasties in China, who were enabled to write children's primers incisively and rhythmically, such as *Three-Character Classics*, *Thousand-Character Verse*, and *Children Regulations*, which are still the classics for the elementary education of Chinese ancient civilization. Why can we not take advantage of the rhythmicity and melodiousness of Chinese in teaching Chinese as a foreign language to our students?

To take advantage of the rhythmicity and melodiousness of Chinese in teaching does not mean that we need to ask our students to recite poems of the Tang Dynasty, lyrics of the Song Dynasty, and verses of the Yuan Dynasty. It does not mean that we will ask our students to learn to do storytelling, comic dialogues, or clapper talks either. Nor does it mean that we will request our students to recite *Three-Character Classics*, *The Hundred Family Surnames*, *Thousand-Character Verse*, or *Children Regulations*. Should we do that, we would violate the pedagogical principle of advancing gradually in due order and the communication principle that should be observed in foreign language teaching. If Chinese language beginners were asked to learn to recite poems before learning to speak, it would not only be very difficult for them to know what they are talking about, but it would also be hardly possible for them to learn to communicate for daily purposes. Based on our teaching experiences and our understanding of commonly used Chinese words and expressions as well as the basic Chinese grammatical concepts Chinese language beginners need to learn, we have written this book *Practical Rhythmic Chinese* with fifty-six lessons of rhythmic passages in a little over four hundred different Chinese characters. With the new approach, we hope that students will find it easy and fun to learn and practice Chinese tones while they learn, understand, and master Chinese daily expressions and the basic Chinese grammatical concepts.

Practical Rhythmic Chinese can be used as supplementary teaching materials for students at the elementary level, no matter what major Chinese language textbook has been adopted. One may use the book to learn Chinese lesson by lesson from the beginning to the end. Alternatively, one may also select suitable contents from the book according to his or her needs. Every passage in the book contains basic vocabulary and sentence patterns commonly used in daily life. They not only serve as source materials for daily communications, but they also form the foundation to improve Chinese language communicative competence. Under the circumstances that no other Chinese language textbooks are available, *Practical Rhythmic Chinese* can also be used as a major Chinese language textbook independently.

The basic procedure for using each rhythmic passage is as follows: 1) listen, 2) listen and repeat, 3) listen and read, 4) listen, read, and speak, 5) read and speak, 6) recite, 7) speak and write. Let students listen to the recording of a rhythmic passage several times as initial "input" to stimulate their desire to repeat after the recording. Students usually start to repeat after the recording while listening to it. After listening to it several times, students can usually speak along. The more students listen, the better and faster they will be able to speak. Now, let students to read the rhythmic passage in Chinese characters while listening to its recording so as to help to establish the link between the sounds and shapes of Chinese characters. After that, students are asked to read the passage in characters out loud while listening. Then, let them read it out loud without listening. Chinese characters in the passage serve as clues. Students should be able to recite the rhythmic passage. If students can recite the rhythmic passage fluently, they should be asked to learn to write down the passage while reciting it.

As each rhythmic Chinese passage is accompanied with percussion background music on a CD, students can practice chanting a passage in "solo", "duet", "chorus", "cantata", or "troll". Semester-end Chinese talent shows and recitation contests can be organized and held for students to chant and recite rhythmic passages as to motivate them to chant them well and eventually learn to speak Chinese with correct pronunciations and tones.

We have found that using rhythmic passages has the following merits:

1) It is easy to increase repeated Chinese "input" without much difficulty; consequently, the efforts students made to imitate and the desire students have for Chinese "output" have also been increased.

2) It is easy to make Chinese language teaching and learning more enjoyable; consequently, the interest and enthusiasm in learning Chinese have been increased.

3) It is easy for students to imitate and memorize rhythmic passages; consequently, the number of students who have learned to master Chinese tones has been increased.

The approach used in *Practical Rhythmic Chinese* was devised on the basis of many years of our research and experiences in teaching American college students. We would like to thank the editors at Foreign Language Teaching and Research Press for their valuable support during the process of publishing this book. We would like to dedicate *Practical Rhythmic Chinese* to those teachers who are working industriously on the front line of Chinese as a foreign language teaching and those students who are learning Chinese enthusiastically despite that Chinese is viewed as a difficult language. We hope that this book, when used in teaching and learning, will reveal the distinctive music features of the Chinese language and will help to make the experiences of teaching and learning Chinese pleasant and enjoyable.

John Yin & Diana Sun

使用建议

教学对象

　　《实用节奏汉语》以母语为英语并初学汉语的大学生和中学生以及成人学生为主要教学对象，小学生也可以使用。本书注重实用，突出汉语的节奏性、音乐性，易于诵读，便于记忆。全书用英语解说，适用于英语国家的大学、中学、周末中文学校和孔子学院。

教学目标

　　《实用节奏汉语》以零起点学生为主要对象，帮助学生通过听说读写了解和掌握汉语拼音、常用汉字、基础语法、日常用语等基础汉语语言知识和汉语交际技能。不仅为有志学好汉语的学生顺利进入中级和高级阶段的汉语学习打下坚实基础，也可以帮助学习时间较少又需要与中国人交往的人士，较快地获得一些汉语的基本知识和交际能力。

教学时段

　　《实用节奏汉语》全书共 56 课。按照学生的接受能力和可以实际安排的教学时间，每课的教学时间大约 1 至 2 小时。课后学生应安排至少一个小时的时间练习听和说，练习时间多多益善。如果每个学期可以安排 14 个星期的教学时间，每个星期上 1 至 2 小时的汉语课，《实用节奏汉语》的内容则可以在 2 至 4 个学期内学完，教学时段为 1 至 2 个学年。

教学安排

　　对于已有较为固定的汉语教材的学校或汉语班来说，《实用节奏汉语》可以作为辅助性教材，根据需要从书中提取适当的内容，配合已经在使用的汉语教材，对初级汉语的教学起丰富补充作用。如果教学时间较少，又没有固定的教材，《实用节奏汉语》也可以独立使用，从头至尾、按部就班地使用书中的内容帮助学生用较少的时间，学习和掌握汉语语言的基础知识和基本技能。

　　《实用节奏汉语》中的每一个段子都有学生在日常用语中会用到的基本词汇和句式，是学生用汉语作日常交际的素材，也是学生提高汉语语言能力的基础。书中每课分为四大部分：一、听与看；二、看与说；

三、理解；四、实践。

教学可以基本按照这四部分的顺序展开，用 1 至 2 课时完成。

第一部分为语言输入期。《实用节奏汉语》配有录音光盘，在课前或在课上要求学生先反复听节奏汉语段子的录音。然后，可以让他们看文字，把声音和文字联系起来。文字部分提供了汉语拼音、汉字、单字英语译文和整句英语译文，方便学生了解每个汉字的字音、字形、字义和在整句中的意义，但不要求全都理解。每课的生字词均用加粗的字体标出，因此省去了单列生字词表的需求。学生通过第一部分的听与看，应该达到耳熟能详，心领神会的境界。

第二部分为模仿输出期。让学生继续听录音，跟着录音边听边说，模仿跟读。同时看只有汉字而没有拼音和英语译文的第二部分。汉字作为一个提示，帮助学生巩固汉字字形与字音之间对应的联系。然后，让学生在没有录音只有汉字的提示下，根据汉字文本一字一板地诵读出来，以此训练学生识读汉字能力。最后，要求学生不用汉字的提示就能模仿说出整个段子。学生通过第二部分的看与说，应该在整体输入的基础上，达到整体输出的能力。也就是说，学生应该能背诵出本课的节奏汉语段子。

第三部分为加深理解期。学生在能机械地但又正确和流利地说出本课节奏汉语段子时，他们对自己所说的内容已经有所了解，但并不一定完全理解。为帮助学生理解段子中以前没有接触过的汉语语音、语法和文化知识，第三部分提供了相关的简明阐释，既可供学生课后阅读，也可以作为教师课上进行简要说明的参考。学生通过第三部分的阅读和教学，应该可以对本课节奏汉语段子的内容，有比较理性的认识，从而增强自己学习汉语的悟性，达到"知其然亦知其所以然"。

第四部分为操作实践期。主要分"对话"、"交际"和"书写"三小部分来帮助学生学以致用。"对话"部分，以本课节奏汉语段子为基础，为学生提供一个会话的实例，让学生能用学过的内容进行比较自然的交谈。学生可以先阅读会话，然后以 A 或 B 的角色完成对话。只要学生熟练掌握了本课节奏汉语的段子，完成对话就比较容易。"交际"部分是任务型的。学生根据具体情景和任务要求，用学过的语言知识和练习过的语言技能，去完成交际任务。完成交际任务的过程就是语言知识和技能运用的过程和语法规则内化的过程。如果时间允许，教师可以给学生安排类似交际任务,增加学生学以致用的机会。"书写"部分提供了"九宫格"让学生抄写本课中出现的生字，给他们一个加深记忆的机会。汉字只看只认而不写是难以记住的，动手动笔，一笔一画地写汉字不仅给学生一个习写汉字的机会，实际上也给了他们一个欣赏汉字艺术的机会。教师可以给学生布置抄写本课节奏汉语段子的课后作业，也可以要求学生在开始学习新课前，不仅能背诵而且还能默写出本课的段子。

　　上述教学安排仅供参考。教师不必拘泥于上述教学安排，可以根据自己学生的具体情况和授课时数灵活安排。在教学中，不要忘了《实用节奏汉语》的目的，就是要让汉语教与学的经历都更加愉悦和欢畅。

印京华　孙怡清

Suggestions for Use

INTENDED USERS

Practical Rhythmic Chinese has native English speaking students in college and high school and other adults who are Chinese language beginners as its intended users, although it may also be used for elementary school children. *Practical Rhythmic Chinese* pays great attention to the practical use of Chinese and takes advantage of the rhythmicity and melodiousness of the Chinese language to make Chinese easy to learn to read and speak. The whole book is written in English. It is, therefore, suitable for colleges, high schools, Chinese weekend schools, and Confucius institutes in English speaking countries.

OBJECTIVES

Practical Rhythmic Chinese strives to help Chinese language beginners to learn Chinese sound system, commonly used Chinese characters, basic Chinese grammar, and frequently used Chinese daily expressions through listening, speaking, reading, and writing. It is not only intended to help to lay a solid foundation for students who are determined to advance to a higher level of Chinese language learning, but it is also intended to help those who have very limited Chinese learning time but need to communicate with Chinese people to acquire some basic Chinese language knowledge and communication ability quickly.

TIME

Practical Rhythmic Chinese contains 56 lessons in all. The instruction of each lesson may need one to two classes, depending on the learning aptitude of students and the available class time. In addition, students need to spend at least one hour after class on listening and speaking, although the more time they spend after class, the better. If there are 14 weeks in one academic semester and students can meet one to two hours each week, then the contents in *Practical Rhythmic Chinese* can be covered and learned in two to four academic semesters. The period of time for learning Chinese by using *Practical Rhythmic Chinese* is one to two academic years.

ARRANGEMENT

For schools or classes that have already adopted a good Chinese language textbook, *Practical Rhythmic Chinese* can be used as supplementary teaching materials to enrich and supplement Chinese language classes accordingly. If the instruction time is limited and no particular Chinese language textbook has been adopted, then *Practical Rhythmic Chinese* can be used independently to help students to learn the Chinese language knowledge and skills one lesson after another from the beginning to the end without wasting time.

Every rhythmic passage in the book has the words and expressions that students will need in daily communications. These words and expressions are the basic source for their daily communications in Chinese, and they also serve as the foundation, on which students improve their communicative competence in Chinese. Each lesson in *Practical Rhythmic Chinese* has four major sections: 1) Listen and Read, 2) Read and Speak, 3) Understand, and 4) Practice.

Instructions can be carried out in accordance with the sequence of these four sections, using one to two classes.

The first section is the input phase. *Practical Rhythmic Chinese* has a CD that contains the rhythmic passages in each lesson. Students are required to listen to the recording of a rhythmic passage as many times as possible before and after class. Then, ask them to look at the passage in Chinese characters so as to establish the link between the shapes and the pronunciations of Chinese characters. The textbook has provided *pinyin*, which is the phonetic alphabet of Chinese, Chinese characters, literal English translation for each character, and English translation for each sentence in the hope that students can be assisted in getting to know the sound, shape, and meaning of each Chinese character by itself and its meaning in a sentence. All the new characters in each lesson are in the bold type, saving the trouble of having a vocabulary list for each lesson. After the first section, students should be very familiar with what they have heard and have grasped the meaning of the rhythmic passage through listening and reading.

The second section is the imitation phase. Let students continue to listen to the recording and imitate while listening. Students should now read the rhythmic passage provided in the second section, which has no English translation and Chinese phonetic transcription. Now Chinese characters serve as clues for students to help themselves to consolidate the connections between the shapes and meanings of the Chinese characters used in the passage. Ask students to read the passage out loud character by character to train their ability to say a Chinese character when seeing it. Finally, ask students to say the whole rhythmic passage without looking at it. After the second section, students should be able to reproduce the whole passage after taking it in as a whole. In other words, students should be able to recite the rhythmic passage by heart.

The third section is the better understanding phase. Very often, students can recite the rhythmic passage fluently and accurately, but they may not really comprehend it completely. To help students to understand the phonetic, syntactic, and cultural knowledge associated with the passage, the third section provides a simple explanation for students to read after class or for instructors to refer to when concise explanations are needed in class. After the third section, students should have a better understanding of the rhythmic passage, and their comprehension and sense of the Chinese language should be improved, as they not only know what something is but also why it is so.

The fourth section is the practice phase. It consists of three parts: Dialogue, Communication, and Writing, helping students to apply what they have learned into practice. The Dialogue Part provides students an example dialogue based on what is learned in the rhythmic passage. Students are expected to use what they have learned to converse naturally. Students can be asked to read the dialogue first and then play the role of A or B to perform the dialogue. As long as students know the rhythmic passage well, they will be able to do the dialogue with ease. The Communication Part is task-oriented. Students are expected to use what they have just learned or have learned in the past to accomplish the communicative tasks according to the given situation and the task requirements. The process of accomplishing the communicative tasks is the process of applying the Chinese language knowledge and skills students are learning, and it is also the process of internalizing the grammatical rules they have been taught. If permitted by time, instructors may assign additional similar communicative tasks to increase the language application opportunities for students. The Writing Part provides writing boxes with grid lines and models of the new characters of the lesson for students to practice writing the new Chinese characters. It is often difficult to memorize a character by looking at it without writing it. Taking a pen and writing it stroke by stroke will not only enhance students' recognition of the character, but will also help them to appreciate Chinese calligraphy as a form of art. Instructors may assign students to write the rhythmic passage out in Chinese characters as homework and may also ask students to be able to recite the passage and write it out by heart before learning the next lesson.

The arrangement and procedure discussed above are only suggestions for reference. Instructors should not rigidly adhere to them; instead, the learning aptitude of students and the available class hours should be taken into considerations, and the teaching arrangement and procedure should be handled with flexibility accordingly. Keep in mind the purpose of *Practical Rhythmic Chinese*: To make our Chinese language teaching and learning experiences ever more joyful and enjoyable.

John Yin & Diana Sun

入门一：现代汉语语音
Introduction One: Modern Chinese Phonetics

To learn to speak Chinese well, you need to know the Chinese sound system well. Once you know how each sound in Chinese is produced by using various parts of your mouth, it will be easier for you to try to produce each sound consciously.

Modern Chinese takes the Beijing pronunciation as its standard. According to the conventional method of analyzing Chinese phonetics, a syllable in Chinese usually consists of three components: an initial, a final, and a tone. For example, the syllable *tā* is formed with the initial *t*, the final *a*, and the tone 2 (the level tone). Now let us look at the initials, the finals, and the tones in the Chinese sound system respectively.

I. Initials

In modern Chinese, there are 21 initials. Initials are consonants at the beginning of syllables. The pronunciation of each of these 21 initials is as follows. Note that the notations of the International Phonetic Alphabet are provided in the square brackets. If you do not know how to read these IPA notations, ask your Chinese language instructor to help you.

Table of Initials

Method / Place	plosive		affricate		fricative		nasal	bilateral
	voiceless		voiceless		Voiceless	Voiced	voiced	voiced
	unaspirated	aspirated	unaspirated	aspirated				
bilabial	*b* [p]	*p* [pʰ]					*m* [m]	
dental-labial					*f* [f]			
blade-alveolar			*z* [ts]	*c* [tsʰ]	*s* [s]			
alveolar	*d* [t]	*t* [tʰ]					*n* [n]	*l* [l]
blade-palatal			*zh* [tʃ]	*ch* [tʃʰ]	*sh* [ʃ]	*r* [z]		
palatal			*j* [tɕ]	*q* [tɕʰ]	*x* [ɕ]			
velar	*g* [k]	*k* [kʰ]			*h* [x]			

Now, let's look at how each of the 21 initials is pronounced more closely. Listen to the recordings for each sound or ask your instructor to pronounce the sound several times for you to listen to and then imitate closely.

    b   Close both lips and hold the air in the mouth, and then open both lips suddenly to release the air. The vocal cords do not vibrate. This is an unaspirated voiceless bilabial plosive, which is pronounced as [p]. Note that it is a voiceless sound and should not be pronounced as "b" in the English word "**be**"; rather, it should be pronounced as "p" in the English word "**space**".

    p   The place of articulation is the same as that of *b*. However, when opening the lips, the air stream is burst out with force, which is usually referred to as "aspiration". The vocal cords do not vibrate. This is an aspirated voiceless bilabial plosive, which is pronounced as $[p^h]$. It is the same as "p" in the English word "**pay**".

    m   Close both lips. When it is pronounced, the soft palate goes down, the air stream goes out from the nasal cavity, and the vocal cords vibrate. This is a voiced bilabial nasal. It is pronounced as [m], which is the same as "m" in the English "**my**."

    f   The upper teeth touches the lower lip, and the air stream goes through the crevices between the teeth and the lip with friction. The vocal cords do not vibrate. This is a voiceless labio-dental fricative, which is pronounced as [f] and is the same as "f" in the English word "**for**."

    d   The tip of the tougue is against the upper alveolar ridge, the air stream is hold inside the mouth, and then move the tip of the tougue downwards suddenly to release the air. The vocal cords do not vibrate. This is an unaspirated voiceless alveolar plosive, which is pronounced as [t]. It is the same as "t" in the English word "**stand**", not the same as "d" in the English word "**do**".

    t   The place of articulation is the same as that of *d*. However, the air stream is burst out with aspiration. The vocal cords do not vibrate. This is an aspirated voiceless alveolar plosive, which is pronounced as $[t^h]$ and is the same as "t" in the English word "**to**".

n   The tip of the tougue is against the upper alveolar ridge. When the sound is pronounced, the soft palate goes down, and the air stream goes out from the nasal cavity. The vocal cords vibrate. This is a voiced alveolar nasal, which is pronounced as [n] and is the same as "n" in the English word "no". This sound may also be combined with a vowel sound to form a nasal final and is pronounced as "n" in the English word "pen".

l   The tip of the tougue is against the upper alveolar ridge, and the soft palate goes down. The air stream goes through the sides of the tougue, and the vocal cords vibrate. This is a voiced alveolar bilateral, which is pronounced as [l] and is the same as "l" in the English word "low".

g   The back of the tougue is against the soft palate, and then let the back of the tougue suddenly leave the soft palate to release the air. The vocal cords do not vibrate. This is an unaspirated voiceless velar plosive, which is pronounced as [k]. It is not pronounced in the same way as "g" in the English word "go"; rather, it is pronounced as "k" in the English word "sky".

k   The place of articulation is the same as that of *g*. However, when the back of the tougue leaves the soft palate suddenly, the air stream is burst out with aspiration. The vocal cords do not vibrate. This is an aspirated voiceless velar plosive, which is pronounced as [kʰ] and is the same as "k" in the English "key".

h   The back of the tougue is close to the soft palate, and the air stream goes out between the back of the tougue and the soft palate with friction. The vocal cords do not vibrate. This is a voiceless velar fricative, which is pronounced as [x] and is the same as "h" in the English word "hot".

z   The tip of the tougue is against the back of lower teeth, and the front part of the tougue touches the back of upper teeth. The air stream goes out from the crevices between the tip of the tougue and the back of teeth with friction. The vocal cords do not vibrate. This is an unaspirated voiceless blade-alveolar affricate, which is pronounced as [ts] and is similar to "ds" in the English word "beds".

c   The place of articulation is the same as that of *z*. However, the air stream is released between the tip of the tougue and the back of teeth with aspiration. The vocal cords do not vibrate. This is an aspirated voiceless blade-alveolar affricate, which is pronounced as [ts^h]. It is pronounced in the same way as "ts" in the English word "bets" except that this sound always occurs at the beginning of a syllable and never ends a syllable in Chinese.

s   The tip of the tougue is close to the back of lower teeth, and the air stream goes through the opening between the surface of the tougue and the back of the upper teeth with friction. The vocal cords do not vibrate. This is a voiceless blade-alveolar fricative, which is pronounced as [s] and is the same as "s" in the English word "so".

zh   The tip of the tougue is curled up to be against the hard palate and hold the air stream in the mouth. Then let it go through between the tip of the tougue and the hard palate with friction. The vocal cords do not vibrate. This is an unaspirated voiceless blade-palatal affricate, which is pronounced as [tʃ]. It is similar to "g" in the English word "germ".

ch   The place of articulation is the same as that of *zh*. However, release the air stream through the tip of the tougue and the hard palate with aspiration. The vocal cords do not vibrate. This is an aspirated voiceless blade-palatal affricate, which is pronounced as [tʃ^h] and is similar to "ch" in the English word "**chirp**".

sh   The tip of the tougue is curled up to be close to the hard palate, and the air stream goes through between the tip of the tougue and the hard palate with friction. The vocal cords do not vibrate. This is a voiceless blade-palatal fricative, which is pronounced as [ʃ] and is similar to "sh" in the English word "**shirt**".

r   The place of articulation is the same as that of *sh*. When the air stream goes through between the tip of the tougue and the hard palate, the vocal cords vibrate. This is a voiced blade-palatal fricative, which is pronounced as [ʐ]. It is not the same as "r" in the English word "**river**"; rather, it is similar to "s" in the English "vision" or "pleasure".

j   The front of the tougue is against the hard palate, and the tip of the tougue is against the back of the lower teeth. The air stream goes through between the front of the tougue and the hard palate with friction. The vocal cords do not vibrate. This is an unaspirated voiceless palatal affricate, which is pronounced as [tɕ]. English does not have this sound. It is close to "j" in the English word "jeep", but you need to say it without curling up the tougue.

    q   The place of articulation is the same as that of *j*. However, when the air stream goes through between the front of the tougue and the hard palate, there is aspiration. The vocal cords do not vibrate. This is an aspirated voiceless palatal affricate, which is pronounced as [tɕʰ]. It is close to "ch" in the English word "cheat", but it needs to be pronounced without curling up the tougue.

    x   The front of the tougue is close to the hard palate, and the air stream goes out between the front of the tougue and the hard palate. The vocal cords do not vibrate. This is a voiceless palatal fricative, which is pronounced as [ɕ]. It is close to "sh" in the English word "sheet"; however, the tougue must not be curled up.

II. Finals

Apart from an initial, there is always a final in a Chinese syllable. Without a final, a syllable cannot be formed. A final can be 1) a simple final with only one vowel sound as *a* in *ma*, 2) a compound final which consists of two or three vowels as *ao* in *mao* or *iao* in *miao*, or 3) one or two vowels with a nasal consonant at the end as *a* and *ng* together in *mang* and *ia* and *n* together in *mian*. In modern Chinese common speech, there are 39 finals.

Table of Finals:

		i [i]	*u* [u]	*ü* [y]
Simple finals	*a* [A]	*ia* [iA]	*ua* [uA]	
	o [o]		*uo* [uo]	
	e [ɤ]			
	ê [ɛ]	*ie* [iɛ]		*üe* [yɛ]
	-i [ɿ], *-i* [ʅ]			
	er [ɚ]			
Compound finals	*ai* [ai]		*uai* [uai]	
	ei [ei]		*uei* [uei]	
	ao [au]	*iao* [iau]		
	ou [əu]	*iou* [iəu]		

实用节奏汉语

(continual)

	an [an]	ian [iɛn]	uan [uan]	üan [yɛn]
Nasal finals	en [ən]	in [in]	uen [uən]	ün [yn]
	ang [ɑŋ]	iang [iɑŋ]	uang [uɑŋ]	
	eng [əŋ]	i(e)ng [iəŋ]	ueng [uəŋ]	
	ong [uŋ]	iong [iuŋ]		

There are five vowel letters in the Chinese phonetic alphabet, called *pinyin*: *a, e, i, o, u,* and *ü*. However, do not take it for granted that each vowel letter represents just one vowel sound. From the above Table of Finals, you can see that each of the six vowel letters can be used alone or in combination with other vowel letters and nasal consonant letters to represent more than one vowel sound in Chinese. For example, the vowel letter *i* represents the sound [i] after the letters *t, d, l,* and *n*, but it represents the sound [ɪ] after the letters *z, c,* and *s*, and the sound [ʅ] after the letters *zh, ch, shi,* and *r*. You need to understand the tougue positions and the mouth shapes and to develop the ability to tell the differences among the different sounds each vowel letter represents on its own or in combination with other letters. Again, you need to listen to the recordings or your instructor first carefully and then imitate closely.

a [A]   The central part of the tougue faces the central part of the hard palate, the mouth is wide open, and the lips are not rounded. This is a front low unrounded vowel. Its pronunciation is the same as "a" in the English "father".

o [o]   The back of the tougue goes up towards the soft palate, the mouth is quite open, and the lips are rounded. This is a back, mid-high, rounded vowel. There is no such a sound in English, but the tougue position for the pronunciation of this sound is between "o" in the English "out" and "o" in the English word "oat."

e [ɤ]   The position of the tougue is a bit high, the mouth is half open, and the lips are not rounded. This is a back, mid-high, unrounded vowel. Its pronunciation is close to "e" in the English word "term".

ê [ɛ]   The tougue goes towards the front, the mouth is half open, and the corners of the mouth are spread to the sides. This is a front, mid-low, unrounded vowel. It is pronounced as "e" in the English word "yes".

i [i]   The tip of the tougue touches the back of the lower teeth, the front of the tougue goes close to the hard palate, the opening of the mouth is narrow, and the lips are spread. This is a front, high, unrounded vowel. It is pronounced as "ee" in the Enlgish "see".

-i [ɿ]   This vowel is never pronounced alone. It appears only after the initials *z, c, s* and is pronounced as their continuation. This is a blade-alveolar high unrounded vowel. English does not have this sound. The tougue position for this sound is between "ee" in the English "seek" and "i" in the English word "sick".

-i [ʅ]   This vowel is never pronounced alone either. It appears only after the initials *zh, ch, shi, r* and is pronounced as their continuation. This is a blade-palatal high unrounded vowel. English does not have this sound. Its pronunciation is close to "ir" in the English word "chirp", but the tougue is a lot closer to the upper hard palate.

u [u]   The back of the tougue is close to the soft palate, the opening of the mouth is narrow, and the lips are rounded. This is a back high rounded vowel. It is similar to "oo" in the English word "zoo".

ü [y]   The position of the tougue is a bit lower than that of *i*, and the lips are stuck out and rounded. This is a front high rounded vowel. English does not have this sound, but to pronounce this sound, stick out the lips and keep them rounded while trying to say *i*.

er [ɚ]   While pronouncing [ə], curl up the tougue. This is a blade-palatal unrounded retroflex vowel. Sometimes, the [ə] sound may be replaced by [ɑ] for certain words in Chinese, such as 二 for "two".

ai   It is formed with [a] and [i]. The opening of the mouth is from wide to narrow. Its pronunciation is the same as that of the English letter "i".

ao   It is formed with [ɑ] and [u]. Its pronunciation is the same as "ou" in the English word "house."

ou   It is formed with mid-high rounded vowel [ə] and [u]. Its pronunciation is the same as that of the name for the English letter "o".

ei   It is formed with mid-high unrounded [e] and [i]. Its pronunciation is the same as that of the name for the English letter "a".

ia   It is formed with [i] and [A]. [i] is soft and short, and [A] is comparatively louder. Its pronunciation is the same as "ya" in the English word "**yard**".

ie   It is formed with [i] and front mid-high unrounded ê [ɛ]. It is pronounced in the same way as "ye" in the English word "**yes**".

ua   It is formed with [u] and [A].

uo   It is formed with [u] and [o].

üe   It is formed with [y] and front mid-high unrounded ê [ɛ].

iao   It is the combination of i [i] and ao [ɑu].

iou   It is the combination of i [i] and ou [əu]. After zero initial, it is written as you. After other initials, it is written as iu.

uai   It is the combination of u [u] and ai [ai].

uei   It is the combination of u [u] and ei [ei]. After zero initial, it is written as wei; and after other initials, it is written as ui.

an   It is formed with front, low, unrounded [a] and the nasal [n].

en   It is formed with middle vowel [ə] and the nasal [n].

in   It is formed with front, high, unrounded vowel [i] and the nasal [n].

ün   It is formed with front, high, rounded vowel [y] and the nasal [n].

ang   It is formed with back, low vowel [ɑ] and the velar nasal [ŋ].

ong   It is formed with back, high, rounded vowel [u] and the velar nasal [ŋ].

eng   It is formed with central vowel [ə] and the velar nasal [ŋ].

ing   It is formed with front, high, unrounded vowel [i] and the velar nasal [ŋ].

ian   It is formed with [i] and [ɛn].

uan   It is formed with [u] and [an].

uen   It is formed with [u] and [ən]. After zero initial, it is written as wen; and after other initials, it is written as un.

üan   It is formed with [y] and [ɛn].

iang   It is the combination of *i* [i] and *ang* [ɑŋ].

iong   It is the combination of *i* [i] and *ong* [uŋ].

uang   It is the combination of *u* [u] and *ang* [ɑŋ].

ueng   It is the combination of *u* [u] and *eng* [əŋ].

In modern Chinese, most of the syllables have initials and finals; however, some syllables have finals only and no initials. Syllables of this kind are called zero initial syllables. For example:

a   e   ao   ou   en   an   ang

However, zero initial syllables with *i* or *u* and no other vowel letters to follow, then add *y* before *i* and add *w* before *u*. For example:

i > yi   in > yin   ing > ying   u > wu

When *ü* is preceded by a zero initial, just change *ü* to *yu*. For example:

ü > yu   üe > yue   üan > yuan   ün > yun

If zero initial syllables with *i* or *u* with other vowel letters to follow, then change *i* to *y* or change *u* to *w*. For example:

ia > ya	*iao > yao*	*ie > ye*	*iou > you*
ian > yan	*iang > yang*	*iong > yong*	
ua > wa	*uo > wo*	*uai > wai*	*uei > wei*
uan > wan	*uen > wen*	*uang > wang*	*ueng > weng*

ü and the finals that begin with *ü* will omit the two dots on top when preceded by *j*, *q*, and *x* and are written as *ju*, *qu*, and *xu*. However, when *ü* is put after *n* and *l*, the two dots on top are kept, and they are written as *nü* and *lü*.

When *iou*, *uei*, and *uen* are preceded with an initial, they are written as -*iu*, -*ui*, and -*un* with the vowel in the middle omitted. For example, *diu*, *dui*, and *dun*.

When the syllables that begin with *a*, *o*, or *e* are placed after another syllable and the distinction of syllables may be confused, the apostrophe is then used to separate the two syllables. For example: *píng'ān* (peaceful) and *xǐ'ài* (be fond of).

III. Tones

Chinese is a tonal language. Tones are the changes in pitch when syllables are pronounced. Like initials and finals, tones have the function of differentiating meanings. When the tone of a syllable is changed, the meaning of the syllable is also changed. For example,

mā (妈 mother)

má (麻 hemp)

mǎ (马 horse)

mà (骂 scold)

The standard Chinese pronunciation has four basic tones:

The 1st tone:　　a high level tone, using – as its tone mark.

The 2nd tone:　　a rising tone, using ´ as its tone mark.

The 3rd tone:　　a low dipping tone, using ˇ as its tone mark.

The 4th tone:　　a falling tone, using ˋ as its tone mark.

The four basic tones in the standard Chinese pronunciation can be graphically displayed in the following diagram with 5 as the highest pitch and 1 as the lowest pitch:

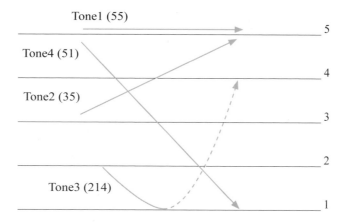

The tone mark is placed over the main vowel in a syllable. For example,

ā   cāo   fēi   jué   kuāi   xiōng

When preceded by initials, the finals *iou*, *uei*, and *uen* omit the vowel in the middle, and the tone mark is place as follows: *liù, tuǐ, sūn*.

The dot over the vowel *i* is omitted when it has a tone mark over it. For example: *tuī, pīng*.

Apart from the afore-mentioned four basic tones, there is a short and soft tone. It is called the neutral tone. For the neutral tone, there is no tone mark. For example:

bàba 爸爸
xièxie 谢谢

Appendix: The Table of the Standard Chinese Pronunciation (1-4)

1

Initials \ Finals	a	o	e	ê	-i	-i	er	ai	ei	ao	ou	an	en	ang	eng	ong
b	ba	bo						bai	bei	bao		ban	ben	bang	beng	
p	pa	po						pai	pei	pao	pou	pan	pen	pang	peng	
m	ma	mo						mai	mei	mao	mou	man	men	mang	meng	
f	fa	fo							fei		fou	fan	fen	fang	feng	
d	da		de					dai	dei	dao	dou	dan		dang	deng	dong
t	ta		te					tai		tao	tou	tan		tang	teng	tong
n	na		ne					nai	nei	nao	nou	nan	nen	nang	neng	nong
l	la		le					lai	lei	lao	lou	lan		lang	leng	long
z	za		ze		zi			zai	zei	zao	zou	zan	zen	zang	zeng	zong
c	ca		ce		ci			cai	cei	cao	cou	can	cen	cang	ceng	cong
s	sa		se		si			sai	sei	sao	sou	san	sen	sang	seng	song
zh	zha		zhe			zhi		zhai	zhei	zhao	zhou	zhan	zhen	zhang	zheng	zhong
ch	cha		che			chi		chai		chao	chou	chan	chen	chang	cheng	chong
sh	sha		she			shi		shai	shei	shao	shou	shan	shen	shang	sheng	
r										rao	rou	ran	ren	rang	reng	rong
j																
q																
x																
g	ga		ge					gai	gei	gao	gou	gan	gen	gang	geng	gong
k	ka		ke					kai	kei	kao	kou	kan	ken	kang	keng	kong
h	ha		he					hai	hei	hao	hou	han	hen	hang	heng	hong
zero	a		e	ê			er	ai	ei	ao	ou	an	en	ang		

Finals / Initials	2									
	i	*ia*	*iao*	*ie*	*iou*	*ian*	*in*	*iang*	*ing*	*iong*
b	bi		biao	bie		bian	bin		bing	
p	pi		piao	pie		pian	pin		ping	
m	mi		miao	mie	miu	mian	min		ming	
f										
d	di		diao	die	diu	dian			ding	
t	ti		tiao	tie		tian			ting	
n	ni		niao	nie	niu	nian	nin	niang	ning	
l	li		liao	lie	liu	lian	lin	liang	ling	
z										
c										
s										
zh										
ch										
sh										
r										
j	ji	jia	jiao	jie	jiu	jian	jin	jiang	jing	jiong
q	qi	qia	qiao	qie	qiu	qian	qin	qiang	qing	qiong
x	xi	xia	xiao	xie	xiu	xian	xin	xiang	xing	xiong
g										
k										
h										
zero	yi	ya	yao	ye	you	yan	yin	yang	ying	yong

Finals / Initials	3									4			
	u	*ua*	*uo*	*uai*	*ue*	*uan*	*un*	*uang*	*ueng*	*ü*	*üe*	*üan*	*ün*
b	bu												
p	pu												
m	mu												
f	fu												
d	du		duo		dui	duan	dun						
t	tu		tuo		tui	tuan	tun						
n	nu		nuo			nuan				nü	nüe		
l	lu		luo			luan	lun			lü	lüe		
z	zu		zuo		zui	zuan	zun						
c	cu		cuo		cui	cuan	cun						
s	su		suo		sui	suan	sun						
zh	zhu	zhua	zhuo	zhuai	zhui	zhuan	zhun	zhuang					
ch	chu		chuo	chuai	chui	chuan	chun	chuang					
sh	shu	shua	shuo	shuai	shui	shuan	shun	shuang					
r	ru		ruo		rui	ruan	run						
j										ju	jue	juan	jun
q										qu	que	quan	qun
x										xu	xue	xuan	xun
g	gu	gua	guo	guai	gui	guan	gun	guang					
k	ku	kua	kuo	kuai	kui	kuan	kun	kuang					
h	hu	hua	huo	huai	hui	huan	hun	huang					
zero	wu	wa	wo	wai	wei	wan	wen	wang	weng	yu	yue	yuan	yun

入门二：现代汉字
Introduction Two: Modern Chinese Characters

Chinese characters are a system of symbols for recording the Chinese language. Chinese characters already have a history of at least more than three thousand years and are one of the oldest written languages in the world. In the Chinese history, Chinese characters made great contributions to the development of politics, economics, and culture as well as the preservation of historical documents and materials. They will continue to play a very important role in all walks of life in China.

If you want to learn Chinese language well, you cannot avoid learning Chinese characters. Mastering Chinese characters is mastering the important tool of the Chinese written language.

The commonly used written languages in the world are of two categories: alphabetic languages and non-alphabetic languages. Chinese belongs to the latter. There is no direct connection between Chinese characters and Chinese pronunciation; in other words, Chinese characters themselves cannot explicitly represent how they are pronounced. For alphabetic languages, as long as you master the alphabet, spelling rules, generally speaking, you can write out a word when you hear it, and by looking at a word, you can pronounce it. However, with Chinese characters, you can do neither.

Chinese characters represent syllables; one character is one syllable. However, some of the words in Chinese contain one syllable; that is, one character. Some other words contain two or more syllables. They must be represented by two or more characters. In the Chinese language, characters are not all equivalent to words.

The Chinese language recorded in characters does not use the system of leaving space between words. Between words, there is no explicit distinction. This is one big difference between the Chinese language and alphabetic languages.

Chinese characters first developed on the basis of pictographic characters; therefore, they have the nature of representing meanings. This nature has determined that the shape and structure of Chinese characters are inevitably more complex than those of alphabetic languages. In order for you to master Chinese character well, the following is a brief introduction to the Chinese characters' strokes, stroke order, radicals, structural forms, and number of Chinese characters.

I. Strokes

The dots and lines that form the shapes and structures of Chinese characters are called strokes. In writing a character, what is written on the paper from the time the pen touches the paper to the time the pen is lifted from the paper is referred to as "one stroke." There are eight basic strokes in Chinese:

Stroke	Name	Example
一	*héng* (horizontal stroke)	十
丨	*shù* (vertical stroke)	王
丿	*piě* (left-falling stroke)	人
乀	*nà* (right-falling stroke)	八
丶	*diǎn* (dot)	文
丿	*tí* (rising stroke)	河
乛乚	*zhé* (turn)	马, 医, ...
乛亅乚...	*gōu* (hook)	写, 小, 儿, ...

Most of the characters are formed with two or more strokes. Because of using several strokes in a connected manner, some more complex strokes have come into use. They are:

Stroke	Name	Example
乛	*héngzhé* (horizontal turn)	口
乛	*héngpiě* (horizontal and left-falling)	又

⌐	*hénggōu* (horizontal hook)	买
コ	*héngzhégōu* (horizontal turn with a hook)	月
㇇	*héngzhétí* (horizontal turn with a rising stroke)	说
㇆	*héngzhéwāngōu* (horizontal turn with a curve and a hook)	九
㇉	*héngzhézhépiě* (horizontal turn with another turn and a left-falling stroke)	建
㇌	*héngzhézhézhégōu* (horizontal turn, turn, turn and a hook)	奶
㇀	*shùtí* (horizontal and rising)	衣
ㄴ	*shùzhé* (vertical turn)	山
㇚	*shùgōu* (vertical hook)	小
㇖	*shùwāngōu* (vertical stroke with a curve and a hook)	儿
㇅	*shùzhézhégōu* (vertical turn with another turn and a hook)	马
㇜	*piědiǎn* (left-falling and a dot)	女
㇛	*piězhé* (left-falling with a turn)	么
)	*wāngōu* (curving hook)	手
㇏	*xiégōu* (slanting hook)	我
㇃	*wògōu* (lying hook)	心

II. Stroke order

For a character that has more than one stroke, the stroke order is about which stroke goes first and which one goes next. The major rules of stroke order are as follows:

Stroke Order Rules	Example	
1. From top to bottom	三 一 二 三	多 ノクタ多多多
2. From left to right	你 ノイイ伊伊佟佟你	明 丨冂冂冃日旧明明明
3. Horizontal first, vertical second	十 一 十	下 一丁下
4. Left-falling first, right-falling second	人 ノ 人	八 ノ 八
5. Horizontal first, left-falling second	厂 一 厂	大 一ナ大
6. From outside to inside	月 ノ 冂月月	凤 ノ 几凡凤
7. Center first, sides second	小 丨 小 小	水 丨 丬水水
8. Outside first, inside next, closure last	日 丨冂円日	四 丨 冂匹四四

III. Radicals

In the shapes and structures of Chinese characters, there are some common components. These common components are referred to as radicals. For example, in 你, 他, and 们, 亻 is a radical. Some of the radicals are characters by themselves, such as 日, 口, and 木; other radicals are not characters by themselves but can be used to form characters. For example, 氵 is not a character, but it can be used to form 汉, 江, 河 and so on. Knowing Chinese character radicals can deepen the understanding of the shapes of Chinese characters, have a better grasp of the Chinese characters, and help look up characters in the dictionaries that are compiled in the order of radicals. Some commonly used radicals are as follows:

Radicals	Name and Meaning	Example
(The following radicals are also characters by themselves.)		
日	*rì zì páng* ("sun" side)	明
月	*yuè zì páng* ("moon" side)	期
木	*mù zì páng* ("wood" side)	树
土	*tǔ zì páng* ("soil" side)	地
禾	*hé mù páng* ("grain" side)	种
女	*nǚ zì páng* ("female" side)	好
心	*xīn zì dǐ* ("heart" bottom)	想
口	*kǒu zì páng* ("mouth" side)	叫
目	*mù zì páng* ("eye" side)	眼
门	*mén zì kuàng* ("door" frame)	问
广	*guǎng zì tóu* ("vast" top)	店
厂	*chǎng zì tóu* ("factory" top)	厅
王	*xié yù páng* ("jade" side)	现

(The following radicals are derived from characters and are not characters by themselves.)

亻 < 人	*dān rén páng* ("person" side)	他

忄 < 心	*shù xīn páng* ("vertical heart" side)	忙
讠 < 言	*yán zì páng* ("speech" side)	说
扌 < 手	*tí shǒu páng* ("hand" side)	打
𧾷 < 足	*zú zì páng* ("foot" side)	路
辶 < 走	*zǒu zhī páng* ("walking" side)	进
氵 < 水	*sān diǎn shuǐ* ("water" side)	汉
灬 < 火	*sì diǎn dǐ* ("fire" bottom)	热
钅 < 金	*jīn zì páng* ("metal" side)	银
刂 < 刀	*lì dāo páng* ("vertical knife" side)	利
竹 < 竹	*zhú zì tóu* ("bamboo" top)	篮
艹 < 艸	*cǎo zì tóu* ("grass" top)	花
纟 < 丝	*jiǎo sī páng* ("silk" side)	红
礻 < 示	*shì zì páng* ("reveal" side)	祝
饣 < 食	*shí zì páng* ("meal" side)	饭
疒 < 病	*bìng zì páng* ("sickness" side)	疼
阝 left < 阜	*zuǒ ěr páng* ("mound" side)	院
阝 right < 邑	*yòu ěr páng* ("settlement" side)	那
犭 < 犬	*fǎn quǎn páng* ("mammal" side)	狗
衤 < 衣	*yī zì páng* ("garment" side)	裤
罒 < 四	*sì zì tóu* ("net" top)	罪
宀	*bǎo gài tóu* ("roof" top)	家
囗	*guó zì kuàng* ("enclosure" frame)	国
彳	*shuāng rén páng* ("intersection" side)	行
攵	*fǎn wén páng* ("hand-with-a-stick" side)	教

IV. Structural Forms

There are eight major structural forms for Chinese characters:

1) Single Structure: A character of this kind cannot be dissected into radicals and is taken as a whole unit. It is referred to as a single-element character. For example: 我，水，山，电.

2) Upper-Lower Structure: A character of this kind can be divided into two parts: upper and lower. For example: 是，爸，花.

3) Upper-Middle-Lower Structure: A character of this kind can be divided into three parts: upper, middle, and lower. For example: 意，草，菜.

4) Left-Right Structure: A character of this kind can be divided into two parts: left and right. For example: 你，好，忙.

5) Left-Middle-Right Structure: A character of this kind can be divided into three parts: left, middle, and right. For example: 谢，哪，树.

6) Half-Enclosing Structure: A character of this kind can be divided into two parts. The outer frame part may be two-sided or three-sided. For example: 问，医，这.

7) Enclosing Structure: A character of this kind can be divided into two parts: outside and inside. The outside part is a enclosing frame. For example: 国，回，团.

8) Triangle-shaped Structure: A character of this kind is formed with three identical parts with one at the top and two side by side at the bottom. For example: 品，众，森.

No matter how many stokes there are, how many radicals there are, and how radicals are placed; every Chinese character is a square, and Chinese characters are, therefore, referred to as block styled characters. To keep the uniformity of these blocks and the proportional balance between radicals in a block, the same radical in different characters may occupy different proportions. For example, the radical 女 is in 好, 要, and 努, and its proportion in the three characters are different.

V. Number of Chinese Characters

There are several dozens of thousand Chinese characters in existence. *The Great Chinese Character Dictionary*, the most inclusive dictionary compiled so far, contains about 60,000 characters. However, only 2,500 of them are commonly used in modern Chinese. Anyone who masters 1,000 to 1,500 commonly used characters will experience no major difficulties in dealing with their work and social life in China or in furthering their study of Chinese language at the advanced level.

Dì–yī   kè   Nǐ   hǎo!

第一课   你好!
Lesson 1   Hello!

一 听与看 Listen and Read

Listen to the recording of the following sentences as many times as possible until you can say it along with the recording. You should also look at the following transcription while listening and try to imitate.

Nǐ hǎo!   Nǐ hǎo!

你 好! 你 好!

you | good | you | good

Hello! Hello!

Nǐ hǎo!   Nǐ hǎo!   Nǐ hǎo!

你 好! 你 好! 你 好!

you | good | you | good | you | good

Hello! Hello! Hello!

二 看与说 Read and Speak

Now, listen to the recording while looking at the following sentences. Then read it out aloud. Finally, recite it by heart to yourself and then to your classmates or instructor.

你好! 你好!

你好! 你好! 你好!

三 理解 Understand

More and more young people in China use the expression 你好 *nǐ hǎo* to greet each other, although the more traditional way of greeting each other often involves asking where the greeted party is heading for or making an assumption about what the greeted party is doing or is going to do to get confirmation. You will learn more expressions to greet other people in the lessons to follow.

Both the word 你 *nǐ* and the word 好 *hǎo* have the 3rd tone (the dipping tone) marked as ˇ. However, no two 3rd tone syllables can be pronounced as the 3rd tone syllable in a row. If a 3rd tone syllable is followed by another 3rd tone syllable, then the tone of the first syllable is pronounced in the 2nd tone (the rising tone).

（四）实践 Practice

1. 对话 Conversation

> A: 你好!
> B: 你好!

2. 交际 Communication

Task 1 Like in most places of the world, in China smiling is a good way to indicate you are approachable and are ready to make friends. Smile to a classmate next to you and say 你好 *nǐ hǎo* to him/her in correct tones.

Task 2 Shaking hands is a common practice on formal occasions and in business contacts. Stand up and shake hands with a classmate and say 你好 *nǐ hǎo* to him/her.

Task 3 Bowing has been a traditional Chinese way to show courtesy. Bow to your instructor and say 你好 *nǐ hǎo* to him/her.

Task 4 Saying 你好 *nǐ hǎo* twice in fast progression shows enthusiasm and friendliness. Wave to a classmate and say 你好 *nǐ hǎo* twice in fast speed.

3. 书写 Writing

yī   one   *Héng.*

一

dì   [prefix for ordinals]   *Piě, héng, diǎn, piě, héng, diǎn; héngzhé, héng, shùzhézhégōu, shù, piě.*

第

kè   lesson   *Diǎn, héngzhétí; shù, héngzhé, héng, héng, héng, shù, piě, nà.*

课

nǐ   you   *Piě, shù; piě, hénggōu, shùgōu, diǎn, diǎn.*

你

hǎo   good   *Piědiǎn, piě, héng; héngpiě, shùgōu, héng.*

好

Dì–èr   kè   Zhèige   hǎo   ma?

第二课   这个 好 吗？

Lesson 2   Is this one good?

一）听与看   Listen and Read

Listen to the recording of the following sentences as many times as possible until you can say it along with the recording. You should also look at the following transcription while listening and try to imitate.

Hǎo ma?   Hǎo ma?

好 吗？ 好 吗？

good | [ques.] | good | [ques.]

Good? Good?

Zhèige   hǎo ma?

这个   好 吗？

this | [meas.] | good | [ques.]

Is this one good?

Hěn hǎo,   hěn hǎo,

很 好， 很 好，

very | good | very | good

Very good, very good,

zhèige   hěn hǎo.

这个   很 好。

this | [meas.] | very | good

this one is very good.

Nèige   ne?   Nèige   ne?

那个 呢？   那个 呢？

that | [meas.] | [elliptical ques.] | that | [meas.] | [elliptical ques.]

How about that one? How about that one?

Nèige   hǎo ma?

那个 好 吗？

that | [meas.] | good | [ques.]

Is that one good?

Yě hěn hǎo,   yě hěn hǎo,
也 很 好，也 很 好，
also | very | good | also | very | good
Also very good, also very good,

liǎng ge dōu hěn hǎo.
两　个 都 很 好。
two | [meas.] | all | very | good
both are very good.

二　看与说　Read and Speak

Now, listen to the recording and look at the following sentences. Then read it out aloud. Finally, recite it by heart to yourself and then to your classmates or instructor.

好吗？好吗？

这个好吗？

很好，很好，

这个很好。

那个呢？那个呢？

那个好吗？

也很好，也很好，

两个都很好。

三 理解 Understand

吗 *ma* is a question word in Chinese. It can be placed at the end of any statement and turn the statement into a yes/no question. For example, you can turn "你好 *nǐ hǎo*！" into "你好吗 *nǐ hǎo ma*？".

呢 *ne* is also a question word in Chinese, but it is an elliptical question word. It is used in an elliptical question. That is, when the same question is asked about somebody else or something else and there is no need to repeat the question, 呢 *ne* is used. The elliptical question "……呢 *ne*?" in Chinese is like the question "How about …?" in English. If someone asks you: 你好吗 *nǐ hǎo ma*? You can answer the question by saying: 很好 *hěn hǎo*, and then ask the same question in turn by saying: 你呢 *nǐ ne*?

In English, we can use "this" to refer to something close to us and "that" for something relatively farther away from us. In Chinese, 这 *zhèi* means "this" and 那 *nèi* means "that". The standard pronunciation for 这 is *zhè*, but its colloquial pronunciation is *zhèi*; the standard pronunciation for 那 is *nà*, and its colloquial pronunciation is *nèi*. We have used their colloquial pronunciations in this lesson, but do not be surprised when you hear some native Chinese speakers say these two words in their standard pronunciations.

个 *ge* is a measure word in Chinese. In English, we also use measure words, such as "piece" and "loaf" for bread, "bottle" and "glass" for water and wine. But in Chinese, everything has a corresponding measure word to be used with 这 *zhèi* "this" and 那 *nèi* "that" as well as with numerals. 个 *ge* is a quite versatile measure word that can be used for many things in Chinese. When a Chinese language learner has not learned enough measure words for various kinds of objects in Chinese, 个 *ge* can be used handily. When you go shopping with a Chinese friend to choose something to buy, you can use 这个 *zhèige* and 那个 *nèige* to mean "this one" and "that one" regardless of what measure word would be appropriate for a certain merchandize.

也 *yě* means "also", and 都 *dōu* means "all". In Chinese, when you want to express the concept of "both are good", you say 两个都很好 *liǎng ge dōu hěn hǎo* "the two are both good".

四 实践 Practice

1. 对话 Conversation

> A: 这个好吗?
> B: 很好。
> A: 那个呢? 那个好吗?
> B: 也很好。两个都很好。

2. 交际 Communication

Task 1 Pretend you are a tourist in China and find something you would like to buy. Use one hand to point at the item you intend to buy by saying 这个 *zhèige* while using your other hand to give your cash to the salesperson.

Task 2 You have just found something that interests you at a street stand. Since the item is a bit far from you, point at it by saying 那个 *nèige* and give your money to the salesperson.

Task 3 Point at two items you intend to buy by saying 两个 *liǎng ge* and pay for them following the price tag amount.

Task 4 Pretend you are shopping with your travel companion in China. Ask your friend for opinion by saying "这个好吗 *zhèige hǎo ma?*". Since your friend loves your taste, the answer you get is always 很好 *hěn hǎo*.

Task 5 You are trying to make decisions about which item to buy. You are trying to ask your travel companion's opinion, but he/she is not much a help since the answer you get is "这个很好 *zhèige hěn hǎo*, 那个也很好 *nèige yě hěn hǎo*, 两个都很好 *liǎng ge dōu hěn hǎo*." You end up paying for both.

3. 书写 Writing

èr   two   *Héng, héng.*

二

ma   [question word]   *Shù, héngzhé, héng; héngzhé, shùzhézhégōu, héng.*

吗

ne   [elliptical question word]   *Shù, héngzhé, héng; héngzhé, héng, piě, piě, shùwāngōu.*

呢

zhè; zhèi   this   *Diǎn, héng, piě, diǎn; diǎn, héngzhézhépiě, píngnà.*

这

nà; nèi   that   *Héngzhégōu, héng, héng, piě; héngpiěwāngōu, shù.*

那

ge   [measure word]   *Piě, nà, shù.*

个

hěn   very   *Piě, piě, shù; hénzhé, héng, héng, shútí, piě, nà.*

很

yě   also   *Héngzhégōu, shù, shùwāngōu.*

也

dōu   all   *Héng, shù, héng, piě, shù, héngzhé, héng, héng; héngpiěwāngōu, shù.*

都								

liǎng   two   *Héng, shù, héngzhégōu, piě, diǎn, piě, diǎn.*

两								

Dì–sān kè　　*Nǐ máng ma?*
第三课　　你 忙 吗?
Lesson 3　　Are you busy?

一) 听与看　Listen and Read

Listen to the recording of the following sentences as many times as possible until you can say it along with the recording. You should also look at the following transcription while listening and try to imitate.

Nǐ máng ma?　　Nǐ máng ma?
你 忙 吗? 你 忙 吗?
you | busy | [ques.] | you | busy | [ques.]
Are you busy? Are you busy?

Hěn máng, hěn máng, hěn máng.
很 忙, 很 忙, 很 忙。
very | busy | very | busy | very | busy
Very busy, very busy, very busy.

Xiànzài wǒ hěn máng.
现在 我 很 忙。
present | at | I | very | busy
Now I am very busy.

Nǐ gē ne?　　Nǐ gē ne?
你 哥 呢? 你 哥 呢?
you | elder brother | [ques.] | you | elder brother | [ques.]
How about your elder brother? How about your elder brother?

Nǐ gē tā máng ma?
你 哥 他 忙 吗?
you | elder brother | he | busy | [ques.]
Is your elder brother (he) busy?

Bù máng, bù máng, bù máng.
不 忙, 不 忙, 不 忙。
not | busy | not | busy | not | busy
Not busy, not busy, not busy.

Wǒ gē tā bù máng.

我 哥 他 不 忙。

I | elder brother | he | not | busy

My elder brother (he) is not busy.

二 看与说 Read and Speak

Now, listen to the recording and look at the following sentences. Then read it out aloud. Finally, recite it by heart to yourself and then to your classmates or instructor.

你忙吗？你忙吗？

很忙，很忙，很忙。

现在我很忙。

你哥呢？你哥呢？

你哥他忙吗？

不忙，不忙，不忙。

我哥他不忙。

三 理解 Understand

In Lesson One, we discussed that the 3rd tone changes to the 2nd tone when a syllable bearing the 3rd tone is followed by another 3rd tone syllable. However, when followed by a non-3rd tone syllable, the 3rd tone syllable will reduce its 3rd tone to an incomplete 3rd tone, which is the first half of the complete 3rd tone. The incomplete 3rd tone is a very low tone. How low can you go without causing any discomfort? That will be the tone you should pronounce when you have a 3rd tone syllable that is followed by a non-3rd tone syllable as in 你忙 *nǐ máng*, 很忙 *hěn máng*, 你哥 *nǐ gē*, and 我哥 *wǒ gē*.

现在 *xiànzài* is a two syllable word, meaning "now". It is an expression indicating a point of time in Chinese. An expression of time is almost always placed at the beginning of a sentence or right after the subject (the doer of an action or the topic) of a sentence. For example, "现在你忙吗 *xiànzài nǐ máng ma*? 你现在忙吗 *nǐ xiànzài máng ma*?". If you put a time expression at the end of a sentence, it then sounds like that you have forgotten to mention the time expression and try to add it later to make yourself clear.

"你哥他忙吗 *nǐ gē tā máng ma*?" is the same as "你哥忙吗 *nǐ gē máng ma*?". In Chinese, when somebody is mentioned as the subject of a sentence, a personal pronoun may be added as an appositive to refer to the same person. For example, "你哥他好吗 *nǐ gē tā hǎo ma*? 我哥他很好 *wǒ gē tā hěn hǎo*".

四 实践 Practice

1. 对话 *Conversation*

> A: 你忙吗?
> B: 很忙。现在我很忙。
> A: 你哥呢? 他忙吗?
> B: 他不忙。

2. 交际 *Communication*

Task 1 You haven't seen your friend for a while. Greet your friend by saying 你好 *nǐ hǎo* and then chat with him/her, asking whether he/she has been busy or not. Since you also know his/her brother, ask about him/her too.

Task 2 You need to get some help from your friend. Find out whether your friend is available at the moment by saying "你现在忙吗 *nǐ xiànzài máng ma*?". Since your friend is very busy at the moment, ask about the availability of his/her brother.

3. 书写 Writing

sān   three   *Héng, héng, héng.*

三

wǒ   I   *Piě, héng, shùgōu, tí, xiégōu, piě, diǎn.*

我

tā   he   *Piě, shù; héngzhégōu, shù, shùwāngōu*

他

gē   elder brother   *Héng, shù, héngzhé, héng, shù, héng, shù, héngzhé, héng, shùgōu.*

哥

bù   not   *Héng, piě, shù, diǎn.*

不

máng   busy   *Diǎn, diǎn, shù; diǎn, héng, shùzhé.*

忙

xiàn   present   *Héng, héng, shù, tí; shù, héngzhé, piě, shùwānggōu.*

现

zài   at   *Héng, piě, shù, héng, shù, héng.*

在

Dì–sì   kè   Zhè   shì   wǒ   bàba.

第四课　这是我爸爸。

Lesson 4　This is my dad.

一　听与看　Listen and Read

Listen to the recording of the following sentences as many times as possible until you can say it along with the recording. You should also look at the following transcription while listening and try to imitate.

1.	Substitution 1	Substitution 2

Zhè shì wǒ bàba.
这 是 我 爸爸。
this | be | I | dad
This is my dad.

	gēge	*jiějie*
	哥哥	姐姐
	elder brother	elder sister

Zhè shì wǒ māma.
这 是 我 妈妈。
this | be | I | mom
This is my mom.

	dìdi	*mèimei*
	弟弟	妹妹
	younger brother	younger sister

Bàba, māma, bàba, māma.
爸爸、妈妈，爸爸、妈妈，
dad | mom | dad | mom
Dad, mom; dad, mom;

	gēge, dìdi	*jiějie, mèimei*
	哥哥、弟弟	姐姐、妹妹
	elder brother	younger brother	elder sister	younger sister

bàba hé māma.
爸爸 和 妈妈。
dad | and | mom
dad and mom.

	gēge hé dìdi	*jiějie hé mèimei*
	哥哥和弟弟	姐姐和妹妹
	elder brother	and	younger brother	elder sister	and	younger sister

2.

Zhè bú shì wǒ bàba,
这 不 是 我 爸爸，
this | not | be | I | dad
This is not my dad,

	māma
	妈妈
	mom

zhè shì tā bàba.
这 是 他 爸爸。
this | be | he | dad
this is his dad.

	māma
	妈妈
	mom

Zhè bú shì wǒ gēge,
这 不 是 我 哥哥，
this | not | be | I | elder brother
This is not my elder brother,

jiějie
姐姐
elder sister

zhè shì wǒ dìdi
这 是 我 弟弟。
this | be | I | younger brother.
this is my younger brother.

mèimei
妹妹
younger sister

二 看与说 Read and Speak

1

这是我爸爸。

这是我妈妈。

爸爸、妈妈，爸爸、妈妈，

爸爸和妈妈。

2

这不是我爸爸，

这是他爸爸。

这不是我哥哥，

这是我弟弟。

三 理解 Understand

是 *shì* is the verb, meaning "to be"; however, in Chinese, 是 *shì* does not change its form as the word "be", which may change to "was", "were", "is", "are," or "will be". It is usually left out when an adjective is used after the subject of a sentence. For example, the Chinese sentence for "I am very busy" is 我很忙 *wǒ hěn máng* rather than 我是很忙 *wǒ shì hěn máng*. However, if 是 *shì* is used before an adjective, then it has an emphatic meaning. As in 我是很忙 *wǒ shì hěn máng*, it means "I am indeed very busy, but ..."

Most of the monosyllabic kinship terms in Chinese can be duplicated as disyllabic words to convey the concept of endearment. For example, 爸 *bà* becomes 爸爸 *bàba*, and 妈 *mā* becomes 妈妈 *māma*. However, the tone of the second syllable is often neutralized. The neutral tone is short and unstressed, but its pitch varies according to the tone of the previous syllable. If we set the highest pitch as the fifth degree and the lowest pitch as the first degree, then the general rule is as follows:

1) When preceded by a 1st (i.e., flat) tone syllable, it is in the second degree (i.e., semi-low) pitch. For example, 妈妈 *māma* and 哥哥 *gēge*.

		5
_____ *mā*	_____ *gē*	4
		3
ma ○	*ge* ○	2
		1

2) When preceded by a 2nd (i.e., rising) tone syllable, it is in the third degree (i.e., middle) pitch. For example, 爷爷 *yéye* (grandpa).

		5
		4
yé	*ye* ○	3
		2
		1

3) When preceded by a 3rd (i.e., dipping) tone syllable, it is in the fourth degree (i.e., semi-high) pitch. For example, 姐姐 *jiějie*.

		5
		4
jie ○		3
		2
jiě		1

4) When preceded by a 4th (i.e., falling) tone syllable, it is in the first degree (i.e., low) pitch. For example, 弟弟 *dìdi* and 妹妹 *mèimei*.

		5
dì	*mèi*	4
		3
		2
di ○	*mei* ○	1

Verbalizing these rules by heart may not be easy, but if you can practice saying these kinship terms by imitating the rhythmic verses in this lesson closely and repeatedly, then being able to speak correctly in line with these rules will be easier.

我爸爸 *wǒ bàba* means "my dad", even though 我 *wǒ* by itself means "I". In fact, the character 的 *de* is usually used after 我 *wǒ* to mean "my" or "mine", but when 我 *wǒ* or other personal pronouns, such as 你 *nǐ* and 他 *tā*, are used together with a kinship term, 的 *de* is omitted.

不 *bù* is a negation word in Chinese, meaning "not". Its original tone is the 4th tone (i.e., the falling tone): *bù*, as in 不忙 *bù máng* "not busy" and 不好 *bù hǎo* "not good". However, when it is followed by another 4th tone syllable, it is pronounced in the 2nd tone. For example, 不是 *bú shì* is pronounced as *bú shì* rather than *bù shì*.

四　实践　Practice

1. 对话 Conversation

A: 你好!

B: 你好!

A: 你现在忙吗?

B: 不忙。你呢?

A: 我也不忙。

(Looking at the photos on the wall)

A: 这是你爸爸吗?

B: 是，那是我爸爸。

A: 这是你妈妈吗?

B: 是，是我妈妈。

　　这是我哥哥，这是我弟弟。

A: 那是你妹妹吗?

B: 不是，是我姐姐。

☞ 2. 交际 Communication

| Task 1 | Your parents have come to see you when you study in China. As you walk into the Foreign Student Hostel, introduce your parents to the front desk attendant. |

| Task 2 | On a shopping day, you run into a friend and another person who resembles your friend closely. Confirm your guess that they might be siblings. |

| Task 3 | When someone thinks your mother is your older sister, you eagerly claim that the assumption is false. |

| Task 4 | Your Chinese language instructor shows you his/her family portrait. Ask questions about the people in the portrait to confirm your guesses about their relationship. |

✎ 3. 书写 Writing

sì　four　*Shù, héngzhé, piě, shùwān, héng.*

| 四 | | | | | | | | | |

shì　be　*Shù, héngzhé, héng, héng, héng, shù, héng, piě, nà.*

| 是 | | | | | | | | | |

bà   dad   *Piě, diǎn, piě, nà; héngzhé, shù, héng, shùwāngōu.*

爸								

mā   mom   *Piědiǎn, piě, héng; héngzhé, shùzhézhégōu, héng.*

妈								

hé   and   *Piě, héng, shù, piě, diǎn; shù, héngzhé, héng.*

和								

dì   younger brother   *Diǎn, piě, héngzhé, héng, shùzhézhégōu, shù, piě.*

弟								

jiě   elder sister   *Piědiǎn, piě, héng; shù, héngzhé, héng, héng, héng.*

姐								

mèi   younger sister   *Piědiǎn, piě, héng; héng, héng, shú, piě, nà.*

妹								

Dì-wǔ kè   Zhè shì shéi de   chē?

第五课　这是谁的车?

Lesson 5   Whose car is this?

一　听与看　Listen and Read

Listen to the recording of the following sentences as many times as possible until you can say it along with the recording. You should also look at the following transcription while listening and try to imitate.

Chē,   chē,   chē,

车，车，车，
car | car | car

Car, car, car,

zhè shì shéi de chē?

这是谁的车?
this | be | who | [aux.] | car

whose car is this?

Chē,   chē,   chē,

车，车，车，
car | car | car

Car, car, car,

zhè shì wǒ de chē.

这是我的车。
this | be | I | [aux.] | car

this is my car.

Shū,   shū,   shū,

书，书，书，
book | book | book

Book, book, book,

zhè shì shéi de shū?

这是谁的书?
this | be | who | [aux.] | book

whose book is this?

Shū, shū, shū,

书，书，书，

book | book | book

Book, book, book,

zhè bú shì wǒ de shū.

这不是我的书。

this | not | be | I | [aux.] | book.

this is not my book.

二　看与说　Read and Speak

Now, listen to the recording while looking at the following sentences. Then read it out aloud. Finally, recite it by heart to yourself and then to your classmates or instructor.

车，车，车，

这是谁的车？

车，车，车，

这是我的车。

书，书，书，

这是谁的书？

书，书，书，

这不是我的书。

(三) 理解 Understand

In Chinese, the auxiliary word 的 *de* is used between somebody and something to indicate ownership. 我的车 *wǒ de chē* is "my car", and 我的书 *wǒ de shū* is "my book". "Your car" is 你的车 *nǐ de chē* in Chinese, and "his book" is 他的书 *tā de shū*. When the owner is in question, the question word 谁 *shuí* (often pronounced as *shéi* in daily conversations) is used. There is no need to change the word order in Chinese, and the question word is just put in the place where the information is requested. Look at the following:

my book	我的书	my ...	我的……	mine	我的
your book	你的书	your...	你的……	yours	你的
his book	他的书	his ...	他的……	his	他的
whose book	谁的书	whose...	谁的……	whose	谁的

Whose book is this?	这是谁的书？
This is my book.	这是我的书。

However, if you talk about someone close to you, such as parents and siblings, 的 *de* is often omitted. So, "my dad" is more often 我爸爸 *wǒ bàba* rather than 我的爸爸 *wǒ de bàba*, and "my mom" is 我妈妈 *wǒ māma* rather than 我的妈妈 *wǒ de māma* in Chinese. How about "Whose father is he?" It should be "他是谁爸爸 *tā shì shéi bàba?*"

(四) 实践 Practice

1. 对话 Conversation

A: 这是谁的车？是你的吗？

B: 不是，是我爸的车。

A: 你爸的车很好！

B: (Looking at a bicycle) 这个是我的车，也很好。

👋 2. 交际 Communication

Task 1 You found a textbook in your classroom. Find out whom it belongs to by asking the people around you.

Task 2 You saw an awesome car parked outside. Ask your friend whom it belongs to. Your friend told you that it belongs to his elder brother. Show your admiration for the car.

Task 3 You are at a bicycle store shopping for a reasonably good bike. Since you have no experience shopping in China, you have brought a Chinese friend for advice. Ask your friend for his/her opinions of different bike models.

Task 4 At a bicycle parking lot, you find somebody trying to unlock your bicycle with his key. Put on a stern face and tell that guy: "This is my bike. Not yours."

✏️ 3. 书写 Writing

wǔ   five   *Héng, shù, héngzhé, héng.*

五									

shuí; shéi   who   *Diǎn, héngzhétí; piě, shù, diǎn, héng, héng, héng, shù, héng.*

谁									

de   [auxiliary word]   *Piě, shù, héngzhé, héng, héng; piě, héngzhégōu, diǎn.*

的									

chē   car; vehicle   *Héng, piězhé, héng, shù.*

车									

shū   book   *Héngzhé, héngzhégōu, shù, diǎn.*

书									

Dì–liù kè   Tā   shì   nǎ   guó   rén?

第六课　他是哪国人？

Lesson 6　　What is his nationality?

一　听与看　Listen and Read

Listen to the recording of the following sentences as many times as possible until you can say it along with the recording. You should also look at the following transcription while listening and try to imitate.

Nà shì shéi?   Nà shì shéi?

那 是 谁？ 那 是 谁？

that | be | who | that | be | who

Who is that? Who is that?

Nà shì wǒmen lǎoshī.

那 是 我们 老师。

that | be | I | [plural] | old | master

That is our teacher.

Nǎ guó rén?   Nǎ guó rén?

哪 国 人？ 哪 国 人？

which | country | person | which | country | person

What nationality? What nationality?

Tā (Tā) shì nǎ guó rén?

他 (她) 是 哪 国 人？

he | (she) | be | which | country | person

What is his (her) nationality?

Zhōngguórén, Zhōngguórén,

中国人， 中国人，

middle | country | person | middle | country | person

Chinese, Chinese,

tā (tā) shì Zhōngguórén.

他 (她) 是 中国人。

he | (she) | be | middle | country | person

he (she) is a Chinese.

Měiguórén, Měiguórén,

美国人， 美国人，

beautiful | country | person | beautiful country | person

American, American,

tā shì Měiguórén.

她 是 美国人。

she | be | beautiful | country | person

she is an American.

Nǎ guó rén?　*Nǎ guó rén?*
哪 国 人？　哪 国 人？
which | country | person | Which | country | person
What nationality? What nationality?

Nǐ shì nǎ guó rén?
你 是 哪 国 人？
you | be | which | country | person
What is your nationality?

Měiguórén,　*Měiguórén,*
美国人，　美国人，
beautiful | country | person | beautiful | country | person
American, American,

wǒ shì Měiguórén.
我 是 美国人。
I | be | beautiful | country | person
I am an American.

二　看与说　Read and Speak

Now, listen to the recording while looking at the following sentences. Then read it out aloud. Finally, recite it by heart to yourself and then to your classmates or instructor.

那是谁？那是谁？

那是我们老师。

哪国人？哪国人？

他(她)是哪国人？

中国人，中国人，

他(她)是中国人。

哪国人？ 哪国人？
你是哪国人？

美国人，美国人，
我是美国人。

三 理解 **Understand**

As mentioned in the previous lesson, a statement and a question use the same word order in Chinese. There is no need to change the word order as many English questions often do. The word order in Chinese for "Who is that?" is "That is who?"

们 *men* is a plural suffix for people and is often used with pronouns to indicate plurality, but not always for nouns indicating people when the context is clear. For example,

He is a Chinese. → 他是中国人。
We are Chinese. → 我们是中国人。 (Not 我们是中国人们。)
three elder brothers → 三个哥哥 (Not 三个哥哥们)

Teachers are viewed as people who are quite close to students. Therefore, 的 *de* can also be omitted. For example:

our teacher → 我们老师
your teacher → 你们老师
their teacher → 他们老师 or 她们老师

四 实践 Practice

1. 对话 Conversation

A: 你好!

B: 你好!

A: 你是哪国人?

B: 我是美国人。

A: 你现在忙吗?

B: 不忙。

A: 那个人是谁?

B: 是我们老师。

A: 她也是美国人吗?

B: 不是。

A: 她是哪国人?

B: 她是中国人。

A: 你们老师好吗?

B: 很好!

2. 交际 Communication

Task 1 At the International Student Dorm lounge, a student greets you in Chinese. You conclude from his/her appearance that the student is non-Chinese. Find out the nationality of that student during your chat.

Task 2 You are involved in a group activity with some Chinese students. Find out if all of them are from Beijing and whether their professors are also from Beijing. Ask them whether they have a busy schedule at school. Tell the Chinese students that your professor is a Chinese citizen from the United States and that your professor is very good.

Task 3 Pretend you are a Chinese-American. When a Chinese student asks you about your family members, tell him/her that your dad is American and your mom is Chinese and you are therefore both Chinese and American. When the Chinese student asks about the professions of your parents, tell him/her that they are both teachers.

3. 书写 Writing

liù   six   *Diǎn, héng, piě, diǎn.*

六									

nǎ   which   *Shù, héngzhé, héng; héngzhégōu, héng, héng, piě; héngpiěwāngōu, shù.*

哪									

guó   country   *Shù, héngzhé, héng, héng, shù, héng, diǎn, héng.*

国									

rén   person   *Piě, nà.*

人									

men   [plural]   *Piě, shù; diǎn, shù, héngzhégōu.*

们									

lǎo   old   *Héng, shù, héng, piě, piě, shùwāngōu.*

老									

实用节奏汉语

shī   master   *Shù, piě; héng, shù, héngzhégōu, shù.*

师									

zhōng   middle   *Shù, héngzhé, héng, shù.*

中									

tā   she   *Piědiǎn,* piě, *héng; héngzhégōu, shù, shùwāngōu.*

她									

měi   beautiful   *Diǎn, piě, héng, héng, shù, héng, héng, piě, nà.*

美									

Dì-qī kè   *Zhè shì shénme?*
第七课   这是什么？
Lesson 7   What is this?

一 听与看 Listen and Read

Listen to the recording of the following sentences as many times as possible until you can say it along with the recording. You should also look at the following transcription while listening and try to imitate.

Shénme?   Shénme?
什么？ 什么？
what | [suffix] | what | [suffix]
What? What?

Zhè shì shénme?
这 是 什么？
this | be | what | [suffix]
What is this?

Jiǎozi,   jiǎozi,
饺子，饺子，
dumpling | [suffix] | dumpling | [suffix]
Dumpling, dumpling,

zhè shì jiǎozi.
这 是 饺子。
this | be | dumpling | [suffix]
this is a dumpling.

Zhè shì shénme jiǎozi?
这 是 什么 饺子？
this | be | what | [suffix] | dumpling | [suffix]
What dumpling is this?

Zhè shì zhūròu jiǎozi.
这 是 猪肉 饺子。
this | be | pig | meat | dumpling | [suffix]
This is a pork dumpling.

Nà shì shénme jiǎozi?
那 是 **什么 饺子**？
that | be | **what** | [suffix] | **dumpling** | [suffix]
What dumpling is that?

Nà shì sùcài jiǎozi.
那 是 **素菜 饺子**。
that | be | **plain** | **vegetable** | **dumpling** | [suffix]
That is a vegetable dumpling.

二　看与说　Read and Speak

Now, listen to the recording while looking at the following sentences. Then read it out aloud. Finally, recite it by heart to yourself and then to your classmates or instructor.

什么？什么？

这是什么？

饺子，饺子，

这是饺子。

这是什么饺子？

这是猪肉饺子。

那是什么饺子？

那是素菜饺子。

三 理解 Understand

什么 *shénme* is another question word in Chinese, meaning "what". When asking "What is this?" and "What dumpling is this?" in Chinese, we still keep the word order of a statement by saying: "This is what?" 这是什么 *zhè shì shénme?* and "That is what dumpling?" 那是什么饺子*nà shì shénme jiǎo zi?* The question word 什么 *shénme* is used in place of the matter that is questioned.

The original meaning of the word 子 *zi* is a baby, and it is used in many words as a suffix to indicate that they are nouns. 饺子 *jiǎozi* is dumplings made with wheat flour wrappers with ground meat or vegetable or both as stuffing.

四 实践 Practice

1. 对话 *Conversation*

A: 你好!

B: 你好!

A: 这是什么?

B: 这是饺子。

A: 这是什么饺子?

B: 这是猪肉饺子。

A: 那个也是猪肉的吗?

B: 不是。那个是素菜饺子。

2. 交际 *Communication*

Task 1 You are at a school cafeteria in China. Find out the ingredients of the food you are interested in trying.

Task 2 You are at a dumpling restaurant. Since you are a vegetarian, find out which kinds of dumplings in the sample window have no meat.

Task 3 You are invited to a Chinese friend's home. At the dinner table, ask what kind of meat and what kind of vegetable each dish is made of. After trying the dishes, compliment the host/hostess on the wonderful food they offer you.

Task 4 You are showing some family photos that you brought from the U.S.. When your Chinese friend spots a car in the background of one photo, he/she asks whom it belongs to and what kind of car it is. Your answer would be that it is your mom's car and that it is a Ford, an American car.

Task 5 One summer afternoon, a Chinese friend of yours is reading an English book in the shade on a campus bench. Walk over to chat with your friend by asking what book it is and comment that the book is very good.

qī   seven   *Héng, shùwāngōu.*

七									

shén   what   *Piě, shù; héng, shù.*

什									

me   [suffix]   *Piě, piězhé, diǎn.*

么									

jiǎo   dumpling   *Piě, hénggōu, shùtí; diǎn, héng, piě, diǎn, piě, nà.*

饺									

zi   [suffix]   *Héngpiě, shùgōu, héng.*

子									

zhū   pig   *Piě, wāngōu, piě; héng, shù, héng, piě, shù, héngzhé, héng, héng.*

猪									

ròu   meat   *Shù, héngzhégōu, piě, diǎn, piě, diǎn.*

肉									

sù   plain   *Héng, héng, shù, héng, piězhé, piězhé, diǎn, shùgōu, diǎn, diǎn.*

素									

cài   vegetable; dish   *Héng, shù, shù; piě, diǎn, diǎn, piě, héng, shù, piě, nà.*

菜									

第八课　谁啊？

一　听与看　Listen and Read

Listen to the recording of the following sentences as many times as possible until you can say it along with the recording. You should also look at the following transcription while listening and try to imitate.

Shéi a?   Shéi a?   Shéi a?

谁啊？ 谁啊？ 谁啊？

who||[aux.]||who||[aux.]||who||[aux.]

Who is it? Who is it? Who is it?

Shì wǒ,   shì wǒ,   shì wǒ.

是我，是我，是我。

be|I|be|I|be|I

It's me, it's me, it's me.

Qǐng jìn,   qǐng jìn,   qǐng jìn.

请进，请进，请进。

please|enter|please|enter|please|enter

Come in, please; come in, please; come in, please.

Xièxie,   xièxie,   xièxie.

谢谢，谢谢，谢谢。

thank|thank|thank

Thanks, thanks, thanks.

Qǐng hē chá,   qǐng hē chá

请喝茶，请喝茶。

please|drink|tea|please|drink|tea

Have some tea, please; have some tea, please.

Xièxie,   xièxie,   xièxie.

谢谢，谢谢，谢谢。

thank|thank|thank

Thanks, thanks, thanks.

Bú kèqi,   bú kèqi,
不客气，不客气，
not | guest | air | not | guest | air
Don't stand on ceremony, don't stand on ceremony,

qǐng bú yào kèqi.
请不要客气。
please | not | need | guest | air
no need to stand on ceremony, please.

Chī táng ma?   Chī táng ma?
吃糖吗？吃糖吗？
eat | candy | [ques.] | eat | candy | [ques.]
Have a candy? Have a candy?

Bù chī,   bù chī,   bù chī.
不吃，不吃，不吃。
not | eat | not | eat | not | eat
No, thanks; no, thanks; no, thanks.

Bié kèqi,   bié kèqi,
别客气，别客气，
don't | guest | air | don't | guest | air
Don't stand on ceremony, don't stand on ceremony,

qǐng nǐ bié   kèqi.
请你别客气。
please | you | don't | guest | air
please do not stand on ceremony.

二 看与说 Read and Speak

Now, listen to the recording while looking at the following sentences. Then read it out aloud. Finally, recite it by heart to yourself and then to your classmates or instructor.

谁啊？谁啊？谁啊？
是我，是我，是我。

请进，请进，请进。

谢谢，谢谢，谢谢。

请喝茶，请喝茶。

谢谢，谢谢，谢谢。

不客气，不客气，

请不要客气。

吃糖吗？吃糖吗？

不吃，不吃，不吃。

别客气，别客气，

请你别客气。

<h2>三 理解 Understand</h2>

啊 *a* is an auxiliary word attached to the end of a sentence or a question to soften the tone. In fact, 啊 *a* may also be pronounced and written as 呀 *ya* due to the influence of the ending vowel sound of the word preceding it. Therefore, it can also be 谁呀 *shéi ya*? In English, when hearing someone knocking on the door, we can ask "Who is it?" In Chinese, we do not ask "这是谁 *zhè shì shéi*?" or "那是谁 *nà shì shéi*?". Instead, we simply say "谁呀 *shéi ya*?". When answering to this question in Chinese, we can simply say 我 *wǒ* or 是我 *shì wǒ*.

请 *qǐng* is a polite word and good to use in Chinese. It is always used at the beginning of a command or request and is never used at its end as "please" in English.

The meaning of the expression 不客气 *bú kèqi* is "you are welcome" and is used as a response to someone who thanks you in Chinese. 请不要客气 *qǐng bú yào kèqi* or 请别客气 *qǐng bié kèqi* is often used to urge someone to make himself or herself feel at home.

不要 *bú yào* and 别 *bié* are the same in meaning.

四　实践　Practice

1. 对话 *Conversation*

A: 谁啊？

B: 是我。

A: 啊，是谢老师！请进，请进。
请喝茶。

B: 谢谢。你这个茶很好。是哪国茶？

A: 是美国茶。老师，请吃糖。

B: 不吃，不吃。

A: 别客气。吃一个吧。这个是美国糖。

B: 好吧。 (After putting it in the mouth) 这个美国糖很好吃。

2. 交际 *Communication*

Task 1 You are in your dorm. When you hear knocking on your door, ask who it is and open the door to let him/her in after learning that it is your friend.

Task 2 You have a Chinese guest at your dorm. Offer some drinks and food to your guest. When your guest declines your offer, insist your offer by telling your guest not to be too polite and that it is food or drink you brought from your home country to China.

Task 3 Before returning to your home country, you want to buy some presents for your family and friends. Ask the teashop sales person about some kinds of tea that look good to you.

Task 4 At a large supermarket, an elegant young lady invites you to sit down at her sales table for a tea tasting ceremony. She gave you several kinds of tea and some snack fruit and nut candies to try. Thank the young hostess, praise the tea and food and ask her the names of the kind of nut candy and the two kinds of tea you set your mind on.

 *3. 书写 Writing*

bā   eight   *Piě, nà.*

八									

a   [auxiliary word]; [interjection]   *Shù, héngzhé, héng; héngpiěwāngōu, shù; héng, shù, héngzhé, héng, shùgōu.*

啊									

qǐng   please   *Diǎn, héngzhétí; héng, héng, shù, héng, shù, héngzhégōu, héng, héng.*

请									

jìn   enter   *Héng, héng, piě, shù; diǎn, héngzhézhépiě, píngnà.*

进									

xiè   thank   *Diǎn, héngzhétí; piě, shù, héngzhégōu, héng, héng, héng, piě; héng, shùgōu, diǎn.*

谢									

实用节奏汉语

hē   drink   *Shù, héngzhé, héng; shù, héngzhé, héng, héng, piě, héngzhégōu, piě, diǎn, shùzhé.*

喝								

chá   tea   *Héng, shù, shù; piě, nà, héng, shùgōu, diǎn, diǎn.*

茶								

kè   guest   *Diǎn, diǎn, hénggōu; piě, héngpiě, nà, shù, héngzhé, héng.*

客								

qì   air; gas   *Piě, héng, héng, héngzhéxiégōu.*

气								

yào   need; demand   *Héng, shù, héngzhé, shù, shù, héng; piědiǎn, piě, héng.*

要								

chī   eat   *Shù, héngzhé, héng; piě, héng, héngzhéwāngōu.*

吃								

táng   candy   *Diǎn, piě, héng, shù, piě, diǎn; diǎn, héng, piě, héngzhé, héng, héng, shù, shù, héngzhé, héng.*

糖								

bié   don't   *Shù, héngzhé, héng, héngzhégōu, piě; shù, shùgōu.*

别								

Dì-jiǔ kè   Nín guìxìng?

第九课　您贵姓？

Lesson 9   What is your noble surname?

一　听与看　Listen and Read

Listen to the recording of the following sentences as many times as possible until you can say it along with the recording. You should also look at the following transcription while listening and try to imitate.

Nín guìxìng? Nín guìxìng?

您 贵 姓? 您 贵 姓?

|respectful form of "you"||noble|surname||respectful form of "you"||noble|surname

What is your noble surname? What is your noble surname?

Miǎn guì,   xìng Lǐ; miǎn guì,   xìng Lǐ;

免 贵，姓李；免 贵，姓李；

remove|noble|surname||[a surname]||remove|noble|surname||[a surname]

Without being noble, I am surnamed Li; without being noble, I am surnamed Li;

miǎn guì,   wǒ xìng Lǐ.

免 贵，我 姓 李。

remove|noble|I|surname||[a surname]

without being noble, I am surnamed Li.

Nín ne? Nín ne? Nín ne?

您 呢? 您 呢? 您 呢?

|respectful form of "you"||[ques.]||respectful form of "you"||[ques.]||respectful form of "you"||[ques.]

How about you? How about you? How about you?

Qǐngwèn,   nín guìxìng?

请问，您 贵姓?

please|ask||respectful form of "you"||noble|surname

May I ask what your noble surname is?

Wǒ yě xìng Lǐ,   wǒ yě xìng Lǐ,

我 也 姓李，我 也 姓 李，

I|also|surname||[a surname]||I|also|surname||[a surname]

I am also surnamed Li, I am also surnamed Li,

wǒmen dōu xìng Lǐ.

我们 都 姓李。

I | [plural] | all | surname | [a surname]

we are all surnamed Li.

Shénme míngzi? Shénme míngzi?

什么 名字？什么 名字？

what | [suffix] | name | character | what | [suffix] | name | character

What name? What name?

Nǐ jiào shénme míngzi?

你 叫 什么 名字？

you | call | what | [suffix] | name | character

What is your name?

Wǒ jiào Lǐ Sì, wǒ jiào Lǐ Sì,

我 叫李 四，我 叫李四，

I | call | [a surname] | four | I | call | [a surname] | four

I am called Li Si, I am called Li Si,

wǒ míng jiào Lǐ Sì.

我 名 叫 李 四。

I | name | call | [a surname] | four

my name is Li Si.

Nǐ ne? Nǐ ne? Nǐ ne?

你 呢？你 呢？你 呢？

you | [ques.] | you | [ques.] | you | [ques.]

How about you? How about you? How about you?

Nǐ jiào shénme míngzi?

你 叫 什么 名字？

you | call | what | [suffix] | name | character

What is your name?

Wǒ jiào Wáng Wǔ, wǒ jiào Wáng Wǔ,

我 叫 王 五，我 叫 王 五，

I | call | [a surname] | five | I | call | [a surname] | five

I am called Wang Wu, I am called Wang Wu,

wǒ míng jiào Wáng Wǔ.

我 名 叫 王 五。

I | name | call | [a surname] | five

my name is Wang Wu.

二 看与说 Read and Speak

Now, listen to the recording while looking at the following sentences. Then read it out aloud. Finally, recite it by heart to yourself and then to your classmates or instructor.

您贵姓？您贵姓？

免贵，姓李；免贵，姓李。

免贵，我姓李。

您呢？您呢？您呢？

请问，您贵姓？

我也姓李，我也姓李，

我们都姓李。

什么名字？什么名字？

你叫什么名字？

我叫李四，我叫李四，

我名叫李四。

你呢？你呢？你呢？

你叫什么名字？

我叫王五，我叫王五，

我名叫王五。

三　理解　Understand

To ask someone's name politely, Chinese people usually use the expression "您贵姓 *nín guìxìng*？", which literally means "What is your noble surname?". It reflects the Chinese traditional custom of being polite to people of another clan with a different surname. To reply to the inquirer politely, the answerer usually uses the expression 免贵 *miǎn guì*, which means "without being noble". In modern China, Chinese people also use a less formal expression to ask for someone's name: "你叫什么名字 *nǐ jiào shénme míngzi*？" (what's your name?) The answer to this question is "我叫 *wǒ jiào* …" (I am called…) or "我名叫 *wǒ míng jiào*…" (My name is …)

In Lesson 8, we have learned that 请 *qǐng* (please) is a polite word to be used when making a request. 请问 *qǐngwèn* (excuse me) is a fixed expression in Chinese that can be used before making an inquiry.

四　实践　Practice

1. 对话 *Conversation*

A: 你好！

B: 你好！

A: 请问，您贵姓？

B: 免贵，姓李。

A: 是吗？我也姓李。我们都姓李。

B: 你叫什么名字？

A: 我叫李四。您呢?
B: 我叫李国。
A: 你是中国人吗?
B: 不是，我是美国人。你呢?
A: 我是中国人。

2. 交际 Communication

Task 1 You meet your Chinese conversation partner for the first time. Introduce yourself in Chinese.

Task 2 You are at an international student party in China. Walk over to somebody to greet him/her and find out his/her family name, full name and nationality.

Task 3 You are eating lunch at the school cafeteria sharing a large table with a Chinese student. Start a conversation with a friendly "hi" and inquire his/her full name. Since you notice the dumplings he/she is eating look delicious, find out the kind of stuffing and say that you are going to buy the same kind from the counter.

Task 4 After the first day of class, ask your roommate who his/her Chinese language teachers are and tell your roommate the family names and full names of your teachers.

3. 书写 Writing

jiǔ nine *Piě, héngzhéwāngōu.*

九											

nín [respectful form of "you"] *Piě, shù, piě, hénggōu, shùgōu, diǎn, diǎn; diǎn, wògōu, diǎn, diǎn.*

您

guì noble; expensive *Shù, héngzhé, héng, shù, héng; shù, héngzhé, piě, diǎn.*

贵

xìng surname *Piědiǎn, piě, héng; piě, héng, héng, shù, héng.*

姓

miǎn exempt; remove *Piě, héngpiě, shù, héngzhé, héng, piě, shùwānggōu.*

免

lǐ [a surname]; plum *Héng, shù, piě, nà; héngpiě, shùgōu, héng.*

李

wèn ask *Diǎn, shù, héngzhégōu; shù, héngzhé, héng.*

问

dōu all *Héng, shù, héng, piě, shù, héngzhé, héng, héng; héngpiěwānggōu, shù.*

都

míng name *Piě, héngpiě, diǎn; shù, héngzhé, héng.*

名

zì character *Diǎn, diǎn, hénggōu; héngpiě, shùgōu, héng.*

字

jiào   call   *Shù, héngzhé, héng; shùtí, shù.*

叫									

wáng   [a surname]; king   *Héng, héng, shù, héng.*

王									

第十课　你住哪儿？
Lesson 10　Where do you live?

一　听与看　Listen and Read

Listen to the recording of the following sentences as many times as possible until you can say it along with the recording. You should also look at the following transcription while listening and try to imitate.

Zhù   nǎr?   Zhù   nǎr?

住 哪儿？ 住 哪儿？

live | which | [suffix] | live | which | [suffix]

Live where? Live where?

Nǐmen   zhù   nǎr?

你们 住 哪儿？

you | [plural] | live | which | [suffix]

Where do you live?

Sùshè,   sùshè,

宿舍，宿舍，

lodge | hut | lodge | hut

The dorm,　the dorm,

wǒmen   zhù   sùshè.

我们 住 宿舍。

I | [plural] | live | lodge | hut

we live in the dorm.

Zài   nǎr?   Zài   nǎr?

在 哪儿？ 在 哪儿？

at | which | [suffix] | at | which | [suffix]

Where?　Where?

Sùshè   zài   nǎr?

宿舍 在 哪儿？

lodge | hut | at | which | [suffix]

Where is the dorm?

Zài nàr,   zài nàr,
在那儿，在那儿，
at | that | [suffix] | at | that | [suffix]
Over there, over there,

sùshè zài nàr.
宿舍在那儿。
lodge | hut | at | that | [suffix]
the dorm is over there.

Duōshao hào? Duōshao hào?
多少 号？多少 号？
much | little | number | much | little | number
What number? What number?

Nǐ zhù duōshao hào?
你 住 多少 号？
you | live | much | little | number
What number do you live in?

Shíyī   hào,   shíyī hào,
十一号，十一号，
ten | one | number | ten | one | number
Number Eleven, Number Eleven,

wǒ zhù shíyī hào.
我 住十一号。
I | live | ten | one | number
I live in Number Eleven.

二 看与说 **Read and Speak**

Now, listen to the recording while looking at the following sentences. Then read it out aloud. Finally, recite it by heart to yourself and then to your classmates or instructor.

住哪儿？住哪儿？

你们住哪儿？

宿舍，宿舍，

我们住宿舍。

在哪儿？在哪儿？

宿舍在哪儿？

在那儿，在那儿，

宿舍在那儿。

多少号？多少号？

你住多少号？

十一号，十一号，

我住十一号。

三 理解 Understand

住 *zhù* is a Chinese word that has two connotations. The first is "to live", and the second is "to stay" in English. Whether you have lived in a place for a long time or for a very short period of time, you can use 住 *zhù* in Chinese to express the meaning of "to live" and the meaning of "to stay". Therefore, "I stay at the dorm" is 我住宿舍 *wǒ zhù sùshè*, and "I live in America" can also use 住 *zhù* as 我住美国 *wǒ zhù Měiguó*.

儿 *ér* is used as a suffix attached to the end of 哪 *nǎ* (which) and 那 *nà* (that), forming 哪儿 *nǎr* to mean "where" and 那儿 *nàr* to mean "there". Likewise, for "here", just put 儿 after 这 *zhè* (this) to form 这儿

zhèr. However, people in the southern part of China often prefer not to use the retroflex "*r*" sound as the dialect they speak does not have this sound. Therefore, instead of saying 哪儿 *nǎr*, 那儿 *nǎr*, and 这儿 *zhèr*, they prefer to say 哪里 *nǎli*, 那里 *nàli*, and 这里 *zhèli*.

在 *zài* appears in the word 现在 *xiànzài* (now), it is now used alone and means "to exist" or "to be located at". There are a lot of Chinese words that have two characters, and each character has its own meaning and can be used alone as a word or combined with another character to form a new word with its meaning contributed to the new meaning of the two character word. 多少 *duōshao* is a good example. 多 *duō* has the meaning of "many" or "much", and 少 *shǎo* has the meaning of "few" or "little". When 多 *duō* and 少 *shǎo* are put together, 多少 *duōshao* becomes a question word, meaning "how many" or "how much."

When asking for a number in English, you use the question word "what": What number is it? However, when asking for a number in Chinese, you do not use the question word 什么 *shénme* (what); instead, you can use the question word 多少 *duōshao* (how many): 多少号 *duōshao hào*?

Chinese numerals are logical. Ten and one is eleven, so you just say 十一 *shíyī*. How about other numbers? Have a look at the following:

twelve	十二	*shí'èr*
thirteen	十三	*shísān*
fourteen	十四	*shísì*
fifteen	十五	*shíwǔ*
sixteen	十六	*shíliù*
seventeen	十七	*shíqī*
eighteen	十八	*shíbā*
nineteen	十九	*shíjiǔ*

四 实践 Practice

1. 对话 Conversation

A: 你好。

B: 你好。

A: 你叫什么名字?

B: 我叫王中书。

A: 我叫李国。

B: 你是美国人吗?

A: 是美国人。

B: 你住哪儿?

A: 我住宿舍。

B: 你住哪个宿舍?

A: 那个。

B: 你们宿舍好吗?

A: 很好。

B: 你住多少号?

A: 十五号。

2. 交际 Communication

Task 1 During a telephone conversation, your Chinese conversation partner said he/she will come to meet you where you live. Tell him/her that you live at the dorm, room 131.

Task 2 Since you live at the International Students' Dorm, you are curious where the Chinese students live and how their dorm is. Ask your Chinese conversation partner these two questions and find out his/her room number.

Task 3 You are at the front desk of a student dorm. Tell the receptionist your Chinese friend's name and inquire his/her room number.

Task 4 You are surprised to find out that your Chinese language instructor lives in the faculty apartment building on campus. Ask where the faculty dorm is and which room your instructor lives in.

3. 书写 Writing

shí   ten   *Héng, shù.*

十							

zhù   live   *Piě, shù; diǎn, héng, héng, shù, héng.*

住							

ér   [suffix]   *Piě, shùwāngōu.*

儿							

sù   lodge   *Diǎn, diǎn, hénggōu; piě, shù; héng, piě, shù, héngzhé, héng, héng.*

宿							

shè   hut   *Piě, nà, héng, héng, shù, shù, héngzhé, héng.*

舍							

duō   much   *Piě, héngpiě, diǎn; piě, héngpiě, diǎn.*

多							

shǎo   little   *Shù, diǎn, diǎn, piě.*

少							

hào   number   *Shù, héngzhé, héng, héng, shùzhézhégōu.*

号							

Dì-shíyī kè   Wǒ yòng yíxiàr, xíng ma?

第十一课　我用一下儿，行吗？

Lesson 11　I will use it for a while, OK?

一　听与看　Listen and Read

Listen to the recording of the following sentences as many times as possible until you can say it along with the recording. You should also look at the following transcription while listening and try to imitate.

Yǔsǎn,　yǔsǎn,

雨伞，雨伞，

rain | umbrella | rain | umbrella

Umbrella, umbrella,

shéi de yǔsǎn?

谁 的 雨伞？

who | [aux.] | rain | umbrella

whose umbrella?

Yǔsǎn,　yǔsǎn,

雨伞，雨伞，

rain | umbrella | rain | umbrella

Umbrella, umbrella,

wǒ de yǔsǎn.

我 的 雨伞。

I | [aux.] | rain | umbrella

my umbrella.

Yòng ma?　Yòng ma?

用 吗？用 吗？

use | [ques.] | use | [ques.]

Use it? Use it?

Xiànzài nǐ yòng ma?

现在 你 用 吗？

present | at | you | use | [ques.]

Do you use it now?

Bú yòng, bú yòng,

不用，不用，

not | use | not | use

No, no,

xiànzài wǒ bú yòng.

现在我不用。

present | at | I | not | use

I don't use it now.

Wǒ yòng yíxiàr, xíng ma?

我用一下儿，行吗？

I | use | one | [meas.] | | [suffix] | OK | [ques.]

I will use it for a while, OK?

Wǒ yòng yíxiàr, xíng ma?

我用一下儿，行吗？

I | use | one | [meas.] | | [suffix] | OK | [ques.]

I will use it for a while, OK?

Yòng ba, yòng ba,

用吧，用吧，

use | | [aux.] | | use | | [aux.]

Use it, use it,

yòng ba, yòng ba.

用吧，用吧。

use | | [aux.] | | use | | [aux.]

use it, use it.

Yǔsǎn, yǔsǎn,

雨伞，雨伞，

rain | umbrella | rain | umbrella

Umbrella, umbrella,

huán nǐ yǔsǎn.

还你雨伞。

return | you | rain | umbrella

I am returning you your umbrella.

Xièxie nǐ,   xièxie nǐ,
谢谢 你， 谢谢 你，
thank | you | thank | you
Thank you, thank you,

fēicháng gǎnxiè nǐ!
非常   感谢你！
un- | common | affect | thank | you
thank you very much!

Bú yòng xiè,   bú yòng xiè,
不 用 谢，不 用 谢，
not | use | thank | not | use | thank
You are welcome, you are welcome,

zhēnde   bú yòng xiè!
真的 不 用 谢！
really | [aux.] | not | use | thank
you are really very welcome!

二 看与说 Read and Speak

Now, listen to the recording while looking at the following sentences. Then read it out aloud. Finally, recite it by heart to yourself and then to your classmates or instructor.

雨伞，雨伞，

谁的雨伞？

雨伞，雨伞，

我的雨伞。

用吗？用吗？

现在你用吗？

不用，不用，

现在我不用。

我用一下儿，行吗？

我用一下儿，行吗？

用吧，用吧，

用吧，用吧。

雨伞，雨伞，

还你雨伞。

谢谢你，谢谢你，

非常感谢你！

不用谢，不用谢，

真的不用谢！

三　理解　Understand

When you want to tell somebody that you do not use something, you say 不用 *bú yòng* (not use) in Chinese to mean "I don't use it" in English. However, when 不用 *bú yòng* is used before another action, it is then used to mean "There is no need to …" For example,

Bú yòng wèn. 不用问。 There is no need to ask.

Bú yòng xiè.
不用谢。
You are welcome. (There is no need to thank.)

一下儿 *yíxiàr* is a fixed expression used after an action to soften the tone, meaning "a little bit". For example,

Wèn　yíxiàr.
问一下儿。
Ask about it a little bit.

Yòng　yíxiàr.
用一下儿。
Use it a little bit.

行吗 *xíng ma* is a question tag, meaning "Is it OK?". It is used at the end of a statement to ask for permission or agreement for the content expressed in the statement. For example,

Wǒ chī tā de jiǎozi,　xíng ma?
我吃他的饺子，行吗？
I will eat his dumplings, is it OK?

Wǒ yòng nǐ de chē,　xíng ma?
我用你的车，行吗？
I will use your car, is it OK?

Bié chī táng,　xíng ma?
别吃糖，行吗？
Don't eat candy, is it OK?

吧 *ba* is an auxiliary word used at the end of a question to assume that the answerer will agree with the inquirer. However, it can also be used at the end of a statement to imply consent or indicate that it is a suggestion, request, or mild command. For example:

Nǐ shì lǎoshī ba?
你是老师吧？ (Assuming that the answerer will agree and say yes)
You are a teacher, aren't you?

Nǐ bú shì lǎoshī ba?
你不是老师吧？ (Assuming that the answerer will agree and say no)
You are not a teacher, are you?

Wǒmen chī jiǎozi ba.
我们吃饺子吧。(Implying a suggestion or request)
Let's eat dumplings.

Nǐ yòng ba.
你用吧。(Indicating consent)
Use it.

非常 *fēicháng* is a two-character word that means "very" or "extraordinarily". If you feel that you need to thank someone by using an expression stronger than 谢谢 *xièxie*, then use the expression 非常感谢 *fēicháng gǎnxiè* (thank you very much).

真的 *zhēnde* is a fixed expression, meaning "real" or "really". For example,

Tā zhēnde shì wǒ bàba.
他真的是我爸爸。
He is really my father.

Wǒ zhēnde bù chī zhūròu.
我真的不吃猪肉。
It is true that I do not eat pork.

四 实践 Practice

1. 对话 Conversation

A: 这是谁的雨伞？
B: 是我的。
A: 你现在用吗？
B: 不用。
A: 我用一下儿，行吗？
B: 用吧！
A: 谢谢你。
B: 别客气。

A: 你好，李中书。

B: 你好。

A: 还你雨伞。

B: 啊，好。

A: 非常感谢你。

B: 不用谢。真的不用谢。

2. 交际 Communication

Task 1 You left your homework at your dorm room. You plan to get it during the recess; however, rain starts to pour down. Borrow your teacher's umbrella and return it afterwards with good manners.

Task 2 You need to do some shopping at the farmers market. Ask your roommate whether he/she can lend his/her bike to you and show gratitude when you return it.

Task 3 You don't have your textbook with you, but just need to check one phrase in it that just slipped off your mind. Ask your classmate to let you use his/her book for a second. Thank him/her for allowing you to use it.

Task 4 Your Chinese boy/girl friend has made some dumplings and a few other dishes for a small home party. Since the dumplings smell so delicious, you simply can not resist asking whether you can have just one dumpling before the party begins.

Task 5 After living at the International Student Dorm for two months, you would like to mingle with the Chinese students more in order to get more speaking practices. Ask your leading professor whether it is OK to live at the Chinese student dorm.

🖎 3. 书写 Writing

yòng　use　*Piě, héngzhégōu, héng, héng, shù.*

用								

xià　[action measure word]; down; below　*Héng, shù, diǎn.*

下								

xíng　OK　*Piě, piě, shù; héng, héng, shùgōu.*

行								

yǔ　rain　*Héng, shù, héngzhégōu, shù, diǎn, diǎn, diǎn, diǎn.*

雨								

sǎn　umbrella　*Piě, nà, diǎn, piě, héng, shù.*

伞								

ba　[auxiliaryword]　*Shù, héngzhé, héng; héngzhé, shù, héng, shùwāngōu.*

吧								

huán　return　*Héng, piě, shù, diǎn; diǎn, héngzhézhépiě, píngnà.*

还								

fēi　un-　*shù, héng, héng, héng, shù, héng, héng, héng.*

非								

cháng   common; often   *Shù, diǎn, piě, diǎn, hénggōu; shù, héngzhé, héng, shù, héngzhégōu, shù.*

常									

gǎn   affect   *Héng, piě, héng, shù, héngzhé, héng, xiégōu, piě, diǎn; diǎn, wògōu, diǎn, diǎn.*

感									

zhēn   really   *Héng, shù, shù, héngzhé, héng, héng, héng, héng, piě, diǎn.*

真									

Dì-shí'èr kè   *Wǒ lái jièshào yíxiàr.*

第十二课   我来介绍一下儿。

Lesson 12   Let me introduce you.

（一）听与看   Listen and Read

Listen to the recording of the following sentences as many times as possible until you can say it along with the recording. You should also look at the following transcription while listening and try to imitate.

Rènshi ma?   Rènshi ma?

认识 吗？**认识** 吗？

recognize | know | [ques.] | recognize | know | [ques.]

Do you know? Do you know?

Nǐmen rènshi ma?

你们 **认识** 吗？

you | [plural] | recognize | know | [ques.]

Do you know each other?

Bú rènshi,   bú rènshi,

不 **认识**，不 **认识**，

not | recognize | know | not | recognize | know

Don't know, don't know,

Wǒmen bú rènshi.

我们 不 **认识**。

I | [plural] | not | recognize | know

we don't know each other.

Jièshào yíxiàr,

介绍 一下儿，

interpose | continue | one | [meas.] | [suffix]

Introduce a little bit,

Jièshào yíxiàr,

介绍 一下儿，

interpose | continue | one | [meas.] | [suffix]

introduce a little bit,

wǒ lái jièshào yíxiàr.

我 来 介绍 一下儿。

I | come | interpose | continue | one | [meas.] | [suffix]

let me introduce you to each other a little bit.

Wǒ tóngxué, wǒ tóngxué,

我 同学，我 同学，

I | same | learn | I | same | learn

My classmate, my classmate,

zhèi shì wǒ tóngxué.

这 是 我 同学。

this | be | I | same | learn

this is my classmate.

Wǒ péngyou, wǒ péngyou,

我 朋友，我 朋友，

I | pal | friend | I | pal | friend

My friend, my friend,

zhèi shì wǒ péngyou.

这 是 我 朋友。

this | be | I | pal | friend

this is my friend.

二 看与说 Read and Speak

Now, listen to the recording while looking at the following sentences. Then read it out aloud. Finally, recite it by heart to yourself and then to your classmates or instructor.

认识吗？认识吗？

你们认识吗？

不认识，不认识，

我们不认识。

介绍一下儿，

介绍一下儿，

我来介绍一下儿。

我同学，我同学，

这是我同学。

我朋友，我朋友，

这是我朋友。

三　理解　Understand

认识 *rènshi* is a Chinese word meaning "have enough knowledge to be able to identify someone or something". The second character 识 *shí* is pronounced as *shí* when used alone, but its tone is neutralized and pronounced as *shi* in the word 认识 *rènshi*.

我来 *wǒ lái*... is an expression we can use when we voluntarily do something. If you volunteer to introduce people to each other, then you can say 我来介绍一下儿 *wǒ lái jièshào yíxiàr* (let me introduce you to each other a little bit).

四　实践　Practice

1. 对话 Conversation

A: 你好，李中书！

B: 你好，王贵！

A: 你们认识吗？

B and C: 不认识。

A: 我来介绍一下儿。这是我同学李中书，这是我中国朋友谢进。

B: 你好!

C: 你好! 你也是美国人吗?

B: 是。我们都是美国人。都住在宿舍151号。

C: 真的!

2. 交际 Communication

Task 1 After you meet your second Chinese friend, ask him/her whether he/she knows your conversation partner, whose name is Wang Peng and who lives in number 5 Chinese students' dorm building.

Task 2 When your Chinese friend sees another American student hanging out at the lobby area, he/she asks you whether you happen to know that American student since you come from the same country. Tell him/her you do know this American student. In fact, you are roommates.

Task 3 Your elder brother has come to China to visit you. When you take your brother shopping, you run into your Chinese language instructor. Take the initiative in introducing them to each other.

Task 4 Since you are traveling alone, you decide to join a tour group in China. After settling down in a back seat, introduce yourself to the person who has sat next to you by starting with 我们认识一下儿 *wǒmen rènshi yíxiàr*, 我叫 *wǒ jiào*...

3. 书写 Writing

lái　come　*Héng, diǎn, piě, héng, shù, piě, nà.*

来									

jiè　interpose　*Piě, nà, piě, shù.*

介									

shào　continue　*Piězhé, piězhé, tí; héngzhégōu, piě, shù, héngzhé, héng.*

绍									

rèn　recognize　*Diǎn, hénzhétí; piě, nà.*

认									

shí　know　*Diǎn, hénzhétí; shù, héngzhé, héng, piě, diǎn.*

识									

tóng　same　*Shù, héngzhégōu, héng, shù, héngzhé, héng.*

同									

xué　learn　*Diǎn, diǎn, piě, diǎn, hénggōu; hénggōu, shùgōu, héng.*

学									

péng　pal　*Piě, héngzhégōu, héng, héng; piě, héngzhégōu, héng, héng.*

朋									

yǒu　friend　*Héng, piě, héngpiě, nà.*

友									

Dì–shísān kè

第十三课

Lesson 13

Mǎi bu mǎi?

买不买？

To buy or not to buy?

一 听与看 Listen and Read

Listen to the recording of the following sentences as many times as possible until you can say it along with the recording. You should also look at the following transcription while listening and try to imitate.

Shuō bu shuō? Shuō bu shuō?

说不说？ 说不说？

speak | not | speak | speak | not | speak

Speak or not? Speak or not?

Tā shuō bu shuō Yīngyǔ?

他 说不说 英语？

he | speak | not | speak | Britain | language

Does he speak English or not?

Shuō.

说。

speak

He does.

Xué bu xué? Xué bu xué?

学不学？ 学不学？

learn | not | learn | learn | not | learn

Lear or not? Learn or not?

Tā xué bu xué Hànyǔ?

他 学不学 汉语？

he | learn | not | learn | Han ethnic group | language

Does he learn Chinese or not?

Xué.

学。

learn

He does.

Qù bu qù? Qù bu qù?
去不去? 去不去?
go | not | go | go | not | go
Go or not? Go or not?

Tā qù bu qù shūdiàn?
他 去不去 书店?
he | go | not | go | book | store
Does he go to a bookstore or not?

Qù.
去。
go
He does.

Mǎi bu mǎi? Mǎi bu mǎi?
买不买? 买不买?
buy | not | buy | buy | not | buy
Buy or not? Buy or not?

Tā mǎi bu mǎi cídiǎn?
他 买不买 词典?
he | buy | not | buy | word | classic
Does he buy a dictionary or not?

Bù mǎi.
不 买。
not | buy
He doesn't.

二 看与说 **Read and Speak**

Now, listen to the recording while looking at the following sentences. Then read it out aloud. Finally, recite it by heart to yourself and then to your classmates or instructor.

说不说? 说不说?

他说不说英语?

说。

学不学？ 学不学？

他学不学汉语？

学。

去不去？ 去不去？

他去不去书店？

去。

买不买？ 买不买？

他买不买词典？

不买。

三 理解 Understand

To be or not to be, that is the question. This is a line repeated by Prince Hamlet in the Shakespearian play Hamlet, as he is troubled with the decision on whether or not he should take the action against his uncle who has usurped the power of the Kingdom and married his mother by murdering his father, the old King. In Chinese, a question can just be formed by putting the affirmative action and the negative action together without any question word. For example, 说 *shuō* (speak) is affirmative, 不说 *bù shuō* (not speak) is negative, and 说不说 *shuō bu shuō* (speak or not) is interrogative in Chinese. If you want to ask someone if he/she speaks Chinese, then you can say: 你说不说汉语 *nǐ shuō bu shuō Hànyǔ?*

Notice that when putting the negative together with the affirmative, the negation word 不 *bù* is neutralized for its tone: 是不是 *shì bu shì?* 去不去 *qù bu qù?* 好不好 *hǎo bu hǎo?*

四 实践 Practice

1. 对话 Conversation

A: 我去书店买书。你去不去?

B: 去。我去看一下他们的词典好不好。

A: 你在美国说不说汉语?

B: 不说。我学汉语。

A: 你妈妈不是中国人吗?

B: 是。我妈妈是中国人，我爸爸是美国人。

A: 你妈妈不和你说汉语吗?

B: 她和我说汉语，我和她说英语。

2. 交际 Communication

| Task 1 | You need to buy a dictionary for your language study. Since you don't have a companion to go with yet, knock on the door of your next-door neighbor at the dorm to ask whether he/she wants to go with you. |

| Task 2 | On your way, you chat with your classmate, who is a Chinese-American. Ask him/her whether his/her parents speak Chinese. The answer you get is that his/her dad's side is Chinese and therefore speaks Chinese and that his/her mom does not speak Chinese. |

| Task 3 | At the bookstore, you find two dictionaries that are about equally good. Ask your friend for opinions in order to make your decision. |

📖 3. 书写 Writing

mǎi   buy   *hénggōu, diǎn, diǎn, héng, piě, diǎn.*

买									

shuō   speak   *Diǎn, héngzhétí, diǎn, piě, shù, héngzhé, héng, piě, shùwāngōu.*

说									

yīng   flower; Britain   *Héng, shù, shù, shù, héngzhé, héng, piě, nà.*

英									

yǔ   language   *Diǎn, héngzhétí, héng, shù, héngzhé, héng, shù, héngzhé, héng.*

语									

hàn   Han ethnic group   *Diǎn, diǎn, tí, héngpiě, nà.*

汉									

qù   go   *Héng, shù, héng, piězhé, diǎn.*

去									

diàn   store   *Diǎn, héng, piě; shù, héng, shù, héngzhé, héng.*

店									

cí   word   *Diǎn, héngzhétí, héngzhégōu, héng, shù, héngzhé, héng.*

词									

diǎn   classic   *Shù, héngzhé, héng, shù, shù, héng, piě, diǎn.*

典									

Dì–shísì   kè   *Tā   zuò   shénme   gōngzuò?*

第十四课   她做什么 工作？
Lesson 14   What work does she do?

一   听与看   Listen and Read

Listen to the recording of the following sentences as many times as possible until you can say it along with the recording. You should also look at the following transcription while listening and try to imitate.

Yǒu méiyou   jiějie?   *Yǒu méiyou   jiějie?*

有 没有 姐姐？ 有 没有 姐姐？

have | not | have | elder sister | have | not | have | elder sister

Have an elder sister or not? Have an elder sister nor not?

Nǐ yǒu méiyou   jiějie?

你 有 没有 姐姐？

you | have | not | have | elder sister

Do you have an elder sister or not?

Wǒ yǒu   jiějie,   wǒ yǒu jiějie,

我 有 姐姐， 我 有 姐姐，

I | have | elder sister | I | have | elder sister

I have an elder sister, I have an elder sister,

wǒ yǒu yí ge jiějie.

我 有 一 个 姐姐。

I | have | one | [meas.] | elder sister

I have one elder sister.

Shénme gōngzuò? *Shénme gōngzuò?*

什么 工作？ 什么 工作？

what | [suffix] | work | labor | what | [suffix] | work | labor

What work? What work?

Tā zuò shénme gōngzuò?

她 做 什么 工作？

she | do | what | [suffix] | work | labor

What work does she do?

Tā shì zhíyuán, tā shì zhíyuán,

她 是 职员 ，她 是 职员 ，

she | be | duty | member | she | be | duty | member

She is a clerk, she is a clerk,

tā zài yínháng gōngzuò.

她 在 银行 工作 。

she | at | silver | trade | work | labor

she works at a bank.

Nǐ xiě xìn ma? Nǐ xiě xìn ma?

你 写 信 吗？你 写 信 吗？

you | write | letter | [ques.] | you | write | letter | [ques.]

Do you write letters? Do you write letters?

Nǐ cháng gěi tā xiě xìn ma?

你 常 给 她 写 信 吗？

you | often | to | her | write | letter | [ques.]

Do you often write letters to her?

Bù cháng xiě xìn, bù cháng xiě xìn,

不 常 写 信 ，不 常 写 信 ，

not | often | write | letter | not | often | write | letter

I do not often write letters, I do not often write letters,

wǒ bù cháng gěi tā xiě xìn.

我 不 常 给 她 写 信 。

I | not | often | to | her | write | letter

I do not often write letters to her.

Dǎ diànhuà ma? Dǎ diànhuà ma?

打 电话 吗？打 电话 吗？

make (a phone call) | electric | words | [ques.] | make (a phone call) | electric | words | [ques.]

Make phone calls? Make phone calles?

Nǐ cháng gěi tā dǎ diànhuà ma?

你 常 给 她 打 电话 吗？

you | often | to | her | make (a phone call) | electric | words | [ques.]

Do you often make phone calls to her?

Cháng dǎ diànhuà, cháng dǎ diànhuà,

常 打 电话， 常 打 电话，

often | make (a phone call) | electric | words | often | make (a phone call) | electric | words

I often make phone calls, I often make phone calls,

wǒ cháng gěi tā dǎ diànhuà.

我 常 给 她 打 电话。

I | often | to | her | make (a phone call) | electric | words

I often make phone calls to her.

二 看与说 Read and Speak

Now, listen to the recording while looking at the following sentences. Then read it out aloud. Finally, recite it by heart to yourself and then to your classmates or instructor.

有没有姐姐？有没有姐姐？

你有没有姐姐？

我有姐姐，我有姐姐，

我有一个姐姐。

什么工作？什么工作？

她做什么工作？

她是职员，她是职员，

她在银行工作。

你写信吗？你写信吗？

你常给她写信吗?

不常写信，不常写信，

我不常给她写信。

打电话吗? 打电话吗?

你常给她打电话吗?

常打电话，常打电话，

我常给她打电话。

三　理解　Understand

有 *yǒu* means "to have" or "to possess". When we need to say "do not have" or "do not possess" something, the negation word to be used is 没 *méi* rather than 不 *bù*. Therefore, we say 没有 *méiyou* (do not have). 不 *bù* is never used with 有 *yǒu*, and they simply do not go together. To form an affirmative-negative question, 有没有 *yǒu méiyou* is used.

给 *gěi* is used to mean "to" or "for". In Chinese, it is more common to place "给 *gěi*" + somebody before an action. For example,

> *Wǒ cháng gěi tā mǎi shū.*
> 我常 给他买书。
> I often buy books for him.

> *Tā cháng gěi péngyou dǎ diànhuà.*
> 她常 给朋友 打电话。
> She often makes phone calls to her friends.

打 *dǎ* means "to hit". However, in this lesson, 打电话 *dǎ diànhuà* does not mean "to hit the phone", rather, it means "to make a phone call". 打 *dǎ* has a lot of different meanings, and you will need to learn its different meanings from its different collocations.

四 实践 Practice

1. 对话 Conversation

A: 你有没有兄 *xiōng* (elder brother) 弟姐妹?

B: 有。我有一个姐姐。

A: 你姐姐也是大学生吗?

B: 不是。她是职员。

A: 她在哪儿工作?

B: 中国银行。

A: 你常给她写信吗?

B: 不常写。我们常打电话。

A: 打电话贵不贵?

B: 不贵。

2. 交际 Communication

Task 1 You are invited to dinner by your host family on a Sunday afternoon. When your host asks you about your family, tell them you do not have any sisters, but you do have one elder brother who works at a bank and one younger brother who is a college student like you.

Task 2 When you chat with you Chinese host family, ask the host family parents 1) where they work 2) whether their jobs are good according to their own standard 3) whether their job keeps them busy.

Task 3 Your Chinese conversation partner and you decide to eat dinner together in a small restaurant. While waiting for your food to be served, your speaking partner asks you how you correspond with your family in the United States. Tell him/her that you do not often make phone calls as it is very expensive to call. Instead you write to them via e-mail. Since you do not know how to say "computer" in Chinese, use your fingers to draw a box in the air and pretend typing while saying "I use 这个 *zhèige* to write letters to my parents".

 3. 书写 *Writing*

zuò   do   *Piě, shù; héng, shù, shù, héngzhé, héng; piě, héng, piě, nà.*

做								

gōng   work   *Héng, shù, héng.*

工								

zuò   labor; compose   *Piě, shù; piě, héng, shù, héng, héng.*

作								

yǒu   have   *Héng, piě, shù, héngzhégōu, héng, héng.*

有								

méi   not   *Diǎn, diǎn, tí; piě, héngzhéwān, héngpiě, nà.*

没								

zhí   duty   *Héng, shù, shù, héng, héng, tí; shù, héngzhé, héng, piě, diǎn.*

职								

yuán   member   *Shù, héngzhé, héng; shù, héngzhé, piě, diǎn.*

员									

yín   silver   *Piě, héng, héng, héng, shùtí; héngzhé, héng, héng, shùtí, piě, nà.*

银									

xiě   write   *Diǎn, hénggōu; héng, shùzhézhégōu, héng.*

写									

xìn   letter   *Piě, shù; diǎn, héng, héng, héng, shù, héngzhé, héng.*

信									

gěi   to   *Piězhé, piězhé, tí; piě, nà, héng, shù, héngzhé, héng.*

给									

dǎ   make (a phone call); hit   *Héng, shùgōu, tí; héng, shùgōu.*

打									

diàn   electric   *Shù, héngzhé, héng, héng, shùwāngōu.*

电									

huà   words   *Diǎn, héngzhétí; piě, héng, shù, shù, héngzhé, héng.*

话									

Dì–shíwǔ   kè   *Duōshao qián?*
第十五课   多少 钱？
Lesson 15   How much is it?

一 听与看 Listen and Read

Listen to the recording of the following sentences as many times as possible until you can say it along with the recording. You should also look at the following transcription while listening and try to imitate.

Duōshao qián? Duōshao qián?

多少 钱？ 多少 钱？

much | little | **money** | much | little | **money**

How much is it? How much is it?

Zhè shū duōshao qián?

这 书 多少 钱？

this | book | much | little | **money**

How much is this book?

Èrshí kuài qián, èrshí kuài qián,

二 十 块 钱， 二 十 块 钱，

two | ten | **buck** | **money** | two | ten | **buck** | **money**

Twenty bucks, twenty bucks,

yì běn   èrshí kuài qián.

一 本 二 十 块 钱。

one | [meas.] | two | ten | **buck** | **money**

twenty bucks a copy.

Nǐ yào jǐ běn? Nǐ yào jǐ běn?

你 要 几 本？ 你 要 几 本？

you | want | **how many** | [meas.] | you | want | **how many** | [meas.]

How many copies do you want? How many copies do you want?

Nǐ yào mǎi jǐ běn?

你 要 买 几 本？

you | want | buy | **how many** | [meas.]

How many copies do you want to buy?

Wǒ yào liǎng běn,　wǒ yào liǎng běn,

我要**两本**，我要**两本**，

I | want | two | [meas.] | I | want | two | [meas.]

I want two copies, I want two copies,

wǒ yào mǎi liǎng běn.

我要买**两本**。

I | want | buy | two | [meas.]

I want to buy two copies.

二　看与说　Read and Speak

Now, listen to the recording while looking at the following sentences. Then read it out aloud. Finally, recite it by heart to yourself and then to your classmates or instructor.

多少钱？多少钱？

这书多少钱？

二十块钱，二十块钱，

一本二十块钱。

你要几本？你要几本？

你要买几本？

我要两本，我要两本，

我要买两本。

三　理解　Understand

When we want to know how much money something costs in Chinese, we use 多少钱 *duōshao qián* (how much money). If your are interested in knowing the price of something, put it at the beginning of a sentence as the topic. For example, if a book is the thing you are interested in knowing the price of, you can point at the book and say: "这书多少钱 *zhè shū duōshao qián*?" (How much is this book?) A reply to this question is often started or ended with a number and a measure word for the thing you ask about. For books, the measure word is 本 *běn* (copy); therefore, the reply is 一本二十块 *yì běn èrshí kuài* (20 bucks a copy) or 二十块一本 *èrshí kuài yì běn* (one copy for 20 bucks).

Two tens are twenty, so when 二 *èr* (two) goes before 十 *shí* (ten) in Chinese, it is 二十 *èrshí* (twenty). What about thirty, forty, fifty, and so on? Well, it should be formed in the same way as twenty in Chinese. Have a look at the following:

thirty	三十	*sānshí*
forty	四十	*sìshí*
fifty	五十	*wǔshí*
sixty	六十	*liùshí*
seventy	七十	*qīshí*
eighty	八十	*bāshí*
ninety	九十	*jiǔshí*

We have learned how to count from 1 to 20, and now we have learned how to count from 20 to 90 by tens. If we are truly good at counting 1 to 20 and then from 20 to 90 by tens, then counting from 1 to 99 in Chinese has become possible for us. Look at the following:

10 *shí*	11 *shíyī*	12 *shí'èr*	13 *shísān*	14 *shísì*
15 *shíwǔ*	16 *shíliù*	17 *shíqī*	18 *shíbā*	19 *shíjiǔ*
20 *èrshí*	21 *èrshíyī*	22 *èrshí'èr*	23 *èrshísān*	24 *èrshísì*
25 *èrshíwǔ*	26 *èrshíliù*	27 *èrshíqī*	28 *èrshíbā*	29 *èrshíjiǔ*
30 *sānshí*	31 *sānshíyī*	32 *sānshí'èr*	33 *sānshísān*	34 *sānshísì*
35 *sānshíwǔ*	36 *sānshíliù*	37 *sānshíqī*	38 *sānshíbā*	39 *sānshíjiǔ*
40 *sìshí*	41 *sìshíyī*	42 *sìshí'èr*	43 *sìshísān*	44 *sìshísì*
45 *sìshíwǔ*	46 *sìshíliù*	47 *sìshíqī*	48 *sìshíbā*	49 *sìshíjiǔ*

| 50 *wǔshí* | 51 *wǔshíyī* | 52 *wǔshí'èr* | 53 *wǔshísān* | 54 *wǔshísì* |
| 55 *wǔshíwǔ* | 56 *wǔshíliù* | 57 *wǔshíqī* | ... | 99 *jiǔshíjiǔ* |

要 *yào* means "want" or "need". When you would like to get something in a store, you can make a request starting with 我要 *wǒ yào...* (I want or need …) or 我要买 *wǒ yào mǎi...* (I want or need to buy…)

What is the difference between 多少 *duōshao* and 几 *jǐ*? Both 多少 *duōshao* and 几 *jǐ* are question words meaning "how many" that can be used to ask for something countable. However, 多少 *duōshao* can also be used to ask for something uncountable, whereas 几 *jǐ* cannot be used for something that is not counted with a Chinese numeral word and a measure word. For example, it is correct to ask 多少钱 *duōshao qián* (how much money), but it is incorrect to replace 多少 *duōshao* with 几 *jǐ* in this question. However, if a measure word like 块 *kuài* (buck) for money is used, then it is all right: 几块钱 *jǐ kuài qián* (how many bucks of money).

四　实践　Practice

1. 对话 Conversation

A: 这书多少钱?
B: 三十五。
A: 那本呢?
B: 十块一本。
A: 三十五块的要一本。
B: 十块的买不买?
A: 买。买两本。
B: 三本书五十五块。
A: 好。给你六十。
B: 您给我六十。这是五块。

☞ 2. 交际 *Communication*

Task 1 You find the books at a book stand very interesting. Since the books there do not have any price tag, ask for the prices of one dictionary and two books.

Task 2 When the book seller tells you that the dictionary is 95 dollars, show your surprise by saying "95 is very expensive" and make a bargain by offering to pay 70 dollars.

Task 3 You lost your umbrella in a movie theater. Since this is the third time you lost an umbrella in a month, you decide to go to a local store to buy the cheapest umbrella you can find. Ask the prices of a few kinds of umbrellas and say you will buy two. Make the payment with a fifty dollar bill and get your change.

✎ 3. 书写 *Writing*

qián   money   *Piě, héng, héng, héng, shùtí; héng, héng, xiégōu, piě, diǎn.*

钱									

kuài   buck (for money)   *Héng, shù, tí; héngzhé, héng, piě, nà.*

块									

běn   [measure word for books]   *Héng, shù, piě, nà, héng.*

本									

jǐ   how many   *Piě, héngzhéwāngōu.*

几								

liǎng   two (used before a measure word)   *Héng, shù, héngzhégōu, piě, diǎn, piě, diǎn.*

两								

Dì–shíliù   kè   *Wǒ yào mǎi lán de.*

第十六课   我要买蓝的。
Lesson 16   I want to buy a blue one.

一 听与看 Listen and Read

Listen to the recording of the following sentences as many times as possible until you can say it along with the recording. You should also look at the following transcription while listening and try to imitate.

Mǎi shénme? Mǎi shénme?

买 什么？ 买 什么？
buy | what | [suffix] | buy | what | [suffix]
What to buy? What to buy?

Nǐ yào mǎi shénme?

你 要 买 什么？
you | want | buy | what | [suffix]
What do you want to buy?

Mǎi yīfu,   mǎi yīfu,

买 衣服， 买 衣服，
buy | garment | attire | buy | garment | attire
Buy clothes, buy clothes,

wǒ yào mǎi   yīfu.

我 要 买 衣服。
I | want | buy | garment | attire
I want to buy clothes.

Mǎi nǎ jiàn? Mǎi nǎ jiàn?

买 哪件？ 买 哪件？
buy | which | [meas.] | buy | which | [meas.]
Which piece? Which piece?

Nǐ yào mǎi nǎ jiàn?

你 要 买 哪件？
you | want | buy | which | [meas.]
Which piece do you want to buy?

Hóng de, lǜ de, hēi de, bái de,
红的、绿的、黑的、白的，
red | [aux.] | green | [aux.] | black | aux.] | white | [aux.]
Red one, green one, black one, and white one,

nǐ yào mǎi nǎ jiàn?
你要买哪件？
you | want | buy | which | [meas.]
which piece do you want to buy?

Lán de, lán de, lán de,
蓝的，蓝的，蓝的，
blue | [aux.] | blue | [aux.] | blue | [aux.]
Blue one, blue one, blue one,

wǒ yào mǎi lán de.
我要买蓝的。
I | want | buy | blue | [aux.]
I want to buy a blue one.

Duìbuqǐ, duìbuqǐ,
对不起，对不起，
correct | not | up | correct | not | up
I am sorry, I am sorry,

wǒmen méiyou lán de.
我们没有蓝的。
I | [plural] | not | have | blue | [aux.]
we do not have any blue one.

Méi guānxi, méi guānxi.
没关系，没关系，
not | concern | tie | not | concern | tie
Never mind, never mind,

wǒ mǎi lǜ de ba.
我买绿的吧。
I | buy | green | [aux.] | [aux.]
I'll buy a green one then.

二 看与说 Read and Speak

Now, listen to the recording while looking at the following sentences.
Then read it out aloud. Finally, recite it by heart to yourself and then to your
classmates or instructor.

买什么？买什么？

你要买什么？

买衣服，买衣服，

我要买衣服。

买哪件？买哪件？

你要买哪件？

红的、绿的、黑的、白的，

你要买哪件？

蓝的，蓝的，蓝的，

我要买蓝的。

对不起，对不起，

我们没有蓝的。

没关系，没关系，

我买绿的吧。

三 理解 Understand

件 *jiàn* is a measure word for clothes in Chinese. However, it is used for such upper garments as jackets, shirts, blouses, overcoats, and sweaters. For pants and skirts, a different measure word (条 *tiáo*) is used.

When we talk about something in different colors, we often add 的 *de* after the name of a color and omit the thing after 的 *de* if it is understood. For example, if it is understood that we are buying clothes and a blue colored piece of clothes is what we want, then we simply say 我要买蓝的 *wǒ yào mǎi lán de* (I want to buy a blue one), omitting 衣服 *yīfu* (clothes) at the end of the sentence.

对不起 *duìbuqǐ* is a fixed apologetic expression said to someone whom you feel that you have let down. To reply to this apologetic expression, you can use the fixed expression that means "never mind": 没关系 *méi guānxi*.

四 实践 Practice

1. 对话 Conversation

A: 您要买什么?

B: 我买一件衣服。

A: 你看哪件好?

B: 那件多少钱?

A: 九十。

B: 六十, 行不行?

A: 不行, 不行。八十给你。

B: 有没有蓝的?

A: 对不起, 没有蓝的。红的、绿的、黑的、白的都有。

B: 没关系, 这件绿的也行。

A: 绿的一件。给你。

B: 这是八十块。

A: 好。谢谢。

2. 交际 Communication

Task 1 You are at a popular tourist spot. A crowd of pedlars have surrounded you, trying to lure you into buying their T-shirts at a "low" price. Tell them you don't want to make any purchase. Insist on your decision by saying you won't buy any even for 10 *kuai* a piece.

Task 2 You are at a fine clothing store in downtown Beijing. You fell in love with the style of a fine sweater. You are disappointed that they don't have your favorite color black. In the end, you decide to buy a blue one since the salesperson apologizes and agrees to give you a 50 *kuai* discount.

Task 3 One of your Chinese friends likes to dress like American youths. He/she took you to a clothes store seeking your opinions of his/her choice. Tell him/her that the 80 dollar one is better than the 90 dollar one and that the green garment is better than the red one.

3. 书写 Writing

lán blue *Héng, shù, shù; shù, shù, piě, héng, diǎn, shù, héngzhé, shù, shù, héng.*

蓝											

yī garment *Diǎn, héng, piě, shùtí, piě, nà.*

衣											

fú　attire　*Piě, héngzhégōu, héng, héng; héngzhégōu, shù, héngpiě, nà.*

服							

jiàn　[measure word for clothes]　*Piě, shù; piě, héng, héng, shù.*

件							

lǜ　green　*Piězhé, piězhé, tí; héngzhé, héng, héng, shùgōu, diǎn, tí, piě, nà.*

绿							

hēi　black　*Shù, héngzhé, diǎn, piě, héng, shù, héng, héng; diǎn, diǎn, diǎn, diǎn.*

黑							

bái　white　*Piě, shù, héngzhé, héng, héng.*

白							

duì　correct　*Héngpiě, diǎn; héng, shùgōu, diǎn.*

对							

qǐ　up; rise　*Héng, shù, héng, shù, héng, piě, nà; héngzhé, héng, shùwāngōu.*

起							

guān　concern; shut　*Diǎn, piě, héng, héng, piě, nà.*

关							

xì　tie; fasten　*Piě, piězhé, piězhé, diǎn, shùgōu, diǎn, diǎn.*

系							

Dì–shíqī   kè   Xiànzài jǐ diǎn?

第十七课　现在几点？
Lesson 17　What time is it now?

一　听与看　Listen and Read

Listen to the recording of the following sentences as many times as possible until you can say it along with the recording. You should also look at the following transcription while listening and try to imitate.

Jǐ diǎn?　Jǐ diǎn?

几点？几点？

how many | o'clock | how many | o'clock

What time is it? What time is it?

Xiànzài jǐ diǎn?

现在几点？

present | at | how many | o'clock

What time is it now?

Liǎng diǎn,　liǎng diǎn,

两点，两点，

two | o'clock | two | o'clock

Two o'clock, two o'clock,

xiànzài liǎng diǎn.

现在两点。

present | at | two | o'clock

it is two o'clock now.

Jǐ diǎn?　Jǐ diǎn?

几点？几点？

how many | o'clock | how many | o'clock

What time is it? What time is it?

Xiànzài jǐ diǎn?

现在几点？

present | at | how many | o'clock

What time is it now?

Liǎng diǎn líng èr,　　liǎng diǎn líng èr,

两 点 零 二， 两 点 零 二，

two | o'clock | zero | two | two | o'clock | zero | two

Two past two, two past two

xiànzài liǎng diǎn líng èr.

现在 两 点 零 二。

present | at | two | o'clock | zero | two

it is two past two now.

Jǐ diǎn?　Jǐ diǎn?

几点？ 几点？

how many | o'clock | how many | o'clock

What time is it? What time is it?

Xiànzài jǐ diǎn?

现在几点？

present | at | how many | o'clock

What time is it now?

Liǎng diǎn yí kè,　liǎng diǎn yí kè,

两 点 一 刻， 两 点 一 刻，

two | o'clock | one | quarter | two | o'clock | one | quarter

A quarter past two, a quarter past two,

xiànzài liǎng diǎn yí kè.

现在 两 点 一 刻。

present | at | two | o'clock | one | quarter

it is a quarter past two now.

Jǐ diǎn?　Jǐ diǎn?

几点？ 几点？

how many | o'clock | how many | o'clock

What time is it? What time is it?

Xiànzài jǐ diǎn?

现在几点？

present | at | how many | o'clock

What time is it now?

Liǎng diǎn bàn, liǎng diǎn bàn,

两　点　半，两　点　半，

two | o'clock | half | two | o'clock | half

Half past two, half past two,

xiànzài liǎng diǎn bàn.

现在　两　点　半。

present | at | two | o'clock | half

it is half past two now.

Jǐ diǎn? Jǐ diǎn?

几点？几点？

how many | o'clock | how many | o'clock

What time is it? What time is it?

Xiànzài jǐ diǎn?

现在几　点？

present | at | how many | o'clock

What time is it now?

Chà wǔ fēn, chà wǔ fēn,

差　五　分，差　五　分，

lack | five | minute | lack | five | minute

Lack five minutes, lack five minutes,

sān diǎn chà wǔ fēn.

三　点差五　分。

three | o'clock | lack | five | minute

it is five to three.

二 看与说 Read and Speak

Now, listen to the recording while looking at the following sentences. Then read it out aloud. Finally, recite it by heart to yourself and then to your classmates or instructor.

几点？几点？

现在几点？

两点，两点，

现在两点。

几点？几点？

现在几点？

两点零二，两点零二，

现在两点零二。

几点？几点？

现在几点？

两点一刻，两点一刻，

现在两点一刻。

几点？几点？

现在几点？

两点半，两点半，

现在两点半。

几点？几点？

现在几点？

差五分，差五分，

三点差五分。

三 理解 Understand

现在几点 *xiànzài jǐ diǎn* is a question we use when we are curious about what time it is now. 几 *jǐ* means "how many". In Chinese, we use 几 *jǐ* (how many) rather than 什么 *shénme* (what) to ask for time because numbers are used to tell time and it is not customary in Chinese to use 什么 *shénme* (what) to ask for numbers. 点 *diǎn* means "dot" or "point", referring to the markings on the dial of a clock; therefore, it also means "o'clock" in Chinese.

We have learned that 两 *liǎng* means "two" and is usually used before a measure word in place of the word 二 *èr* in Chinese. When telling time in Chinese, two o'clock is 两点 *liǎng diǎn* rather than 二点 *èr diǎn*, which is awkward and sounds funny to a native Chinese speaker's ear. However, for twelve o'clock, it is correct to say 十二点 *shí'èr diǎn* as 两 *liǎng* is never used to represent two at the end of a non-single digit. Please also note that in Chinese, it is customary to add 零 *líng* (zero) after the hour and before a single digit number for minutes; consequently, for 2 minutes past 2 o'clock, we say 两点零二 *liǎng diǎn líng èr*, using 二 *èr* instead of 两 *liǎng* after 零 *líng*. 分 *fēn* can be omitted as long as the number for minutes requires more than one syllable to say it.

When telling the time 2:15 in Chinese, we can say 两点十五(分) *liǎng diǎn shíwǔ (fēn)*, we can also say 两点一刻 *liǎng diǎn yí kè* (a quarter past two). 一刻 *yí kè* is a quarter of an hour, and two quarters of hour equal to half an hour. If we want to express "half past two" in Chinese, then we either say 两点三十(分) *liǎng diǎn sānshí (fēn)* or 两点半 *liǎng diǎn bàn*, and it is incorrect to say 两点两刻 *liǎng diǎn liǎng kè*.

差 *chà* means "be short of" and is often used to tell the time that is less than 30 minutes close to the next hour. For example, for 2:55, we can say 两点五十五(分) *liǎng diǎn wǔshíwǔ (fēn)*, and we can also say 三点差五分 *sān diǎn chà wǔ fēn* or 差五分三点 *chà wǔ fēn sān diǎn*. What about 2:45? According to what has been explained above, we have three ways of telling this time: 1) 两点四十五(分) *liǎng diǎn sìshíwǔ (fēn)*, 2) 两点三刻 *liǎng diǎn sān kè*, and 3) 三点差一刻 *sān diǎn chà yí kè* or 差一刻三点 *chà yí kè sān diǎn*.

四　实践　Practice

1. 对话 Conversation

A: 现在几点?

B: 两点一刻。

A: 我两点半要跟朋友去买衣服。

B: 你们去哪儿买?

A: 红蓝黑。

B: 我跟你们去，行吗?

A: 行啊。我们现在去我朋友那儿吧。

B: 我去一下儿宿舍。五分钟。

A: 好吧。

2. 交际 Communication

Task 1 After eating an elaborate, prolonged dinner at your Chinese friend's home, you feel it is time to leave. Do it appropriately by first asking what time it is and then say you need to go back to your dorm to call your parents. Make sure you leave comments to the host family about how great their food is and how fine their tea is.

Task 2 Your next-door American friend tells you he/she is going to buy a bicycle. Ask what time and where he/she is going to do the shopping. Ask to go along since you want to take a look at the bicycles available in China and that you are planning to buy an inexpensive bike.

Task 3 An American classmate of yours says he/she is going to the bank. When you hear that, tell him/her that since the time is 8:00, the Bank of China doesn't have anybody working. At 8:30 bank clerks will start working.

3. 书写 Writing

diǎn   o'clock; dot   *Shù, héng, shù, héngzhé, héng; diǎn, diǎn, diǎn, diǎn.*

点

líng   zero   *Héng, diǎn, hénggōu, shù, diǎn, diǎn, diǎn, diǎn; piě, nà, diǎn, héngpiě, diǎn.*

零

kè   quarter (of an hour); engrave   *Diǎn, héng, piězhé, piě, piě, diǎn; shù, shùgōu.*

刻

bàn   half   *Diǎn, piě, héng, héng, shù.*

半

chà   short of   *Diǎn, piě, héng, héng, héng, piě, héng, shù, héng.*

差

fēn   minute; divide; cent   *Piě, nà; héngzhégōu, piě.*

分

Dì-shíbā   kè   Wǒmen   qù   kàn   jǐ   diǎn   de   diànyǐng?

第十八课   我们去看几点的电影?
Lesson 18   What time's movie are we going to see?

一 听与看 Listen and Read

Listen to the recording of the following sentences as many times as possible until you can say it along with the recording. You should also look at the following transcription while listening and try to imitate.

Yǒu kòngr ma?   Yǒu kòngr ma?

有空儿吗? 有空儿吗?
have | leisure | [suffix] | [ques.] | have | leisure | [suffix] | [ques.]

Will you have leisure time? Will you have leisure time?

Míngtiān wǎnshang yǒu kòngr ma?

明天   晚上 有空儿吗?
bright | day | evening | up | have | leisure | [suffix] | [ques.]

Will you have leisure time tomorrow evening?

Yǒu kòngr,   Yǒu kòngr,

有空儿, 有空儿,
have | leisure | [suffix] | have | leisure | [suffix]

I will, I will,

míngtiān wǎnshang wǒ yǒu kòngr.

明天   晚上 我有空儿。
bright | day | evening | up | I | have | leisure | [suffix]

I will have leisure time tomorrow evening.

Kàn diànyǐng,   Kàn diànyǐng,

看 电影 , 看 电影 ,
look | electric | shadow | look | electric | shadow

See a movie, see a movie,

wǒmen qù kàn diànyǐng ba.

我们去看 电影吧。
I | [plural] | go | look | electric | shadow | [aux.]

let's go to see a movie.

Jǐ diǎn de?   Jǐ diǎn de?
几点的？ 几点的？
how many | o'clock | [aux.] | how many | o'clock | [aux.]
What time's movie? What time's movie?

Wǒmen qù kàn jǐ diǎn de?
我们去看几点的？
I | [plural] | go | look | how many | o'clock | [aux.]
What time's movie are we going to see?

Bā diǎn de,   Bā diǎn de,
八点的， 八点的，
eight | o'clock | [aux.] | eight | o'clock | [aux.]
The movie at eight o'clock, the movie at eight o'clock,

wǒmen qù kàn bā diǎn de.
我们去看八点的。
I | [plural] | go | look | eight | o'clock | [aux.]
we are going to see the movie at eight o'clock.

Hǎo a,   hǎo a,
好啊， 好啊，
good | [aux.] | good | [aux.]
Good, good,

qī diǎn bàn,   zàijiàn.
七点半， 再见。
seven | o'clock | half | again | see
see you at seven thirty.

二 看与说 Read and Speak

Now, listen to the recording while looking at the following sentences. Then read it out aloud. Finally, recite it by heart to yourself and then to your classmates or instructor.

有空儿吗？ 有空儿吗？

明天晚上有空儿吗？

有空儿，有空儿，

明天晚上我有空儿。

看电影，看电影，

我们去看电影吧。

几点的？几点的？

我们去看几点的？

八点的，八点的，

我们去看八点的。

好啊，好啊，

七点半，再见。

三 理解 Understand

明天晚上有空儿吗 *míngtiān wǎnshang yǒu kòngr ma* is a question in Chinese to ask if someone has any leisure time tomorrow evening. Notice three things: 1) the 2nd person pronoun 你 *nǐ* (you) is often omitted when it is obvious, just as we omit "you" in English when giving a command, such as "close the door"; 2) the time expression 明天晚上 *míngtiān wǎnshang* (tomorrow evening) appears at the beginning of the sentence, and it would be incorrect to have the time expression placed at the end of the sentence as commonly done in English; and 3) whether it is now or in the future, the verb form of 有 *yǒu* remains the same. The concept of time for an action or event is expressed and understood mainly through time expressions, context, and sentence structures with auxiliary words, which we will learn in this book later.

With 吧 *ba* at the end of the statement, 我们去看电影吧 *wǒmen qù kàn diànyǐng ba* is a suggestion, and from the context, it can be understood that the action of seeing a movie is suggested for tomorrow evening. As the specific time of seeing a movie tomorrow evening needs to be clarified, the question 我们去看几点的电影 *wǒmen qù kàn jǐ diǎn de diànyǐng* (which time's movie are we going to see) is raised. The question could have been phrased as 我们几点去看电影 *wǒmen jǐ diǎn qù kàn diànyǐng* (at what time are we going to see a movie), but when there is a schedule for movie shows, the question is about which time's movie to see. Because 电影 *diànyǐng* is understood as the topic of the conversation, it is omitted in the question: 我们去看几点的 *wǒmen qù kàn jǐ diǎn de*?

再见 *zàijiàn* is a commonly used expression, meaning "goodbye". We can also say 明天见 *míngtiān jiàn*, meaning "see you tomorrow".

四 实践 Practice

1. 对话 Conversation

A: 明天晚上你有空儿吗？

B: 有空儿。

A: 明天我们去看一个电影吧！

B: 什么电影？

A:《老人国》。

B: 多少钱？

A: 一个人二十五。

B: 我们看几点的？

A: 八点的。

B: 好啊！我几点去你宿舍？

A: 七点半，行吗？

B: 行。再见。

👆 2. 交际 Communication

Task 1 It is Friday night. You are happy that you don't have to worry about homework and tests for a while. Call a Chinese friend for his/her availability for an 8:00 o'clock movie and invite him/her to see a popular American movie that is just released.

Task 2 After a delicious dinner and a relaxing movie, invite your Chinese friends to your dorm room to chat in Chinese while drinking tea and eating American candies you brought from home.

Task 3 After a month's study, you feel that your old dictionary is no longer good enough for your level of learning. Call your Chinese-speaking partner to see if he/she is available the next day to go to 贵友书店 *Guìyǒu Shūdiàn* with you for a better dictionary. Ask your Chinese friend what time tomorrow he/she is free and say that you will go to his dorm to meet him/her at a mutually convenient time.

✏️ 3. 书写 Writing

kàn look *Piě, héng, héng, piě; shù, héngzhé, héng, héng, héng.*

看									

kòng leisure; empty *Diǎn, diǎn, hénggōu, piě, diǎn; héng, shù, héng.*

空									

míng bright *Shù, héngzhé, héng, héng; piě, héngzhégōu, héng, héng.*

明									

tiān　day　*Héng, héng, piě, nà.*

天

wǎn　evening; late　*Shù, héngzhé, héng, héng; piě, héngpiě, shù, héngzhé, héng, piě, shùwāngōu.*

晚

shàng　up　*Shù, héng, héng.*

上

yǐng　shadow　*Shù, héngzhé, héng, héng; diǎn, héng, shù, héngzhé, héng, shùgōu, diǎn, diǎn; piě, piě, piě.*

影

zài　again　*Héng, shù, héngzhégōu, shù, héng, héng.*

再

jiàn　see　*Shù, héngzhé, piě, shùwāngōu.*

见

Dì–shíjiǔ   kè   *Wǒmen   zěnme   qù?*

第十九课   我们怎么去？

Lesson 19   How are we going there?

一 听与看 Listen and Read

Listen to the recording of the following sentences as many times as possible until you can say it along with the recording. You should also look at the following transcription while listening and try to imitate.

Chāoshì, Chāoshì,

超市，超市，
super | market | super | market
Supermarket, supermarket,

wǒmen qù chāoshì.

我们去超市。
I | [plural] | go | super | market
we are going to a supermarket.

Zěnme qù? Zěnme qù?

怎么去？怎么去？
how | [suffix] | go | how | [suffix] | go
How to go there? How to go there?

Wǒmen zěnme qù?

我们怎么去？
I | [plural] | how | [suffix] | go
How are we going there?

Zuò chē qù,   zuò chē qù,

坐 车 去， 坐 车 去，
sit | vehicle | go | sit | vehicle | go
Go there by bus, go there by bus,

wǒmen zuò chē qù.

我们坐 车 去。
I | [plural] | sit | vehicle | go
we are going there by bus.

Gōngyuán, gōngyuán,

公园，公园，

public | garden | public | garden

Park, park,

wǒmen qù gōngyuán.

我们去 公园 。

I | [plural] | go | public | garden

we are going to a park.

Zěnme qù? Zěnme qù?

怎么去？怎么去？

how | [suffix] | go | how | [suffix] | go

How to go there? How to go there?

Wǒmen zěnme qù?

我们 怎么去？

I | [plural] | how | [suffix] | go

How are we going there?

Qí chē qù, qí chē qù,

骑车去，骑车去，

ride | vehicle | go | ride | vehicle | go

Go there by bike, go there by bike,

wǒmen qí chē qù.

我们骑车去。

I | [plural] | ride | vehicle | go

we are going there by bike.

Fànguǎnr, fànguǎnr,

饭馆儿，饭馆儿，

meal | hall | [suffix] | meal | hall | [suffix]

Restaurant, restaurant,

wǒmen qù fànguǎnr.

我们去饭馆儿。

I | [plural] | go | meal | hall | [suffix]

we are going to a restaurant.

Zěnme qù?   Zěnme qù?

怎么去？怎么去？

how | [suffix] | go | how | [suffix] | go

How to go there? How to go there?

Wǒmen zěnme qù?

我们怎么去？

I | [plural] | how | [suffix] | go

How are we going there?

Zǒu lù qù,   zǒu lù qù,

走路去，走路去，

walk | road | go | walk | road | go

Go there on foot, go there on foot,

wǒmen zǒu lù qù.

我们走路去。

I | [plural] | walk | road | go

we are going there on foot.

Jīchǎng,   jīchǎng,

机场，机场，

machine | open space | machine | open space

Airport, airport,

wǒmen qù jīchǎng.

我们去机场。

I | [plural] | go | machine | open space

we are going to the airport.

Zěnme qù?   Zěnme qù?

怎么去？怎么去？

how | [suffix] | go | how | [suffix] | go

How to go there? How to go there?

Wǒmen zěnme qù?

我们怎么去？

I | [plural] | how | [suffix] | go

How are we going there?

Dǎ dī qù,   Dǎ dī qù,
打的去，打的去，
hit | **taxi** | go | hit | **taxi** | go
Go there by taxi, go there by taxi,

wǒmen dǎ dī qù.
我们打的去。
I | [plural] | hit | **taxi** | go
we are going there by taxi.

二 看与说 Read and Speak

Now, listen to the recording while looking at the following sentences. Then read it out aloud. Finally, recite it by heart to yourself and then to your classmates or instructor.

超市，超市，

我们去超市。

怎么去？怎么去？

我们怎么去？

坐车去，坐车去，

我们坐车去。

公园，公园，

我们去公园。

怎么去？怎么去？

我们怎么去?
骑车去，骑车去，
我们骑车去。

饭馆儿，饭馆儿，
我们去饭馆儿。
怎么去？怎么去？
我们怎么去？
走路去，走路去，
我们走路去。

机场，机场，
我们去机场。
怎么去？怎么去？
我们怎么去？
打的去，打的去，
我们打的去。

三　理解　Understand

We have learned many question words in Chinese so far. It is a good time to review them:

吗 *ma* (yes-no question): 你忙吗?

呢 *ne* (elliptical question): 我很忙。你呢?

吧 *ba* (confirmation question): 这是你的书吧?

谁 *shuí/shéi* (who): 他是谁?

什么 *shénme* (what): 他要吃什么?

哪 *nǎ* (which): 他是哪国人?

哪儿 *nǎr* (where): 他要去哪儿?

多少 *duōshao* (how many / how much): 这本书多少钱?

几 *jǐ* (how many): 他要买几本书?

The first three question words (吗 *ma*, 呢 *ne*, and 吧 *ba*) appear at the end of a sentence or a phrase and turn the sentence or the phrase into a question. The rest of the question words (谁 *shéi*, 什么 *shénme*, 哪 *nǎ*, 哪儿 *nǎr*, 多少 *duōshao*, and 几 *jǐ*) are different because a question is formed by inserting one of them in a sentence at a place where information is needed without the trouble of changing the original sentence order. To answer the question formed by one of these question words, we usually just provide the needed information in place of the question word in the question.

Q: 他是**谁**?　　　　　　A: 他是**我朋友**。

Q: 他要吃**什么**?　　　　A: 他要吃**饺子**。

Q: 他是**哪**国人?　　　　A: 他是**中**国人。

Q: 他要去**哪儿**?　　　　A: 他要去**书店**。

Q: 这本书**多少**钱?　　　A: 这本书**二十块**钱。

Q: 他要买**几**本书?　　　A: 他要买**两**本书。

怎么 *zěnme* (how) in this lesson is another question word in Chinese. We use it to ask for ways to get something done or find out the manner of an action. If we go somewhere and we want to know how we will get there, we can ask: 我们怎么去 *wǒmen zěnme qù*? To answer this question, we simply provide the needed information in place of the question word 怎么 *zěnme* in the question. There are several ways that people can go from one place to another. The following four can be used to answer the question:

坐车 *zuò chē* (by bus)   →   我们坐车去。
骑车 *qí chē* (by bike)   →   我们骑车去。
走路 *zǒu lù* (on foot)   →   我们走路去。
打的 *dǎ dī* (by taxi)   →   我们打的去。

车 *chē* in Chinese is a generic term for all things that have wheels and help people to travel. As sitting (坐 *zuò*) is considered by Chinese as the usual way of taking a bus, taking a bus in Chinese is 坐车 *zuò chē*. Likewise, as riding (骑 *qí*) is what people do when traveling with a bike, riding a bike in Chinese is 骑车 *qí chē*. When no vehicle is used, people walk (走 *zǒu*) on the road (路 *lù*). Traveling on foot in Chinese is 走路 *zǒu lù*. A colloquial expression for taking a taxi is 打的 *dǎ dī*. 打 *dǎ* is a versatile Chinese word that can be used to refer to many different actions, and it means "taking" here. 的 is pronounced *dī* rather than de in this expression, and it is an abbreviated transliteration word in Cantonese for 的士 *dīshì* (taxi). So, 打的 *dǎ dī* is to take a taxi.

四 实践 Practice

1. 对话 Conversation

A: 明天我有一个美国朋友要来。
B: 你去机场要打的吗?
A: 不用打的。我坐车去。
B: 回大学呢?
A: 回大学我跟朋友打的。
B: 明天晚上你们做什么?
A: 我们要去超市。

B: 我也要去。你们几点去?
A: 六点。
B: 我跟你们去，行吗?
A: 好啊! 你要坐车去吗?
B: 不坐。我们走路去吧。
A: 行。

☞ 2. 交际 Communication

Task 1 Finally the weekend is here. You invite your Chinese friend to go to a park. When he/she asks you about the time to leave and the transportation means, say that you will leave at 9 o'clock and suggest that you go by bus instead of by taxi since it costs just one dollar to take the bus.

Task 2 You plan to go to the local supermarket. Try to borrow your roommate's bike. Tell him/her what time you will need the bus and what time you will return it.

Task 3 Your Chinese friend invites you to see a Chinese movie. Ask him/her the name of the movie, the time of the movie and how you are planning to get there.

3. 书写 Writing

zěn   how   *Piě, héng, shù, héng, héng; diǎn, wògōu, diǎn, diǎn.*

怎								

chāo   super; surpass   *Héng, shù, héng, shù, héng, piě, nà; héngzhégōu, piě, shù, héngzhé, héng.*

超								

shì   market; municipality   *Diǎn, héng, shù, héngzhégōu, shù.*

市									

zuò   sit   *Piě, diǎn, piě, diǎn, héng, shù, héng.*

坐									

gōng   public   *Piě, nà, piězhé, diǎn.*

公									

yuán   garden   *Shù, héngzhé, héng, héng, piě, shùwāngōu, héng.*

园									

qí   ride   *Héngzhé, shùzhézhégōu, tí; héng, piě, diǎn, héng, shù, héngzhé, héng, shùgōu.*

骑									

fàn   meal   *Piě, hénggōu, shùtí; piě, piě, héngpiě, nà.*

饭									

guǎn   hall   *Piě, hénggōu, shùtí; diǎn, diǎn, hénggōu, shù, héngzhé, héng, héngzhé, héng.*

馆									

zǒu   walk   *Héng, shù, héng, shù, héng, piě, nà.*

走									

lù   road   *Shù, héngzhé, héng, shù, héng, shù, tí; piě, héngpiě, nà, shù, héngzhé, héng.*

路									

jī   machine   *Héng, shù, piě, diǎn; piě, héngzhéwāngōu.*

机								

chǎng   open space   *Héng, shù, tí; héngzhézhézhégōu, piě, piě.*

场								

第二十课   每天你几点起床？
Lesson 20   When do you get up every day?

一 听与看   Listen and Read

Listen to the recording of the following sentences as many times as possible until you can say it along with the recording. You should also look at the following transcription while listening and try to imitate.

Měi tiān, měi tiān,
每天，每天，
every | day | every | day
Every day, every day,

nǐ jǐ diǎn qǐ chuáng?
你几点 起 床 ？
you | how many | o'clock | rise | bed
when do you get up?

Liù diǎn qǐ chuáng,
六 点 起 床 ，
six | o'clock | rise | bed
Get up at six o'clock,

wǒ liù diǎn qǐ chuáng.
我六点 起 床 。
I | six | o'clock | rise | bed
I get up at six o'clock.

Měi tiān,   měi tiān,
每天，每天，
every | day | every | day
Every day, every day,

nǐ jǐ diǎn chī zǎofàn?
你几点 吃早饭？
you | how many | o'clock | eat | early | meal
when do you have breakfast?

Qī diǎn chī zǎofàn,

七点 吃早饭，

seven | o'clock | eat | **early** | meal

Have breakfast at seven o'clock,

wǒ qī diǎn chī zǎofàn.

我七点 吃早饭。

I | seven | o'clock | eat | **early** | meal

I have breakfast at seven o'clock.

Měi tiān, měi tiān,

每天，每天，

every | day | **every** | day

Every day, every day,

nǐ jǐ diǎn shàng kè?

你几点 上 课?

you | how many | o'clock | have | class

when do you have a class?

Bā diǎn shàng kè,

八点 上 课，

eight | o'clock | have | class

Have a class at eight o'clock,

wǒ bā diǎn shàng kè.

我八点 上 课。

I | eight | o'clock | have | class

I have a class at eight o'clock.

Měi tiān, měi tiān,

每天，每天，

every | day | **every** | day

Every day, every day,

nǐ jǐ diǎn shuì jiào?

你几点 睡 觉?

you | how many | o'clock | **sleep** | a sleep

when do you sleep?

Shíyī diǎn,   shíyī diǎn,
十一点，十一点，
ten | one | o'clock | ten | one | o'clock
Eleven o'clock, eleven o'clock,

wǒ   shíyī diǎn shuì   jiào.
我十一点 睡 觉。
I | ten | one | o'clock | sleep | a sleep
I go to bed at eleven o'clock.

二　看与说　Read and Speak

　　Now, listen to the recording while looking at the following sentences. Then read it out aloud. Finally, recite it by heart to yourself and then to your classmates or instructor.

每天，每天，
你几点起床？
六点起床，
我六点起床。

每天，每天，
你几点吃早饭？
七点吃早饭，
我七点吃早饭。

每天，每天，

你几点上课?

八点上课,

我八点上课。

每天,每天,

你几点睡觉?

十一点,十一点,

我十一点睡觉。

三 理解 Understand

In Chinese, the words and phrases expressing a point of time are always placed before the action and after the doer or the topic of a sentence. However, they can also be placed at the very beginning of a sentence. It would be incorrect in Chinese to place them after the action or at the end of a sentence as in English.

我每天六点起床。(correct)
每天我六点起床。(correct)
每天六点我起床。(correct)
*我每天起床八点。(wrong)
*我八点起床每天。(wrong)
*我起床每天八点。(wrong)

四　实践　Practice

🎧 1. 对话 Conversation

A: 你做什么工作?

B: 我不工作。我在大学学习。

A: 你学习什么?

B: 我学习汉语。

A: 你们在大学忙吗?

B: 很忙。

A: 你每天几点起床?

B: 六点半起床。

A: 几点吃早饭?

B: 七点吃。

A: 几点上课?

B: 八点上课。

A: 你坐车去吗?

B: 不用坐。我走路去。

A: 你晚上几点睡觉?

B: 十一点睡。

🤝 2. 交际 Communication

> **Task 1**　When you visit your host family, they ask you about your daily life at your home university. Tell them that you often go to bed at 12:00 p.m.. When they show their surprise, tell them that you often get up at 9:00 since you do not have 8:00 class.

Task 2 On a hot summer evening, you and your Chinese friend are in a bar savoring the freshly-made pure fruit cold drink. Your Chinese friend asks you what kind of food you eat for breakfast in your home country. Say that you get up at 10 o'clock and do not eat breakfast. When you ask the same question to your Chinese friend, he/she says he/she gets up at 7 o'clock but doesn't eat breakfast either. He/she just eats candy and drinks tea.

Task 3 You are on a bus going to a tourist spot. Since you are sitting next to a female Chinese language instructor, you decide to chat with her to practice your Chinese and at the same time learn about her daily life. Ask 1) whether the job keeps her busy, 2) what time she usually gets up, 3) what she often eats for breakfast, 4) what transportation means she uses to get to school, 5) whether her workload is heavy (many classes), and 6) what time she usually goes to bed.

3. 书写 Writing

měi   every   *Piě, héng, piězhé, héngzhégōu, diǎn, héng, diǎn.*

每								

chuáng   bed   *Diǎn, héng, piě; héng, shù, piě, nà.*

床								

zǎo   early   *Shù, héngzhé, héng, héng; héng, shù.*

早								

shuì   sleep   *Shù, héngzhé, héng, héng, héng; piě, héng, shù, héng, shù, shù, héng, héng.*

睡									

jiào   a sleep   *Diǎn, diǎn, piě, diǎn, hénggōu; shù, héngzhé, piě, shùwāngōu.*

觉									

Dì-èrshíyī   kè   Měi tiān   qǐ chuáng   yǐhòu,   nǐ zuò shénme?

第二十一课 每天起床以后，你做什么？
Lesson 21   **What do you do after getting up every day?**

一 听与看 Listen and Read

Listen to the recording of the following sentences as many times as possible until you can say it along with the recording. You should also look at the following transcription while listening and try to imitate.

Měi tiān qǐ chuáng yǐhòu,   nǐ zuò shénme?
每天起床以后，你做什么？
every | day | rise | bed | [prefix] | back | you | do | what | [suffix]
What do you do after getting up every day?

Wǒ qù duànliàn.
我去锻炼。
I | go | forge | smelt
I go to have a workout.

Měi tiān duànliàn yǐhòu,   nǐ zuò shénme?
每天锻炼以后，你做什么？
every | day | forge | smelt | [prefix] | back | you | do | what | [suffix]
What do you do after having a workout every day?

Wǒ qù xǐ zǎo.
我去洗澡。
I | go | wash | bath
I go to take a bath.

Měi tiān xǐ zǎo yǐhòu,   nǐ zuò shénme?
每天洗澡以后，你做什么？
every | day | wash | bath | [prefix] | back | you | do | what | [suffix]
What do you do after taking a bath every day?

Wǒ qù chī fàn.
我去吃饭。
I | go | eat | meal
I go to eat a meal.

Měi tiān chī fàn yǐhòu,　　nǐ zuò shénme?

每 天 吃饭 以后， 你 做 什么？

every | day | eat | meal | [prefix] | back | you | do | what | [suffix]

What do you do after eating a meal every day?

Wǒ qù shàng kè.

我 去 上 课。

I | go | up | class

I go to attend a class.

Měi tiān xià kè yǐhòu,　　nǐ zuò shénme?

每 天 下 课 以后， 你 做 什么？

every | day | down | class | [prefix] | back | you | do | what | [suffix]

What do you do after the class is over every day?

Wǒ chūqù wánr.

我 出去 玩 儿。

I | exit | go | play | [suffix]

I go out to have fun.

二　看与说　Read and Speak

Now, listen to the recording while looking at the following sentences. Then read it out aloud. Finally, recite it by heart to yourself and then to your classmates or instructor.

每天起床以后，你做什么？

我去锻炼。

每天锻炼以后，你做什么？

我去洗澡。

每天洗澡以后，你做什么？

我去吃饭。

每天吃饭以后，你做什么？

我去上课。

每天下课以后，你做什么？

我出去玩儿。

三　理解　Understand

以后 *yǐhòu* means "after" in Chinese. However, unlike the word "after" in English, it is attached to the end of a word, phrase, or clause. In English we say "after getting up everyday", but in Chinese we say 每天起床以后 *měi tiān qǐ chuáng yǐhòu*. If the English word order with "after" is used in Chinese, then it is wrong. For example,

> *měi tiān　qǐ chuáng　yǐhòu*
> 每天 起 床 以后 (correct)

> *yǐhòu　měi tiān　qǐ chuáng*
> 以后每天 起 床 (wrong)

Since any word, phrase, or clause attached with 以后 *yǐhòu* at its end expresses a time, it has to be placed before the major action of the sentence, and it is awkward to put it after the major action. Again, it is all right to put the subject or the doer before or after the time expression. For example,

> *Měi tiān　qǐ chuáng yǐhòu,　wǒ qù duànliàn.*
> 每天 起 床 以后，我去锻炼。 (correct)

> *Wǒ měi tiān　qǐ chuáng yǐhòu,　qù duànliàn.*
> 我每天 起 床 以后，去锻炼。 (correct)

> *Wǒ qù duànliàn　měi tiān　qǐ chuáng yǐhòu.*
> 我去锻炼 每天 起 床 以后。 (wrong)

四 实践 Practice

1. 对话 Conversation

A: 你每天几点起床?

B: 六点半。你几点起床?

A: 九点。你起床以后做什么?

B: 去锻炼。

A: 你怎么锻炼?

B: 我走路,骑车。

A: 锻炼以后,你做什么?

B: 洗澡,吃早饭。

A: 我起床很晚,不吃早饭。

B: 有人说,不吃早饭不好。

A: 我妈也说不好。你们几点上课?

B: 八点上。十二点下课。

A: 下午有课吗?

B: 没有。

A: 那我们出去玩儿,好吗?

B: 好啊。

2. 交际 Communication

Task 1 You slept in on a Saturday morning. After lunch you feel that you want to find somebody to see a movie. Call a Chinese friend to ask if he/she has some free time after dinner. If the answer is positive, invite him/her to see a movie with you.

Task 2 During your class recess time, ask a classmate whether he/she would like to go to the bookstore with you when class is over. Say that you need to buy a new dictionary.

Task 3 It is about 8:00 a.m. on a Sunday morning. You are waken up by the ringing of your phone. When you pick up the phone, you find that it is your Chinese speaking partner who has called to invite you to go to a local park with a few Chinese students. Ask 1) if they can wait till after you take a shower 2) if they are all riding their bikes to the park.

 3. 书写 Writing

yǐ [prefix for localizers] *Shùtí, diǎn, piě, diǎn.*

以									

hòu back; behind *Piě, piě, héng, shù, héngzhé, héng.*

后									

duàn forge *Piě, héng, héng, héng, shùtí; piě, shù, héng, héng, tí; piě, héngzhéwān, héngpiě, nà,.*

锻									

liàn smelt *Diǎn, piě, piě, diǎn; héng, piězhé, héngzhégōu, diǎn, diǎn.*

炼									

xǐ wash *Diǎn, diǎn, tí; piě, héng, shù, héng, piě, shùwāngōu.*

洗									

zǎo bath *Diǎn, diǎn, tí; shù, héngzhé, héng, shù, héngzhé, héng, shù, héngzhé, héng, héng, shù, piě, nà.*

澡

chū exit *Shùzhé, shù, shù, shùzhé, shù.*

出

wán play; have fun *Héng, héng, shù, tí; héng, héng, piě, shùwāngōu.*

玩

Dì-èrshí'èr   kè   Nín yào hē diǎnr   shénme?

第二十二课　您要喝点儿什么？

Lesson 22   What would you like to drink?

一　听与看　Listen and Read

Listen to the recording of the following sentences as many times as possible until you can say it along with the recording. You should also look at the following transcription while listening and try to imitate.

Hē diǎnr shénme? Hē diǎnr shénme?

喝点儿什么？喝点儿什么？

drink | dot | [suffix] | what | [suffix] | drink | dot | [suffix] | what | [suffix]

Something to drink? Something to drink?

Nín yào hē diǎnr shénme?

您 要喝点儿什么？

[respectful form of "you"] | want | drink | dot | [suffix] | what | [suffix]

Would you like something to drink?

Hóngchá háishi lǜchá?

红茶 还是绿茶？

red | tea | also | be | green | tea

Black tea or green tea?

Kělè   háishi Xuěbì?

可乐还是雪碧？

able | delight | also | be | snow | bluish green

Coke or Sprite?

Lái bēi kāfēi,   lái bēi kāfēi,

来杯咖啡，来杯咖啡，

come | cup | transliteration (coffee) | come | cup | transliteration (coffee)

A cup of coffee, please; a cup of coffee, please;

gěi wǒ lái bēi kāfēi.

给我来杯咖啡。

to | me | come | cup | transliteration (coffee)

a cup of coffee for me, please.

Bù hǎoyìsi,   bù hǎoyìsi,

不好意思，不好意思，

not | good | intention | thinking | not | good | intention | thinking

I am sorry, I am sorry,

Wǒmen méiyou kāfēi.

我们 没有咖啡。

I | [plural] | not | have | transliteration (coffee)

we do not have coffee.

Nà ...,   nà ...,

那……，那……，

that | that

Then…, then…,

lái píng píjiǔ,   lái píng píjiǔ,

来瓶啤酒，来瓶啤酒，

come | bottle | beer | alcohol | come | bottle | beer | alcohol

a bottle of beer, please; a bottle of beer, please;

lái píng píjiǔ ba.

来瓶啤酒吧。

come | bottle | beer | alcohol | [aux.]

a bottle of beer, please.

二 看与说 **Read and Speak**

Now, listen to the recording while looking at the following sentences. Then read it out aloud. Finally, recite it by heart to yourself and then to your classmates or instructor.

喝点儿什么？喝点儿什么？

您要喝点儿什么？

红茶还是绿茶？

可乐还是雪碧?

来杯咖啡，来杯咖啡，

给我来杯咖啡。

不好意思，不好意思，

我们没有咖啡。

那……，那……，

来瓶啤酒，来瓶啤酒，

来瓶啤酒吧。

三 理解 Understand

点儿 *diǎnr* is used as a quantifier, meaning "a little bit of". It is used to soften the tone. "I want to have some tea" in Chinese is 我要喝点儿茶 *wǒ yào hē diǎnr chá*. If what to drink is in question, then use 什么 *shénme* in place of 茶 *chá* like this: 喝点儿什么 *hē diǎnr shénme*?

还是 *háishi*, which means "or", is used to form an alternative question. For example,

---

Xiànzài liǎng diǎn háishi sān diǎn?
现在 两 点还是三点?
Is it two o'clock **or** three o'clock now?

Nǐ shì gēge háishi dìdi?
你是哥哥还是弟弟?
Are you an elder brother **or** a younger brother?

Nǐ yào chī zhūròu jiǎozi háishi sùcài jiǎozi?
你要吃猪肉饺子还是素菜饺子?
Do you want to eat pork dumplings **or** vegetable dumplings?

Because 还是 *háishi* is used exclusively to form questions in Chinese, do not use it to mean "or" in a statement. For "or" in a statement in Chinese, we have to use another word: 或者 *huòzhě*. For example,

> *Wǒ měi tiān liù diǎn **huòzhě** qī diǎn qǐchuáng.*
> 我每天六点 **或者**七点 起床。
> I get up at six **or** seven o'clock everyday.

杯 *bēi* (cup) and 瓶 *píng* (bottle) are also measure words. "One cup of coffee" in Chinese is 一杯咖啡 *yì bēi kāfēi*, and "one bottle of beer" is 一瓶 啤酒 *yì píng píjiǔ*. If the numeral is one before a measure word, then it can be omitted when used after an action. For example,

> *Hē píng píjiǔ.*
> 喝瓶啤酒。
> Drink a bottle of beer.

> *Mǎi jiàn yīfu.*
> 买件衣服。
> Buy a piece of clothing.

来 *lái* originally means "come", but it is often used when ordering food or drinks, meaning "bring". Therefore, "a cup of coffee, please" in Chinese is 来杯咖啡 *lái bēi kāfēi*.

不好意思 *bù hǎoyìsi* is a fixed phrase that means "feeling embarrassed" and is often used as an apologetic expression.

那 *nà* means "that", but it can also be used to mean "then" or "in that case", leading out an alternative solution.

四　实践　Practice

1. 对话 Conversation

A: 您好!
B: 你好。三个人。

A: 跟我来。请！ 您要喝点儿什么？

B: 你们都有什么？

A: 红茶、绿茶、可乐、雪碧 ……

B: 有咖啡吗？

A: 不好意思，没有。

B: 那 ……，来瓶啤酒吧！

A: 您要吃点儿什么？

B: 我看看。

A: 好。

B: 这个要一个，这个要两个。

A: 好。

2. 交际 Communication

Task 1 For your Chinese friend's birthday, you decide to take him/her out to an elegant bar. Ask the waiter about the kinds of drinks available and order one drink for your friend and one for yourself.

Task 2 After eating at the school cafeteria for a whole week, you decide you should try some local restaurants within the vicinity of your host Chinese university area. Order some vegetarian dumplings. For other entries which you have not learned how to say their names, just look at the photos on the menu and point at the most appealing food and order by saying this one, this one and that one.

Task 3 Before leaving China, you plan to buy some tea for your friends as presents. Among the many kinds of green tea, you would like to buy the kind you drank at your host family's apartment. When you find out that kind is out of stock, ask if any will be in stock tomorrow. If yes, say you will come to buy it tomorrow. If not, show your hesitation by saying 那 *nà*... and then point at your second choice green tea and say you will buy that one instead.

3. 书写 Writing

kě able *Héng, shù, héngzhé, héng, shùgōu.*

可

lè delight *Piě, shùzhé, shùgōu, diǎn, diǎn.*

乐

xuě snow *Héng, diǎn, hénggōu, shù, diǎn, diǎn, diǎn, diǎn; héngzhé, héng, héng.*

雪

bì bluish green *Héng, héng, shù, tí; piě, shù, héngzhé, héng, héng; héng, piě, shù, héngzhé, héng.*

碧

bēi cup *Héng, shù, piě, diǎn; héng, piě, shù, diǎn.*

杯

kā [transliteration] *Shù, héngzhé, héng; héngzhégōu, piě; shù, héngzhé, héng.*

咖

fēi [transliteration] *Shù, héngzhé, héng; héng, héng, héng, shù, shù, héng, héng, héng.*

啡

yì intention *Diǎn, héng, diǎn, piě, héng; shù, héngzhé, héng, héng; diǎn, wògōu, diǎn, diǎn.*

意

sī thinking *Shù, héngzhé, héng, shù, héng; diǎn, wògōu, diǎn, diǎn.*

思

píng   bottle   *Diǎn, piě, héng, héng, piě, shù; héng, shùtí, héngzhéwāngōu, diǎn.*

瓶

pí   beer   *Shù, héngzhé, héng; piě, shù, héngzhé, héng, héng, piě, héng, shù.*

啤

jiǔ   alcohol   *Diǎn, diǎn, tí; héng, shù, héngzhé, piě, shùwān, héng, héng.*

酒

Dì–èrshísān   kè   *Dàifu   bú ràng tā hē.*

第二十三课 大夫不让他喝。
Lesson 23   **The doctor does not allow him to drink.**

一 听与看 Listen and Read

Listen to the recording of the following sentences as many times as possible until you can say it along with the recording. You should also look at the following transcription while listening and try to imitate.

Chī ròu,   chī ròu,
吃肉，吃肉，
eat | meat | eat | meat
Eat meat, eat meat,

tā tè ài chī ròu.
他特爱吃肉。
he | **especially** | **love** | eat | meat
he especially loves to eat meat.

Chī ròu,   chī ròu,
吃肉，吃肉，
eat | meat | eat | meat
Eat meat, eat meat,

wǒ qǐng tā chī ròu.
我请他吃肉。
I | invite | him | eat | meat
I treat him to meat.

Wènwen dàifu,   wènwen dàifu,
问问大夫，问问大夫，
ask | **big** | **man** | ask | **big** | **man**
Ask the doctor, ask the doctor,

nǐ qù wènwen dàifu.
你去问问大夫。
you | go | ask | **big** | **man**
you go and ask the doctor.

Bié qǐng tā chī,   bié qǐng tā chī,
别 请 他 吃，别 请 他 吃，
don't | invite | he | eat | don't | invite | he | eat
Don't treat him to meat, don't treat him to meat,

dàifu   bú ràng tā chī.
大夫不让他吃。
big | man | not | allow | him | eat
the doctor does not allow him to eat it.

Hē jiǔ,   hē jiǔ,
喝 酒，喝 酒，
drink | alcohol | drink | alcohol
Have a drink, have a drink,

tā tè   ài hē jiǔ.
他特爱喝酒。
he | especially | love | drink | alcohol
he especially loves to have a drink.

Hē jiǔ,   hē jiǔ,
喝 酒，喝 酒，
drink | alcohol | drink | alcohol
Have a drink, have a drink,

wǒ qǐng tā hē jiǔ.
我请他喝酒。
I | invite | him | drink | alcohol
I treat him to a drink.

Wènwen yīshēng,   wènwen yīshēng,
问问 医生，问问 医生，
ask | cure | person | ask | cure | person
Ask the doctor, ask the doctor,

nǐ qù wènwen yīshēng.
你去问问 医生。
you | go | ask | cure | person
you go and ask the doctor.

Bié qǐng tā hē,   bié qǐng tā hē,
别 请他喝，别 请他喝，
don't | invite | he | drink | don't | invite | he | drink
Don't treat him to a drink, don't treat him to a drink,

yīshēng bú ràng tā hē.
医生不让他喝。
cure | person | not | allow | him | drink
the doctor does not allow him to drink.

二 看与说 Read and Speak

Now, listen to the recording while looking at the following sentences. Then read it out aloud. Finally, recite it by heart to yourself and then to your classmates or instructor.

吃肉，吃肉，

他特爱吃肉。

吃肉，吃肉，

我请他吃肉。

问问大夫，问问大夫，

你去问问大夫。

别请他吃，别请他吃，

大夫不让他吃。

喝酒，喝酒，

他特爱喝酒。

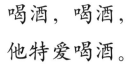

喝酒，喝酒，

我请他喝酒。

问问医生，问问医生，

你去问问医生。

别请他喝，别请他喝，

医生不让他喝。

三　理解　Understand

请 *qǐng* means "please" as in 请进 *qǐng jìn* (please come in). 请 *qǐng* can also be used to mean "to invite", which is to ask somebody to do something politely. For example,

Wǒ qǐng nǐ chī fàn.
我请你吃饭。
I'll **invite** you to have dinner.

Tā qǐng wǒ kàn diànyǐng.
他请我看电影。
He'll **invite** me to see a movie.

However, 请 *qǐng* often has the connotation of treating someone to something in Chinese. If the word 请 *qǐng* is used, it implies that the invitee will not make any payment and the inviter will pay for the cost. Therefore, the previous two example sentences may be translated as:

Wǒ qǐng nǐ chī fàn.
我请你吃饭。
I'll **treat** you to a meal.

Tā qǐng wǒ kàn diànyǐng.
他请我看电影。
He'll **treat** me to a movie.

When we ask a question in Chinese, we use the word 问 *wèn* (ask); however, when we ask somebody to do something, then 问 *wèn* is not an appropriate word to use as it is used exclusively for asking questions. Instead, 让 *ràng* is the right word to use. For example,

I **ask** him to buy a dictionary.
我让他买词典。(correct)
我问他买词典。(wrong)

He **asks** me to learn Chinese.
他让我学汉语。(correct)
他问我学汉语。(wrong)

If we put the negation word 不 *bù* before 让 *ràng*, then the meaning is "do not allow" or "do not let". Please note that the tone for 不 *bù* becomes *bú* when followed by 让 *ràng*.

Tā bú ràng wǒ hē jiǔ.
他不让我喝酒。
He **does not allow** me to drink alcohol.

问问 *wènwen* is not a typo. It is a grammatical function in Chinese to have a verb (an action word) reduplicated to soften the tone of the speaker. Instead of saying 你去问大夫 *nǐ qù wèn dàifu*, which sounds too abrupt, we can make it sound less abrupt and intrusive by reduplicating the verb 问 *wèn* in the sentence: 你去问问大夫 *nǐ qù wènwen dàifu*. Please note the tone of the second syllable in the reduplicated verb is neutralized.

四 实践 Practice

1. 对话 Conversation

A: 明天没有课，我请你出去吃饭。
B: 不好意思，让你请我。
A: 我们是朋友。

B: 大夫不让我喝啤酒。

A: 那我们喝茶。

B: 好吧。

A: 你爱吃肉，我请你吃美国牛肉。

B: 不行，不行。大夫也不让我吃肉。

A: 那我们别出去吃了。我请你出去玩儿吧。

B: 别、别、别！你吃肉，我吃素菜。

A: 吃饭以后，我请你看电影。

B: 不行，不行。你请我吃饭，让我来请你看电影。

A: 好吧。电影是几点的?

B: 我打电话问问。七点的。

A: 明天我们五点走，行不行?

B: 行。你来以前，给我打个电话。

A: 好。

2. 交际 Communication

Task 1	You are getting along very well with your Chinese roommate. Since your roommate has treated you several times to dinner in local small restaurants, you insist on paying for the bill at a nice western restaurant by saying: "You have often treated me. Now let me treat you."
Task 2	Around noontime, you see your roommate getting ready to head to the school cafeteria. Tell him/her not to eat at the cafeteria since you want to take him/her out.
Task 3	Since you want to take both your Chinese roommate and his/her girlfriend/boyfriend to a movie, ask your roommate to ask his/her girlfriend/boyfriend what time tomorrow he/she will be free.

3. 书写 Writing

dà; dài   big   *Héng, piě, nà.*

大								

fū   man   *Héng, héng, piě, nà.*

夫								

ràng   let; allow   *Diǎn, héngzhétí, shù, héng, héng.*

让								

tè   especially   *Piě, héng, shù, tí, héng, shù, héng, héng, shùgōu, diǎn.*

特								

ài   love   *Piě, diǎn, diǎn, piě, diǎn, hénggōu; héng, piě, héngpiě, nà.*

爱								

yī   cure   *Héng, piě, héng, héng, piě, diǎn, shùzhé.*

医								

shēng   person; born; unfamiliar   *Piě, héng, héng, shù, héng.*

生								

Dì–èrshísì   *kè*   *Jīntiān   jǐ   yuè   jǐ   hào?*

第二十四课   今天几月几号？

Lesson 24   What is the date and month today?

一   听与看   Listen and Read

Listen to the recording of the following sentences as many times as possible until you can say it along with the recording. You should also look at the following transcription while listening and try to imitate.

Jǐ yuè jǐ hào?

几月几号？

how many | **month** | how many | date

What is the date and month?

Jīntiān jǐ yuè jǐ hào?

今天几月几号？

present | day | how many | **month** | how many | date

What is the date and month today?

Èryuè bā hào,

二月八号，

two | **month** | eight | date

February the eighth,

jīntiān Èryuè bā hào.

今天二月八号。

present | day | two | **month** | eight | date

it is February the eighth today.

Xīngqī jǐ?   Xīngqī jǐ?

星期几？星期几？

star | period | how many | star | period | how many

What day is it?   What day is it?

Jīntiān xīngqī jǐ?

今天星期几？

present | day | star | period | how many

What day is it today?

Xīngqī liù,   Xīngqī liù,

星 期 六 ，星 期 六 ，

star | period | six | star | period | six

Saturday, Saturday,

Jīntiān Xīngqī liù.

今 天 星 期 六 。

present | day | star | period | six

it is Saturday today.

Shēngrì,   shēngrì,

生 日 ，生 日 ，

born | day | born | day

Birthday, birthday,

jǐn tiān shì wǒ shēngrì.

今 天 是 我 生 日 。

present | day | be | I | born | day

today is my birthday.

Kuàilè,   kuàilè,

快 乐 ，快 乐 ，

rapid | delight | rapid | delight

Happy, happy,

zhù nǐ shēngrì   kuài lè !

祝 你 生 日 快 乐 !

wish | you | born | day | rapid | delight

happy birthday to you!

二 看与说 Read and Speak

Now, listen to the recording while looking at the following sentences. Then read it out aloud. Finally, recite it by heart to yourself and then to your classmates or instructor.

几月几号？

今天几月几号？

二月八号，

今天二月八号。

星期几？星期几？

今天星期几？

星期六，星期六，

今天星期六。

生日，生日，

今天是我生日。

快乐，快乐，

祝你生日快乐！

三 理解 Understand

In Chinese, the word for "month" is 月 *yuè*, which literally means "moon". All twelve months in a year are numbered. January is month one, February is month two, and so on. However the numbers go before 月 *yuè*.

January	*Yīyuè* 一月	February	*Èryuè* 二月
March	*Sānyuè* 三月	April	*Sìyuè* 四月

May	*Wǔyuè* 五月	June	*Liùyuè* 六月
July	*Qīyuè* 七月	August	*Bāyuè* 八月
September	*Jiǔyuè* 九月	October	*Shíyuè* 十月
November	*Shíyīyuè* 十一月	December	*Shí'èryuè* 十二月

The word for "date" is 日 *rì*, which literally means "sun". In daily conversations, the word 号 *hào*, which literally means "number" is often used in place of 日 *rì* for "date". Therefore, 一号 *yī hào*, 二号 *èr hào*, 三号 *sān hào*, 四号 *sì hào*... 三十一号 *sānshíyī hào* are what you hear and say in daily conversations about dates. However, on newspapers and in formal letters, you will read and write 一日 *yī rì*, 二日 *èr rì*, 三日 *sān rì*, 四日 *sì rì*... 三十一日 *sānshíyī rì*.

In Chinese, bigger time units go first. January 1st or the 1st of January is written as 一月一日 *Yīyuè yī rì* and is said as 一月一号 *Yīyuè yī hào*. What about the last date of the last month, December 31st or the 31st of December in Chinese? It is formally 十二月三十一日 *Shí'èryuè sānshíyī rì* and informally 十二月三十一号 *Shí'èryuè sānshíyī hào*.

The word for "week" is 星期 *xīngqī*, which literally means "star period". All seven days of the week are also numbered. Monday is the first day of the week, so it is 星期一 *Xīngqīyī*; Tuesday is the second day of the week, so it is 星期二 *Xīngqī'èr*. However, don't assume that Sunday is 星期七 *Xīngqīqī*, which is unheard of in Chinese. It should really be 星期日 *Xīngqīrì* formally and 星期天 *Xīngqītiān* informally.

Monday	*Xīngqīyī* 星期一
Tuesday	*Xīngqī'èr* 星期二
Wednesday	*Xīngqīsān* 星期三

Thursday	*Xīngqīsì* 星期四
Friday	*Xīngqīwǔ* 星期五
Saturday	*Xīngqīliù* 星期六
Sunday	*Xīngqīrì* *Xīngqītiān* 星期日 or 星期天

Because all dates, months, and days are numbered in Chinese, when we ask what date, month, or day of the week it is, we use the question word 几 *jǐ* (how many). For example,

Jīntiān jǐ hào?
今天几号？
What is the date today?

Xiànzài jǐ yuè?
现在几月？
What month is it now?

Jīntiān xīngqī jǐ?
今天星期几？
What day is it today?

四 实践 Practice

1. 对话 Conversation

A: 今天几月几号？

B: 二月八号。

A: 明天是你生日！

B: 是啊，明天星期六是我生日。

A: 祝你生日快乐！

B: 谢谢你。来我宿舍喝酒吧!

A: 不行，不行! 我请你出去吃饭。

B: 那不好意思。

A: 谁让我是你朋友呢? 别客气。我请你吃饺子。

2. 交际 Communication

Task 1 When you find out that tomorrow is your Chinese language teacher's birthday, first offer your birthday good wishes, and then tell him/her that you and your classmates offer to take him/her out to have dinner at an American restaurant. When your teacher follows the Chinese manner to turn down your offer for formality reason, insist on your offer.

Task 2 Your Chinese friend tells you that she and a few friends are planning to have an outing day at a local park next Saturday. She asks whether you want to go with them. Ask her what date is next Saturday and tell her you would like to go since your language instructor says this park is very beautiful.

Task 3 You are very excited to tell your Chinese friend that your parents have called you saying that they are coming to visit you. When your friend asks what day they are coming, say that they are coming this Sunday, February 8th.

3. 书写 Writing

jīn　present　*Piě, nà, diǎn, héngzhé.*

今									

yuè　month　*Piě, héngzhégōu, héng, héng.*

月									

xīng   star   *Shù, héngzhé, héng, héng; piě, héng, héng, shù, héng.*

星									

qī   period   *Héng, shù, shù, héng, héng, héng, piě, diǎn; piě, héngzhégōu, héng, héng.*

期									

rì   day; sun   *Shù, héngzhé, héng, héng.*

日									

kuài   fast; rapid   *Diǎn, diǎn, shù; héngzhé, héng, piě, nà.*

快									

zhù   wish   *Diǎn, héngpiě, shù, diǎn; shù, héngzhé, héng, piě, shùwāngōu.*

祝									

Dì–èrshíwǔ   kè   Zhè shì shéi gěi nǐ mǎi de   huār?

第二十五课　这是谁给你买的花儿？
Lesson 25　Who is it that bought you the flowers?

一　听与看　Listen and Read

Listen to the recording of the following sentences as many times as possible until you can say it along with the recording. You should also look at the following transcription while listening and try to imitate.

Shéi mǎi de   huār?

谁 买 的 花 儿 ？
who | buy | [aux.] | **flower** | [suffix]
Who bought the flowers?

Shéi mǎi de   huār?

谁 买 的 花 儿 ？
who | buy | [aux.] | **flower** | [suffix]
Who bought the flowers?

Zhēn hǎokàn,   zhēn hǎokàn.

真 好 看 ， 真 好 看 。
really | good | look | really | good | look
Really beautiful, really beautiful.

Zhè shì shéi gěi nǐ mǎi de   huār?

这 是 谁 给 你 买 的 花 儿 ？
this | be | who | for | you | buy | [aux.] | **flower** | [suffix]
Who is it that bought you the flowers?

Wǒ péngyou mǎi de   huār,

我 朋 友 买 的 花 儿 ，
I | pal | friend | buy | [aux.] | **flower** | [suffix]
The flowers my friend bought,

wǒ péngyou mǎi de   huār,

我 朋 友 买 的 花 儿 ，
I | pal | friend | buy | [aux.] | **flower** | [suffix]
the flowers my friend bought.

shì　hǎokàn,　shì　hǎokàn.
是 好看，是 好看。
be | good | look | be | good | look
beautiful indeed, beautiful indeed.

Zhè shì wǒ péngyou gěi wǒ mǎi de huār.
这是我 朋友 给我买的花儿。
this | be | I | pal | friend | for | I | buy | [aux.] | **flower** | [suffix]
These are the flowers my friend bought for me.

Shéi zuò de fàn?
谁 做 的 饭？
who | make | [aux.] | meal
Who cooked the meal?

Shéi zuò de fàn?
谁 做 的 饭？
who | make | [aux.} | meal
Who cooked the meal?

Zhēn hǎochī, zhēn hǎochī.
真 好吃，真 好吃。
really | good | eat | really | good | eat
Really delicious, really delicious.

Zhè shì shéi gěi nǐ zuò de fàn?
这 是 谁 给你做的饭？
this | be | who | for | you | make | [aux.] | meal
Who is it that cooked the meal for you?

Wǒ māma zuò de fàn,
我妈妈做的饭，
I | mom | make | [aux.] | meal
The meal my mom cooked,

wǒ māma zuò de fàn,
我妈妈做的饭，
I | mom | make | [aux.] | meal
the meal my mom cooked,

shì hǎochī,   shì hǎochī.

是 好吃，是 好吃。

be | good | eat | be | good | eat

delicious indeed, delicious indeed.

Zhè shì wǒ māma gěi wǒ zuò de fàn.

这是我妈妈给我做的饭。

this | be | I | mom | for | I | make | [aux.] | meal

This is the meal my mom cooked for me.

二 看与说 Read and Speak

Now, listen to the recording while looking at the following sentences.
Then read it out aloud. Finally, recite it by heart to yourself and then to your
classmates or instructor.

谁买的花儿?

谁买的花儿?

真好看，真好看。

这是谁给你买的花儿?

我朋友买的花儿，

我朋友买的花儿，

是好看，是好看。

这是我朋友给我买的花儿。

谁做的饭？

谁做的饭？

真好吃，真好吃。

这是谁给你做的饭？

我妈妈做的饭，

我妈妈做的饭，

是好吃，是好吃。

这是我妈妈给我做的饭。

三 理解 Understand

Compare the following two sentences for their English and Chinese versions:

> 1) This is my book.
>
> *Zhè shì wǒ de shū.*
> 这是我的书。

> 2) This is the book that I bought.
>
> *Zhè shì wǒ mǎi de shū.*
> 这是我买的书。

We can see that in the Chinese version of the first sentence, the auxiliary word 的 *de* helps to show that 我 *wǒ* (I) possesses 书 *shū* (book), and 的 *de* serves the function of the possessive case. So, 我 *wǒ* means "I", and 我的 *wǒ de* means "my". In the Chinese version of the second sentence, the auxiliary word 的 *de* separates 我买 *wǒ mǎi* (I buy) from 书 *shū* (book), and 的 *de* serves as the function of relative pronouns, such as that, who, and which. Although in English, a relative pronoun sometimes can be omitted, 的 *de* is never omitted in Chinese. Look at the following examples:

the bus **that** goes to the bookstore	去书店的车
the dorm **which** they stay at	他们住的宿舍
the coffee he drank	他喝的咖啡
the dictionary I used	我用的词典
the friend **who** made a phone call to me	给我打电话的朋友
the teacher **who** loves to read books	爱看书的老师
the doctor he introduced to me	他给我介绍的大夫
the classmate I know	我认识的同学

好 *hǎo* means "good", and new words can be formed by adding an mono-syllabic action word after 好 *hǎo*. In a new word formed this way, 好 *hǎo* either continues to mean "good" or takes on the meaning of "easy". Look at the following examples:

好看	*hǎokàn*	good-looking, pretty
好吃	*hǎochī*	delicious (good to eat)
好喝	*hǎohē*	tasty (good to drink)
好玩儿	*hǎowánr*	fun
好学	*hǎo xué*	easy to learn
好写	*hǎo xiě*	easy to write
好买	*hǎo mǎi*	easy to buy
好做	*hǎo zuò*	easy to make
好洗	*hǎo xǐ*	easy to wash

All these words formed with 好 *hǎo* are adjectives (i.e., describing words). We know that we do not need 是 *shì* when making statements with adjectives. For example,

I am busy. 我很忙。
I am well. 我很好。

This book is expensive. 这书很贵。

The meal your mom cooked is delicious. 你妈做的饭很好吃。

However, 是 shì can be added only if we want to emphasize and confirm that these statements are true. For example,

我是很忙。I am **indeed** busy.

我是很好。I am **indeed** well.

这书是很贵。This book is **indeed** expensive.

你妈做的饭是很好吃。The meal your mom cooked is **indeed** delicious.

四 实践 Practice

1. 对话 Conversation

A: 谁啊?

B: 是我，李贵。

A: 啊，李贵! 请进，请进!

B: 你的宿舍很大啊!

A: 是很大。这个大学很好。

B: 这个花儿真好看!

A: 是我昨天买的。

B: 哪儿买的?

A: 你看，那个店。

B: 多少钱?

A: 十块。

B: 十块不贵。明天我也去买。

A: 来，我们吃饭吧。

B: 好。

A: 请!

B: 谢谢。真好吃。是你做的吗?
A: 不是，是饭馆儿做的。

🤝 2. 交际 Communication

Task 1 When one student excitedly yells in the hallway that there will be no class tomorrow, walk out immediately to ask him whether it is your language instructor who said it. When the answer was that he heard it from another student, say that you will call your instructor to ask her if it is true.

Task 2 When you return your classmate's dictionary, comment that it is an excellent dictionary. Ask him where she bought it and how much it is. When you hear that the price is very reasonable, say that you are going to buy a copy yourself.

Task 3 When eating dinner at your host family's home, you are delighted by the great variety of dishes they prepared. Say it is delicious. Ask if they are takeaway cooked by a restaurant. When the hostess says that everything is cooked by her, exclaim "Really? All cooked by you? Really delicious!"

3. 书写 Writing

huā   flower   *Héng, shù, shù; piě, shù, piě, shùwāngōu.*

花									

Dì–èrshíliù kè   Zhè shì wǒ de jiā.

第二十六课　这是我的家。
Lesson 26　This is my home.

一　听与看　Listen and Read

Listen to the recording of the following sentences as many times as possible until you can say it along with the recording. You should also look at the following transcription while listening and try to imitate.

Jiā,   jiā,   jiā,

家，家，家，

home | home | home

Home, home, home,

zhè shì wǒ de jiā.

这是我的家。

this | be | I | [aux.] | home

this is my home.

Qiánbian shì kètīng,

前边　是客厅，

front | side | be | guest | hall,

In the front is the living room,

hòubian shì shūfáng,

后边是书房，

back | side | be | book | side room

at the back is the study,

zuǒbian shì cèsuǒ,

左边　是厕所，

left | side | be | toilet | place

on the left is the bathroom,

yòubian shì chúfáng.

右边是厨房。

right | side | be | kitchen | side room

on the right is the kitchen.

Jiārén, jiārén, jiārén,
家人，家人，家人，
home | person | home | person | home | person
Family, family, family,

zhè shì wǒ jiārén.
这是我家人。
this | be | I | home | person
this is my family.

Qiánbian shì wǒ mèi,
前边 是我妹，
front | side | be | I | younger sister
In the front is my sister,

hòubian shì wǒ gē,
后边 是我哥，
back | side | be | I | elder brother
at the back is my elder brother,

zuǒbian shì wǒ bà,
左边 是我爸，
left | side | be | I | dad
on the left is my father,

yòubian shì wǒ mā.
右边 是我妈。
right | side | be | I | mom
on the right is my mother.

二 看与说 Read and Speak

Now, listen to the recording while looking at the following sentences. Then read it out aloud. Finally, recite it by heart to yourself and then to your classmates or instructor.

家，家，家，
这是我的家。

前边是客厅，

后边是书房，

左边是厕所，

右边是厨房。

家人，家人，家人，

这是我家人。

前边是我妹，

后边是我哥，

左边是我爸，

右边是我妈。

三　理解　Understand

Talking about positions and locations in English, we have to use such prepositions as "in", "on", "at" and so on. In Chinese, we can use 在 *zài* (be located at) for all if we put the position words at the end of a sentence or use no prepositions at all if we put the position words at the begining of a sentence. Look at the following:

At the beginning of a sentence:

In the front...	前边……
At the back...	后边……
On the right...	右边……
On the left...	左边……

On top…	上边……
At the bottom…	下边……

At the end of a sentence:

…in the front	……在前边
…at the back	……在后边
…on the right	……在右边
…on the left	……在左边
…on top	……在上边
…at the bottom	……在下边

四 实践 Practice

1. 对话 Conversation

A: 请进!

B and C: 李老师好!

A: 来, 坐, 坐。

B: 李老师, 这是我们给您的花儿。

A: 啊, 真好看! 谢谢! 谢谢!

C: 李老师, 你们家真好, 真大!

A: 还行吧。电影里边, 你们美国人的家都很大。

B: 那是电影。有的美国人家也不大。

A: 来, 你们看看。这是客厅, 这是书房。

B: 左边是不是厨房?

A: 是。右边是厕所。

B: 这是您的家人吗?

A: 是啊。前边两个是我爸妈。

C: 后边两个呢?

A: 是我哥和我妹。

👐 2. 交际 Communication

Task 1 Show your Chinese friend your family photo that you brought from your home country. Tell your friend who is the person on the left, who is on the right, who are in the front.

Task 2 A new international student arrives at your Chinese university campus. Show him/her around and tell him/her the names and functions of the important buildings on campus according to their locations.

Task 3 Share a photo of your house in the United States to your Chinese friends. When they ask you about the details of your house, tell them the locations of different rooms.

🖊 3. 书写 Writing

jiā home *Diǎn, diǎn, hénggōu; héng, piě, wāngōu, piě, piě, piě, nà.*

家									

qián front *Diǎn, piě, héng, shù, héngzhégōu, héng, héng, shù, shùgōu.*

前									

biān side *Héngzhégōu, piě; diǎn, héngzhézhépiě, píngnà.*

边									

tīng hall *Héng, piě; héng, shùgōu.*

厅									

fáng   house; side room   *Diǎn, héngzhé, héng, piě; diǎn, héng, héngzhégōu, piě.*

房

zuǒ   left   *Héng, piě, héng, shù, héng.*

左

cè   toilet   *Héng, piě; shù, héngzhé, piě, diǎn, shù, shùgōu.*

厕

suǒ   place   *Piě, piě, héngzhé, héng; piě, piě, héng, shù.*

所

yòu   right   *Héng, piě, shù, héngzhé, héng.*

右

chú   kitchen   *Héng, piě; héng, shù, héngzhé, héng, diǎn, piě, tí; héng, shùgōu, diǎn.*

厨

Dì-èrshíqī   kè   Wǒ jiā yǒu yí ge dà fángzi.

第二十七课   我家有一个大房子。
Lesson 27   My home has a big house.

一 听与看 Listen and Read

Listen to the recording of the following sentences as many times as possible until you can say it along with the recording. You should also look at the following transcription while listening and try to imitate.

Wǒ jiā yǒu yí ge dà fángzi,

我家有一个大房子,

my | home | have | one | [meas.] | big | house | [suffix]

My home has big house.

fáng lǐ yǒu yí ge dà wūzi,

房里有一个大屋子,

house | inside | have | one | [meas.] | big | room | [suffix]

there is a big room in the house,

wū lǐ yǒu yí ge dà zhuōzi,

屋里有一个大桌子,

room | inside | have | one | [meas.] | big | table | [suffix]

there is a big table in the room,

zhuō shàng yǒu yí ge dà bēizi,

桌上有一个大杯子,

table | up | have | one | [meas.] | big | cup | [suffix]

there is a big cup on the table,

bēi lǐ yǒu yí ge xiǎo sháozi.

杯里有一个小勺子。

cup | inside | have | one | [meas.] | small | spoon | [suffix]

there is a small spoon in the cup.

二 看与说 Read and Speak

Now, listen to the recording while looking at the following sentences. Then read it out aloud. Finally, recite it by heart to yourself and then to your classmates or instructor.

我家有一个大房子，

房里有一个大屋子，

屋里有一个大桌子，

桌上有一个大杯子，

杯里有一个小勺子。

三 理解 Understand

子 zǐ originally means "child", but it has several other extended meanings that you will learn as you continue to learn Chinese. In this lesson, there are quite a few words that ended with 子 zi, which does not have any particular meaning and is just used as a suffix, turning a monosyllabic word into disyllabic one:

房 → 房子 屋 → 屋子 桌 → 桌子 杯 → 杯子 勺 → 勺子

In modern Chinese, there is a tendency to use disyllabic words and phrases by expanding those that are monosyllabic and shortening those that are polysyllabic. For example,

房子里边	→ 房里	(in the house)
屋子里边	→ 屋里	(in the room)
桌子上边	→ 桌上	(on the table)
杯子里边	→ 杯里	(in the cup)

In this lesson and the previous lesson, we have seen two similar sentence structures:

Position Word/Phrase + 是 + Something
Position Word/Phrase + 有 + Something

The sentence structure with 是 *shì* aims to identify what or who it is at a particular location and the sentence with 有 *yǒu* pays attention to what a particular location physically has.

四 实践 Practice

1. 对话 Conversation

A: 你那个中国朋友家大吗?

B: 不大也不小。

A: 他家有几个卧室?

B: 两个。大的他爸妈住，小的是他的。

A: 客厅和厨房怎么样?

B: 厨房小，客厅大。

A: 客厅里有什么?

B: 有一个大桌子。桌子上有几个杯子。

A: 你常去他家玩儿吗?

B: 不常去。

2. 交际 Communication

Task 1 When you chat with your host family during a visit, they ask you about your dorm room at your Chinese university. Tell them that your room is very big. It has two beds, two tables, one TV and one telephone. On your table there are a few books and CD's.

Task 2 One day, you and a few other international students are shopping in the downtown area. One student urgently needs to use the restroom. Since you are pretty familiar with the shopping district, give him/her the direction by saying: Straight ahead of you, on the left there is a bookstore and on the right there is a tea store. Behind the tea store there is a restroom.

Task 3 Since you eat out a lot, when a few of you are trying to decide where to go out for a Saturday dinner, tell them that there is a small restaurant on the right side of the school gate. The Sichuan dishes they cook are delicious and inexpensive.

3. 书写 Writing

lǐ   inside   *Shù, héngzhé, héng, héng, héng, shù, héng.*

里

wū   room   *Héngzhé, héng, piě; héng, piězhé, diǎn, héng, shù, héng.*

屋

zhuō   table   *shù, héng, shù, héngzhé, héng, héng; héng, shù, piě, nà.*

桌

xiǎo   small   *Shùgōu, diǎn, diǎn.*

小

sháo   spoon   *Piě, héngzhégōu, diǎn.*

勺

第二十八课   你干什么呢?
Lesson 28   What are you doing?

一   听与看   Listen and Read

Listen to the recording of the following sentences as many times as possible until you can say it along with the recording. You should also look at the following transcription while listening and try to imitate.

Wéi,   wéi,   wéi,
喂, 喂, 喂,
hello | hello | hello
Hello, hello, hello,

nín shì nǎ yí wèi?
您是哪一位?
[respectful form of "you"] | be | which | one | [meas.]
may I know who this is speaking?

Nǐ cāi wǒ shì shéi.
你猜我是谁。
you | guess | I | be | who
Please guess who I am.

Nǐ shì Zhāng Xiǎomèi.
你是 张 小妹。
you | be | [a surname] | small | younger sister
You are Zhang Xiaomei.

Duì,   duì,   duì.
对, 对, 对。
correct | correct | correct
Correct, correct, correct.

Nǐ zài xiūxi ma?
你在休息吗?
you | at | rest | breath | [ques.]
Are you having a rest?

Wǒ méi zài xiūxi.

我没在休息。

I | not | at | **rest** | **breath**.

I am not having a rest.

Nǐ zài xuéxí ma?

你在学习吗?

you | at | learn | **practice** | [ques.]

Are you studying?

Wǒ méi zài xuéxí.

我没在学习。

I | not | at | learn | **practice**

I am not studying.

Nǐ gàn shénme ne?

你干什么呢?

you | **do** | what | [suffix] | [ques.]

What are you doing?

Wǒ kàn diànshì ne!

我看电视呢!

I | look | electric | **vision** | [aux.]

I am watching TV.

二 看与说 Read and Speak

Now, listen to the recording while looking at the following sentences. Then read it out aloud. Finally, recite it by heart to yourself and then to your classmates or instructor.

喂,喂,喂,

您是哪一位?

你猜我是谁?

你是张小妹。

对，对，对。

你在休息吗？

我没在休息。

你在学习吗？

我没在学习。

你干什么呢？

我看电视呢！

三 理解 Understand

Saying 喂 *wéi* is a very common way of starting a conversation over the telephone. The word 喂 *wèi* can also take the rising tone, so many people start a phone conversation by saying wéi instead of wèi. If we do not know who is on the phone, we can say: 喂，您是哪一位 *wéi, nín shì nǎ yí wèi*, which can be translated literally as "Hello, you are which one?" A better English translation is: "Hello, may I know who this is speaking?"

位 *wèi* is a honorific measure word for people. It is used to show respect for the person or people addressed or referred to. We can use it when we introduce people. For example,

Wǒ lái jièshao yíxiàr.   Zhè wèi shì Lǐ dàifu,   zhè wèi shì Wáng lǎoshī.
我来介绍一下儿。这位是李大夫，这位是王老师。
Let me introduce a bit. This is Dr. Li, and this is Professor Wang.

What is more important in this lesson is to understand and learn how an action in progress is expressed in Chinese. To indicate that an action is going on, we can have the following options:

1) Use 在 *zài* before an action word. For example,

> *Wǒ zài xiūxi.*
> 我在休息。
> (I am taking a rest.)

> *Tā zài xǐ zǎo.*
> 他在洗澡。
> (He is taking a bath.)

> *Wǒmen zài kàn shū.*
> 我们在看书。
> (We are reading books.)

2) Use 呢 *ne* at the end of a sentence. For example,

> *Wǒ xiūxi ne.*
> 我休息呢。
> (I am taking a rest.)

> *Tā xǐ zǎo ne.*
> 他洗澡呢。
> (He is taking a bath.)

> *Wǒmen kàn shū ne.*
> 我们看书呢。
> (We are reading books.)

3) Use both 在 *zài* and 呢 *ne* in a sentence. For example,

> *Wǒ zài xiūxi ne.*
> 我在休息呢。
> (I am taking a rest.)

> *Tā zài xǐ zǎo ne.*
> 他在洗澡呢。
> (He is taking a bath.)

> *Wǒmen zài kàn shū ne.*
> 我们在看书呢。
> (We are reading books.)

For any of the three options listed above, if we want to emphasize that an action is right in the middle of progress, we can add 正 *zhèng* before 在 *zài*. If 在 *zài* is not used, then add 正 *zhèng* before the action word. For example,

> Wǒ   zhèngzài   xiūxi.
> 我 正在 休息。
> (I am right in the middle of taking a rest.)

> Wǒ zhèng xiūxi ne.
> 我 正休息呢。
> (the same as above)

> Wǒ   zhèngzài   xiūxi ne.
> 我 正在 休息呢。
> (the same as above)

For negation of an action that is in progress, 没 *méi* is used before 在 *zài*, and 呢 *ne* should be omitted. For example,

> Wǒ méi zài xiūxi.
> 我没在休息。
> (I am not taking a rest.)

> Tā méi zài xǐ zǎo.
> 他没在洗澡。
> (He is not taking a bath.)

> Wǒmen méi zài kàn shū.
> 我们没在看书。
> (We are not reading books.)

四 实践 Practice

1. 对话 Conversation

A: 喂，您是哪一位？
B: 你好，李贵。
A: 你好。

B: 知道我是谁吗?

A: 你是……

B: 你猜猜。

A: 王二?

B: 不是。

A: 王三。

B: 也不是，我是王四。

A: 啊，王四，你好，你好。

B: 你干什么呢? 你在学习呢吗?

A: 没有。我在这儿看电视呢。

B: 我去你那儿坐坐，行吗?

A: 行!

2. 交际 Communication

Task 1 You get bored from studying for the test tomorrow. So you dial your Chinese friend's number and find that he/she is watching TV instead of studying at the moment. Invite your friend to take a walk.

Task 2 When your Chinese friend calls to ask you to see a movie, tell him/her that you are eating dinner and that you will go to his/her dorm (to meet him/her) after eating dinner.

Task 3 While you are watching a fun movie at a movie theater, your cell phone starts to vibrate showing a number you cannot ignore. Whisper to the caller that you are seeing a movie right now and will call him/her after you finish seeing the movie.

3. 书写 Writing

gàn   do   *Héng, héng, shù.*

干									

wéi; wèi   hey; feed   *Shù, héngzhé, héng; shù, héngzhé, héng, shù, héng, héng, shùtí, piě, nà.*

喂									

wèi   [honorific measure word for people]   *Piě, shù; diǎn, héng, diǎn, piě, héng.*

位									

cāi   guess   *Piě, wānggōu, piě; héng, héng, shù, héng, shù, héngzhégōu, héng, héng.*

猜									

zhāng   [a surname]; piece   *Héngzhé, héng, shùzhézhégōu; piě, héng, shùtí, nà.*

张									

xiū   rest   *Piě, shù; héng, shù, piě, nà.*

休									

xī   breathe stop;   *Piě, shù, héngzhé, héng, héng, héng; diǎn, wògōu, diǎn, diǎn.*

息									

xí   practice   *Héngzhégōu, diǎn, tí.*

习									

shì vision *Diǎn, héngpiě, shù, diǎn; shù, héngzhé, piě, shùwāngōu.*

视								

Dì-èrshíjiǔ kè   *Chī fàn de shíhou, tā kàn bào.*

第二十九课   吃饭的时候，他看报。

Lesson 29   At the time of meals, he reads newspapers.

一 听与看 Listen and Read

Listen to the recording of the following sentences as many times as possible until you can say it along with the recording. You should also look at the following transcription while listening and try to imitate.

*Chī fàn de **shíhou**, tā kàn bào.*

吃 饭 的 **时 候**， 他 看 报。

eat | meal | [aux.] | **time** | **condition** | he | look | newspaper

At the time of meals, he reads newspapers.

*Shàng kè de **shíhou**, tā shuì jiào.*

上 课 的 **时 候**， 他 睡 觉。

up | class | [aux.] | **time** | **condition** | he | sleep | a sleep

At the time of a class, he sleeps.

*Xǐ zǎo de **shíhou**, tā chàng gē.*

洗 澡 的 **时 候**， 他 唱 歌。

wash | bath | [aux.] | **time** | **condition** | he | sing | song

At the time of a bath, he sings songs.

*Kàn shū de **shíhou**, tā dà jiào.*

看 书 的 **时 候**， 他 大 叫。

look | book | [aux.] | **time** | **condition** | he | big | call

At the time of reading books, he shouts.

二 看与说 Read and Speak

Now, listen to the recording while looking at the following sentences. Then read it out aloud. Finally, recite it by heart to yourself and then to your classmates or instructor.

吃饭的时候，他看报。

上课的时候，他睡觉。

洗澡的时候，他唱歌。

看书的时候，他大叫。

三 理解 Understand

When 时 *shí* and 候 *hòu* are put together to form a disyllabic word, the tone for hòu is neutralized. Therefore, it is 时候 *shíhou*. We use 时候 *shíhou* like the word "when" or "at the time" in English, and 的 de is used before 时候 *shíhou* to separate it from its modifier. For example,

我吃饭的时候 → When I have meals
我上课的时候 → When I have a class
我洗澡的时候 → When I take a bath
我看书的时候 → When I read books

If no subject is specified, then it means "at the time". For example,

吃饭的时候 → At the time of meals
上课的时候 → At the time of a class
洗澡的时候 → At the time of a bath
看书的时候 → At the time of reading books

If two different actions have two different doers, then specify the doer for each action. For example,

我吃饭的时候，他看报。 → When I have meals, he reads newspapers.

Compare these two sentences and try to understand the differences in meaning:

他吃饭的时候看报。 → When he has meals, he reads newspapers.
吃饭的时候，他看报。 → At the time of meals, he reads newspapers.

Note that because "...的时候 *de shíhou*" is a time expression, it should always be placed at the beginning of a sentence.

四　实践 Practice

1. 对话 Conversation

A: 我们班有一个人，特有意思。

B: 是吗？怎么有意思？

A: 朋友出去吃饭的时候，他看报。上课的时候，他老 ("always" in a negative sense) 睡觉。

B: 晚上他不睡吗？

A: 不睡。

B: 那他干什么？

A: 打电话、看电视。

B: 谁跟他住一个宿舍？

A: 我。早上洗澡的时候，他唱歌。

B: 他什么时候看书啊？

A: 看书？我们学的书，他不看。

B: 那他看什么书啊？

A: 他老看小店儿买的书。看的时候，还大叫。

2. 交际 Communication

Task 1 During a chat with your host family, they ask about transportation in your home country. Tell them that when you are in your home country, you do not often take the bus or taxi.

> You love riding a bike, but not to commute to school. When you go to a local park, you ride your bike. When you go to school everyday, you drive (开车 *kāi chē*).

Task 2 When your instructor in China asks you what language your home university instructor employs in teaching, say that he/she uses both English and Chinese when you have Chinese language class.

Task 3 When your Chinese friend asks about how your roommate is, say that he/she is a nice person, however, his/her parents always call him/her when you are sleeping.

3. 书写 Writing

shí   time   *Shù, héngzhé, héng, héng; héng, shùgōu, diǎn.*

时								

hòu   condition; wait   *Piě, shù, shù, héngzhé, héng, piě, héng, héng, piě, nà.*

候								

bào   newspaper; report   *Héng, shùgōu, tí; héngzhégōu, shù, héngpiě, nà.*

报								

chàng   sing   *Shù, héngzhé, héng; shù, héngzhé, héng, héng; shù, héngzhé, héng, héng.*

唱								

gē   song   *Héng, shù, héngzhé, héng, shù, héng, shù, héngzhé, héng, shùgōu; piě, hénggōu, piě, nà.*

歌								

Dì–sānshí kè   *Wǒ zuò fàn zuò de hěn hǎo.*

第三十课   我做饭做得很好。

Lesson 30   I cook very well.

一   听与看   Listen and Read

Listen to the recording of the following sentences as many times as possible until you can say it along with the recording. You should also look at the following transcription while listening and try to imitate.

Qǐ chuáng, qǐ chuáng,

起 床， 起 床，

rise | bed | rise | bed

Get up, get up,

nǐ qǐ de zǎo bu zǎo?

你起得早不早？

you | rise | [**aux.**] | early | not | early

do you get up early?

Hěn zǎo, hěn zǎo,

很早，很早，

very | early | very | early

Very early, very early,

wǒ qǐ chuáng qǐ de hěn zǎo.

我起 床 起得很早。

I | rise | bed | rise | [**aux.**] | very | early

I get up very early.

Shuì jiào, shuì jiào,

睡 觉，睡 觉，

sleep | a sleep | sleep | a sleep

Sleep, sleep,

nǐ shuì de wǎn bu wǎn?

你睡得晚不晚？

you | sleep | [aux.] | late | not | late

do you sleep late?

Bù wǎn,　bù wǎn,

不晚，不晚，

not | late | not | late

Not late, not late,

wǒ shuì jiào shuì de bù wǎn.

我睡觉睡得不晚。

I | sleep | a sleep | sleep | [aux.] | not | late

I do not sleep late.

Kàn shū, kàn shū,

看书，看书，

look | book | look | book

Read books, read books,

nǐ kàn de duō bu duō?

你看得多不多？

you | look | [aux.] | many | not | many

do you read a lot?

Bù duō,　bù duō,

不多，不多，

not | many | not | many

Not a lot, not a lot,

wǒ kàn shū kàn de bù duō.

我看书看得不多。

I | look | book | look | [aux.] | not | many

I do not read a lot.

Zuò fàn,　zuò fàn,

做饭，做饭，

make | meals | make | meals

Cook meals, cook meals,

nǐ zuò de hǎo bu hǎo?
你做**得**好 不 好？
you | make | [**aux.**] | good | not | good
do you cook well?

Hěn hǎo, hěn hǎo,
很 好，很 好，
very | good | very | good
Very well, very well,

wǒ zuò fàn zuò de hěn hǎo.
我做饭做**得**很 好。
I | make | meals | make | [**aux.**] | very | good
I cook very well.

二　看与说　Read and Speak

Now, listen to the recording while looking at the following sentences. Then read it out aloud. Finally, recite it by heart to yourself and then to your classmates or instructor.

起床，起床，

你起得早不早？

很早，很早，

我起床起得很早。

睡觉，睡觉，

你睡得晚不晚？

不晚，不晚，

我睡觉睡得不晚。

看书，看书，
你看得多不多？
不多，不多，
我看书看得不多。

做饭，做饭，
你做得好不好？
很好，很好，
我做饭做得很好。

三 理解 Understand

If we want to ask whether someone is a good cook, our question in English can simply be "Do you cook well?" You can answer to this question affirmatively by saying, "I cook very well." We put the phrase "very well" after the action word "cook". We can also do that in Chinese, but we must add the auxiliary word 得 *de* between the action word and the word or phrase we use to describe the action, such as 很好 *hěn hǎo* (very well): 我做得很好 *wǒ zuò de hěn hǎo*. However, 做 *zuò* only means "make", and "to cook" in Chinese is 做饭 *zuò fàn* (make meals). As the second syllable 饭 *fàn* means "meals" and is not an action, 得 *de* cannot be placed after it. It is wrong to say: 我做饭得很好 *wǒ zuò fàn de hěn hǎo*. It is also wrong to say 我做得饭很好 *wǒ zuò de fàn hěn hǎo* because 得 *de* should not be placed before 饭 *fàn* either since it is not a word or phrase to describe the action 做 *zuò*. To make the sentence grammatically correct, we will have to say: 我做饭做得很好 *wǒ zuò fàn zuò de hěn hǎo.*

So, whenever the action has a receiver, state the doer, the action, and the receiver of the action, and then repeat the action word before 得 *de* and the word or phrase to describe the action. For example,

Tā chàng gē chàng de hěn hǎo.
他唱歌唱得很好。
(He sings very well.)

Tā chī fàn chī de bù duō.
他吃饭吃得不多。
(He does not eat much.)

Tā hē chá hē de hěn kuài lè.
他喝茶喝得很快乐。
(He drinks tea happily.)

Tā qí chē qí de hěn kuài.
他骑车骑得很快。
(He rides his bike fast.)

四 实践 Practice

1. 对话 *Conversation*

A: 你在美国做饭吗?

B: 做!

A: 你做得好不好?

B: 我妈说我做得很好。

A: 你常给家里人做吗?

B: 不常做。

A: 给你自己做得多吗?

B: 晚饭每天都自己做。

A: 午饭呢?
B: 午饭在大学餐厅吃。
A: 早饭吃不吃?
B: 不吃。我起得很晚。
A: 起得晚，睡得也晚吧?
B: 是，每天都十二点以后睡。

2. 交际 Communication

Task 1 When a couple of Chinese friends and you are discussing which restaurant to go to for your Saturday dinner, recommend your favorite restaurant by stating that their dishes are cooked extremely well and are not expensive.

Task 2 Your Chinese friend is hanging out at your dorm one evening. When he/she spots one of your homework sheets, he/she asks whether it is your homework. Cover it quickly and say that you didn't do well and feel embarrassed to let your friend see it.

Task 3 You have just moved into a new apartment with a few other international students. You are planning to have an apartment warm-up party. Tell your friends that you don't cook well but you will buy Coke and Sprite and sing English songs for your Chinese friends.

3. 书写 Writing

de [auxiliary word]; gain　*Piě, piě, shù; shù, héngzhé, héng, héng, héng, héng, shùgōu, diǎn.*

得									

Dì-sānshíyī   kè   Nǐ yào qù nǎr?

第三十一课 你要去哪儿？

Lesson 31   **Where do you want to go?**

一 听与看 Listen and Read

Listen to the recording of the following sentences as many times as possible until you can say it along with the recording. You should also look at the following transcription while listening and try to imitate.

Qù nǎr?   Qù nǎr?

去哪儿？去哪儿？

go | which | [suffix] | go | which | [suffix]

Where to go? Where to go?

Nǐ yào qù nǎr?

你要去哪儿？

you | want | go | which | [suffix]

Where do you want to go?

Yào qù shāngdiàn ma?

要去 商 店吗？

want | go | **business** | store | [ques.]

Do you want to go to a store?

Yào qù,   yào qù,

要去， 要去，

want | go | want | go

I want to go, I want to go,

xiànzài jiù yào qù.

现在就要去。

present | at | **at once** | want | go

I want to go right now.

Qù nǎr?   Qù nǎr?

去哪儿？去哪儿？

go | which | [suffix] | go | which | [suffix]

Where to go? Where to go?

Nǐ xiǎng qù nǎr?

你 想 去 哪儿?

you | **think** | go | which | [suffix]

Where would you like to go?

Xiǎng qù Zhōngguó ma?

想 去 中国 吗?

think | go | middle | country | [ques.]

Would you like to go to China?

Hěn xiǎng qù, hěn xiǎng qù,

很 想 去, 很 想 去,

very | **think** | go | very | **think** | go

I would love to go, I would love to go,

hěn xiǎng qù kànkan.

很 想 去 看看。

very | **think** | go | look

I would love to go and have a look.

Qù nǎr? Qù nǎr?

去哪儿? 去哪儿?

go | which | [suffix] | go | which | [suffix]

Where to go? Where to go?

Nǐ néng qù nǎr?

你 能 去 哪儿?

you | **able** | go | which | [suffix]

Where can you go?

Néng qù Huǒxīng ma?

能 去 火星 吗?

able | go | **fire** | star | [ques.]

Can you go the Mars?

Bù néng, bù néng,

不 能 , 不 能 ,

not | **able** | not | **able**

I cannot, I cannot,

xiànzài hái bù néng.

现在还不能。

present | at | still | not | **able**

I cannot yet now.

Zuò shénme? Zuò shénme?

做什么？做什么？

do | what | [suffix] | do | what | [suffix]

What to do? What to do?

Nǐ huì zuò shénme?

你会做什么？

you | **know how** | do | what | [suffix]

What do you know how to do?

Nǐ huì kāi chē ma?

你会开车吗？

you | **know how** | **open** | vehicle | [ques.]

Do you know how to drive?

Huì kāi, huì kāi,

会开，会开，

know how | open | know how | open

I know how to, I know how to,

kāi de hái búcuò.

开得还不错。

open | [aux.] | still | not | **wrong**

I drive quite well.

Zuò shénme? Zuò shénme?

做什么？做什么？

do | what | [suffix] | do | what | [suffix]

What to do? What to do?

Nǐ kěyǐ zuò shénme?

你可以做什么？

you | able | [prefix] | do | what | [suffix]

What are you allowed to do?

Kěyǐ   xī yān ma?

可以吸烟吗？

able | [prefix] | inhale | smoke | [ques.]

Are you allowed to smoke?

Bù kěyǐ,   bù kěyǐ,

不可以，不可以，

not | able | [prefix] | not | able | [prefix]

I may not, I may not,

shìnèi bù   kěyǐ.

室内不可以。

room | inner | not | able | [prefix]

I may not smoke in the room.

Zuò shénme? Zuò shénme?

做什么？做什么？

do | what | [suffix] | do | what | [suffix]

What to do? What to do?

Nǐ yīnggāi zuò shénme?

你应该做什么？

you | should | should | do | what | [suffix]

What should you do?

Yīnggāi hē jiǔ ma?

应该 喝酒吗？

should | should | drink | alcohol | [ques.]

Should drink alcohol?

Bù yīnggāi,   bù yīnggāi,

不应该，不应该，

not | should | should | not | should | should

I should not, I should not,

xuésheng bù   yīnggāi.

学生 不 应该。

learn | person | not | should | should

students should not.

二 看与说 Read and Speak

Now, listen to the recording while looking at the following sentences. Then read it out aloud. Finally, recite it by heart to yourself and then to your classmates or instructor.

去哪儿？去哪儿？

你要去哪儿？

要去商店吗？

要去，要去，

现在就要去。

去哪儿？去哪儿？

你想去哪儿？

想去中国吗？

很想去，很想去，

很想去看看。

去哪儿？去哪儿？

你能去哪儿？

能去火星吗？

不能，不能，

现在还不能。

做什么？做什么？
你会做什么？
你会开车吗？
会开，会开，
开得还不错。

做什么？做什么？
你可以做什么？
可以吸烟吗？
不可以，不可以，
室内不可以。

做什么？做什么？
你应该做什么？
应该喝酒吗？
不应该，不应该，
学生不应该。

三 理解 Understand

There are six auxiliary verbs used in this lesson: 要 *yào*, 想 *xiǎng*, 能 *néng*, 会 *huì*, 可以 *kěyǐ*, and 应该 *yīnggāi*. The first two (要 *yào* and 想 *xiǎng*) are also often used as regular verbs. Regular verbs are those that denote actions, and auxiliary verbs are helping words used before regular verbs to indicate intention, wishes, ability, possibility, permission, obligation of carrying out these actions denoted by the regular verbs.

1) [要 *yào* + verb] means "desire to do something". For example,

> *Wǒ yào xué Hànyǔ.*
> 我要学汉语。
> I **want** to learn Chinese.

2) [想 *xiǎng* + verb] means "would like to do something". It emphasizes the wish or planning of carrying out an action and [要 *yào* + verb] stresses the urge or will of carrying out an action. For example,

> *Wǒ xiǎng qǐng tā kàn diànyǐng.*
> 我 想 请她看 电影。
> I **would like to** invite her to see a movie.

If the wish is strong, 很 *hěn* (very) may be added before 想 *xiǎng*. For example,

> *Wǒ hěn xiǎng qǐng tā kàn diànyǐng.*
> 我很 想 请她看 电影。
> I **would very much like to** invite her to see a movie.

If the wish is so strong that it has become a will, then use 要 *yào*. However, 很 *hěn* is never used with 要 *yào*.

> *Wǒ yào qǐng tā kàn diànyǐng.*
> 我要请她看 电影。
> I **will** invite her to see a movie.

3) [能 *néng* + verb] means "can or be able to do something". Like "can" in English, 能 *néng* denotes two types of "ability": a) internal ability that is on the part of a person, and b) ability conditioned by external factors. For example,

> *Tā néng shuō Hànyǔ.*
> 他能 说 汉语。(personal ability)
> He **can** speak Chinese.

> *Jīntiān tā yǒu kòngr,　néng qù kàn diànyǐng.*
> 今天她有空儿，能去看 电影。(circumstantial ability)
> Today she is free and **can** go to see a movie.

If this ability is on the part of a person rather than conditioned by external factors, then 很 *hěn* can be added before 能 *néng* to mean "very capable of doing something". For example,

> *Tā hěn néng hē jiǔ.*
> 他很能 喝酒。
> He **is very capable of** drinking (without getting drunk).

4) [会 *huì* + verb] means "know how to do something". For example,

> *Tā huì zuò Zhōngguó fàn.*
> 他会做 中国 饭。
> He **knows how to** cook Chinese meals.

> *Tā bú huì yòng cídiǎn.*
> 他不会用词典。
> He **does not know how to** use a dictionary.

很 *hěn* can also be added before 会 *huì* to form 很会 *hěn huì*, and the meaning is "be very good at". For example,

> *Tā hěn huì zuò Zhōngguó fàn.*
> 他很会做 中国 饭。
> He **is very good at** cooking Chinese meals.

[会 *huì* + verb] has another meaning: "be likely or possible to do something". Note that if 会 *huì* takes on this meaning, then 很 *hěn* should not be added. For example,

> *Tā huì lái shàngkè ma?*
> 他会来上课吗?
> Is he **likely to** come to have a class?

5) [可以 *kěyǐ* + verb] in its affirmative form has the same meaning as [能 *néng* + verb]. Therefore, in their affirmative forms, they can be used interchangeably without affecting the meaning. Both of them can be used to ask for permission. However, [可以 *kěyǐ* + verb] is more often used when asking for and giving permission than [能 *néng* + verb]. Both forms use 不能 *bù néng* as their negative form to express the meaning of "unable to do something", and both forms use 可以 *kěyǐ* as their positive form to give positive permissions. For example,

> *Tā néng shuō Hànyǔ ma?*
> 他能 说 汉语 吗?
> **Is** he **able** to speak Chinese?

> *Bù néng.*
> 不能。(ability)
> He's **not**.

> *Tā kěyǐ shuō Hànyǔ ma?*
> 他可以说 汉语 吗?
> **Is** he **able** to speak Chinese?

> *Bù néng.*
> 不能。(ability)
> He's **not**.

> *Wǒ kěyǐ yòng yíxiàr nǐ de diànhuà ma?*
> 我可以用一下儿你的电话吗?
> **May** I use your telephone?

> *Kěyǐ.*
> 可以。(permission)
> You **may**.

> *Wǒ néng yòng yíxiàr nǐ de diànhuà ma?*
> 我能 用一下儿你的电话吗?
> **Can** I use your telephone?

> *Kěyǐ.*
> 可以。(permission)
> You **can**.

6) [应该 *yīnggāi* + verb] means "should or ought to do something." For example,

> *Wǒmen yīnggāi gǎnxiè lǎoshī.*
> 我们**应该**感谢老师。
> We **should** thank our teacher.

四 实践 Practice

1. 对话 Conversation

A: 明天是星期六，你想去哪儿？

B: 我想出去玩儿玩儿。

A: 你要不要去西山？

B: 好啊！ 李贵有车，他能不能去？

A: 我现在就给他打一个电话。

B: 他说能不能去？

A: 不能。可是他说我可以开他的车去。

B: 你会开车吗？

A: 会啊！

B: 你开得好不好？

A: 在美国我开得很不错。

B: 在中国呢？

A: 明天我开开让你看看。

B: 我看，我们还是坐车去吧。

2. 交际 Communication

Task 1 During the 10-minute class recess, you chat with your Chinese instructor. Tell him/her that your parents and your younger brother are scheduled to come to China to see you. When your instructor asks whether your younger brother is also learning Chinese, tell him/her that he really would like to learn it, but he is a middle school student now and his school does not offer Chinese language classes.

Task 2 The garment you bought yesterday at a small store has a problem. Since you feel that your Chinese is not good enough, you make a phone call to a Chinese friend to explain the situation and to ask if he/she can go to the store with you to talk with the salesperson.

Task 3 When a new international student asks you whether smoking is allowed, tell him/her that smoking is not allowed indoors and that it is allowed outdoors.

 *3. 书写 Writing*

shāng   business   *Diǎn, héng, diǎn, piě, shù, héngzhégōu, piě, diǎn, shù, héngzhé, héng.*

商								

jiù   at once   *Diǎn, héng, shù, héngzhé, héng, shùgōu, diǎn, diǎn; héng, piě, shùwāngōu, diǎn.*

就								

xiǎng   think; would like to   *Héng, shù, piě, diǎn; shù, héngzhé, héng, héng, héng; diǎn, wògōu, diǎn, diǎn.*

想								

néng   able   *Piězhé, diǎn, shù, héngzhégōu, héng, héng; piě, shùwāngōu, piě, shùwāngōu.*

能								

huǒ   fire   *Diǎn, piě, piě, nà.*

火								

huì   know how; be likely to   *Piě, nà, héng, héng, piězhé, diǎn.*

会								

kāi open; drive *Héng, héng, piě, shù.*

开

cuò wrong *Piě, héng, héng, héng, shùtí; héng, shù, shù, héng, shù, héngzhé, héng, héng.*

错

xī inhale *Shù, héngzhé, héng; piě, héngzhézhépiě, nà.*

吸

yān smoke *Diǎn, piě, piě, diǎn; shù, héngzhé, héng, piě, diǎn, héng.*

烟

shì room *Diǎn, diǎn, hénggōu; héng, piězhé, diǎn, héng, shù, héng.*

室

nèi inner *Shù, héngzhégōu, piě, diǎn.*

内

yīng should; respond *Diǎn, héng, piě; diǎn, diǎn, piě, héng.*

应

gāi should; deserve *Diǎn, héngzhétí; diǎn, héng, piězhé, piě, piě, diǎn.*

该

Dì-sānshí'èr   kè   *Wǒ yòu kànle   yì běn shū.*

第三十二课   我又看了一本书。
Lesson 32   I read another book.

一　听与看　Listen and Read

Listen to the recording of the following sentences as many times as possible until you can say it along with the recording. You should also look at the following transcription while listening and try to imitate.

Zuótiān zǎoshang,   nǐ kàn mei kàn shū?

昨天 早上，你看 没 看书？
past | day | early | up | you | look | not | look | book
Yesterday morning, did you read any book?

Wǒ kànle   yì běn shū.

我 看了一本书。
I | look | [aux.] | one | [meas.] | book
I read one book.

Kàn shū yǐhòu,   nǐ hē mei hē shuǐ?

看 书以后，你喝没喝水？
look | book | [prefix] | back | you | drink | not | drink | water
After reading, did you drink any water?

Wǒ hēle   yì bēi shuǐ.

我 喝了一杯 水。
I | drink | [aux.] | one | cup/glass | water
I drank one glass of water.

Hē shuǐ yǐhòu,   nǐ chī mei chī miàn?

喝水以后，你吃没吃 面 ？
drink | water | [prefix] | back | you | eat | not | eat | noodle
After drinking water, did you eat any noodles?

Wǒ chīle   yì wǎn miàn.

我吃了一碗 面 。
I | eat | [aux.] | one | bowl | noodle
I ate one bowl of noodle.

Chī miàn yǐhòu,   nǐ shuì mei shuì jiào?
吃 面 以后，你 睡 没 睡 觉？
eat | **noodle** | [prefix] | back | you | sleep | not | sleep | a sleep
After eating noodles, did you get any sleep?

Wǒ shuìle   yíhuìr   jiào.
我 睡 了 一会儿 觉。
I | sleep | [aux.] | one | while | [suffix] | a sleep
I slept for a while.

Shuìxǐng yǐhòu,   nǐ kàn mei kàn shū?
睡 醒 以后，你 看 没 看 书？
sleep | **awake** | [prefix] | back | you | look | not | look | book
After waking up, did you read any book?

Wǒ yòu kànle   yì běn shū.
我 又 看 了 一本书。
I | **again** | look | [aux.] | one | [meas.] | book
I read another book.

二 看与说 Read and Speak

Now, listen to the recording while looking at the following sentences. Then read it out aloud. Finally, recite it by heart to yourself and then to your classmates or instructor.

昨天早上，你看没看书？

我看了一本书。

看书以后，你喝没喝水？

我喝了一杯水。

喝水以后，你吃没吃面？

我吃了一碗面。

吃面以后，你睡没睡觉？

我睡了一会儿觉。

睡醒以后，你看没看书？

我又看了一本书。

三　理解　Understand

In our daily life, there are three different time contexts in which an action takes place: past, present, and future. In each of the three time frames (i.e., tenses), an action can be in different action stages (i.e., aspects). It may be in its progress, in its continuation, or in its completion. To indicate an action in a time frame or in a stage in a particular time frame, different languages have different ways. In English, verbs are inflected for the present and the past, and an auxiliary word is added to indicate the future. For example,

Past	Present	Future
drank	drink	shall/will drink
ate	eat	shall/will eat
slept	sleep	shall/will sleep

In English, verbs in their continuous stage and in their completive stage are indicated by having an auxiliary word and inflected verbs. For example,

	Past	Present	Future
Continuous:	were eating	are eating	shall/will be eating
Completive:	had eaten	have eaten	shall/will have eaten
Cont. + Compl.:	had been eating	have been eating	shall/will have been eating

In Chinese, verbs are not inflected for different time frames. The time frame in which an action takes place is either sensed from the context or indicated by adding a time expression or a particular sentence structure. Stages of an action are often indicated by adding auxiliary words. In Lesson 28, we have learned to add 在 *zài* right before a verb and/or 呢 *ne* at the end of a sentence to indicate that the action denoted by the verb or stated in the sentence is in progress. In this lesson, we are learning to use 了 *le* right after a verb to indicate the action denoted by the verb is accomplished. For example,

> *Tā mǎile liǎng bě̌n shū.*
> 他买了 两 本书。
> He **has bought** two books.

> *Tā hēle sān bēi shuǐ.*
> 他喝了三杯水。
> He **has drunk** three glasses of water.

了 *le* right after a verb is an accomplishment or realization indicator and is not a past time marker. In Chinese, the past time frame is indicated by time expressions; however, in English, an accomplished action is often expressed as a past action, giving us the false impression that 了 *le* right after verb is a past time marker. Therefore, no matter what time frame it may be or how it may be marked in English, if an action is accomplished, use 了 *le* right after the verb denoting the action. For example,

> *Zuótiān tā mǎile liǎng bě̌n shū.*
> 昨天他买了 两 本书。
> **Yesterday** he **bought** one book.

> *Zuótiān tā hēle sān bēi shuǐ.*
> 昨天他喝了三杯水。
> **Yesterday** he **drank** three glasses of water.

没 *méi* is the negation word for an action that has not been accomplished. It is placed before the verb. Note that the accomplishment marker 了 *le* attached after the verb is not needed in negation. For example,

> *Tā méi mǎi liǎng bě̌n shū.*
> 他没买 两 本书。
> He **has not bought** two books.

*Zuótiān tā **méi** hē sān bēi shuǐ.*
昨天他**没**喝三杯水。
Yesterday he **did not drink** three glasses of water.

When questioning whether an action is accomplished or not, we can use the affirmative-negative question format: verb 没 *méi* verb. For example,

Nǐ mǎi mei mǎi shū?
你买没买书？
Have you **bought** any books?

Zuótiān nǐ mǎi mei mǎi shū?
昨天你买没买书？
Did you **buy** any books **yesterday**?

四　实践　Practice

1. 对话 Conversation

A: 星期天你出去了吗？

B: 没出去。我在宿舍呆 *dāi* (stay) 了一天。

A: 你怎么没出去玩儿？

B: 我看了一本特有意思的书。

A: 什么好书？

B: 《红星下的中国》。

A: 中午吃没吃饭？

B: 吃了。吃了一大碗面，还喝了一杯水。

A: 你这午饭可不怎么好。

B: 书好啊！

A: 你一天看了一本书，累不累？

B: 还行。中午我睡了一会儿。

2. 交际 Communication

Task 1 Your Chinese instructor knew that you planned to go shopping over the weekend. When she sees you in class, she asks what you bought. Tell her that you bought two books, three bottles of water, one pack (包 bāo) of tea, and one piece (块 kuài) of meat.

Task 2 Your Chinese friend lives very close to campus. One day when you hang out at her house, it happens to be around lunch time. They insist in having you eat lunch with them at their house. Thank them for their hospitality and tell them that you really ate lunch and you are not just trying to be polite. Say that you and your roommate today ate four dishes and drank two big bottles of beer.

Task 3 When you return to class from a long weekend, your classmates are talking about their activities. Say that you didn't go anywhere and stayed at your dorm for three days and read five books, three English ones and two Chinese ones.

3. 书写 Writing

yòu   again   *Héngpiě, nà.*

又								

le   [auxiliary word]   *Héngpiě, shùgōu.*

了								

zuó   yesterday; past   *Shù, héngzhé, héng; héng, piě, héng, shù, héng, héng.*

昨								

shuǐ　water　*Shùgōu, héngpiě, piě, nà.*

水

wǎn　bowl　*Héng, piě, shù, héngzhé, héng; diǎn, diǎn, hénggōu, piě, héngpiě, diǎn, héngzhégōu, shùwāngōu.*

碗

miàn　noodle; flour　*Héng, piě, shù, héngzhé, shù, shù, héng, héng, héng.*

面

xǐng　awake　*Héng, shù, héngzhé, piě, shùwān, héng, héng; shù, héngzhé, héng, héng, piě, héng, héng, shù, héng.*

醒

Dì-sānshísān kè   *Nǐ qù nǎr le?*

第三十三课   你去哪儿了?
Lesson 33   **Where did you go?**

一   听与看   Listen and Read

Listen to the recording of the following sentences as many times as possible until you can say it along with the recording. You should also look at the following transcription while listening and try to imitate.

Zuótiān shàngwǔ ,

昨天 上午,

past | day | up | **noon**

Yesterday morning,

nǐ qù nǎr le?

你去哪儿了?

you | go | which | [suffix] | [aux.]

where did you go?

Túshūguǎn, túshūguǎn,

图书馆,图书馆,

chart | book | hall | **chart** | book | hall

Library, library,

wǒ qù túshūguǎn le.

我去图书馆了。

I | go | **chart** | book | hall | [aux.]

I went to the library.

Zuótiān xiàwǔ ,

昨天下午,

past | day | down | **noon**

Yesterday afternoon,

nǐ qù nǎr le?

你去哪儿了?

you | go | which | [suffix] | [aux.]

where did you go?

Kàn diànyǐng, kàn diànyǐng,

看 电影，看 电影，

look | electric | shadow | look | electric | shadow

See a movie, see a movie,

wǒ qù kàn diànyǐng le.

我去看 电影 了。

I | go | look | electric | shadow | [aux.]

I went to see a movie.

Zuótiān wǎnshang,

昨天 晚上，

past | day | late | up

Yesterday evening,

nǐ qù nǎr le?

你去哪儿了？

you | go | where | [suffix] | [aux.]

where did you go?

Méi qù nǎr,   méi qù nǎr,

没去哪儿，没去哪儿，

not | go | where | [suffix] | not | go | where | [suffix]

I went nowhere, I went nowhere,

wǒ huí jiā qù shuì jiào le.

我回家去睡 觉了。

I | **return** | home | go | sleep | a sleep | [aux.]

I went back home to sleep.

二 看与说 Read and Speak

Now, listen to the recording while looking at the following sentences. Then read it out aloud. Finally, recite it by heart to yourself and then to your classmates or instructor.

昨天上午，

你去哪儿了？

图书馆，图书馆，

我去图书馆了。

昨天下午，

你去哪儿了？

看电影，看电影，

我去看电影了。

昨天晚上，

你去哪儿了？

没去哪儿，没去哪儿，

我回家去睡觉了。

三 理解 Understand

In this lesson, we see that 了 *le* is placed in a different place. It is not placed right after verbs, but at the end of sentences. When 了 *le* is right after a verb, it indicates the action denoted by the verb is in the completion stage. When 了 *le* is put at the end of a sentence, it means the whole thing stated in the sentence has occurred, and it is a new situation and new information to be given to the listener by the speaker. Again, an event that has occurred is usually a past event; therefore, it is often expressed and indicated by an inflected verb in the past tense in English. Look at the following sentences. To native English speakers, "where has he gone" and "where did he go" have two different time frames and stages. However, native Chinese speakers just use one same question 他去哪儿了 *tā qù nǎr le* for the two English questions.

Tā qù nǎr le?
他去哪儿了？
Where **has** he **gone**? (He has not come back yet.)

Tā qù shūdiàn le.
他去书店了。
He **has gone** to the bookstore.

Tā qù nǎr le?
他去哪儿了？
Where **did** he go? (He went out but has come back now.)

Tā qù shūdiàn le.
他去书店了。
He **went** to the bookstore.

Zuótiān tā qù nǎr le?
昨天他去哪儿了？
Where **did** he **go yesterday**?

Zuótiān tā méi qù shūdiàn, tā qù túshūguǎn le.
昨天他没去书店，他去图书馆了。
Yesterday he **did not** go to the bookstore; he **went** to the library.

四 实践 Practice

1. 对话 Conversation

A: 昨天晚上，你去哪儿了？
B: 我去看电影了。
A: 我找了你半天！

B: 对不起，对不起！真对不起！

A: 你怎么没给我打个电话？

B: 我去得晚了一点儿，真的没空儿给你打。

A: 我想你是不是去图书馆了。我去看了，你没在。

B: 上午我还真的去图书馆了。

A: 看电影以后，你怎么也没给我打电话？

B: 我特想睡觉，就回宿舍睡觉去了。

A: 让我找了半天。你应该请我看电影吧？

B: 好，我请你看两个电影！

2. 交际 Communication

Task 1 You are on an outing with a few Chinese friends on a Sunday morning. After eating lunch, you did not feel well and rush to a restroom nearby. When you come back, your friends ask where you have been. Explain the situation to them.

Task 2 When you come back to your dorm, your Chinese roommate asks where you have been since your mom called three times. Tell him/her that you went to the library. Since tomorrow you have an exam, you stayed at the library the whole afternoon.

Task 3 During the 10-minute recess, one of your classmates decides to go back to his/her dorm room since he/she only slept for three hours last night. When your instructor returns, explain the situation to him/her on behalf of your classmate.

3. 书写 Writing

wǔ   noon   *Piě, héng, héng, shù.*

午									

tú   chart   *Shù, héngzhé, piě, héngpiě, nà, diǎn, diǎn, héng.*

图								

huí   return   *Shù, héngzhé, shù, héngzhé, héng, héng.*

回								

第三十四课   电影 就要 开始了。
Lesson 34   The movie is about to start.

一   听与看   Listen and Read

Listen to the recording of the following sentences as many times as possible until you can say it along with the recording. You should also look at the following transcription while listening and try to imitate.

Kuài zǒu ba,   kuài zǒu ba,
快 走 吧，快 走 吧，
fast | walk | [aux.] | fast | walk | [aux.]
Let's walk quickly, let's walk quickly,

diànyǐng jiù yào kāishǐ le.
电影 就要 开始了。
electric | shadow | at once | want | open | **begin** | [aux.]
the movie is about to start.

Kuài pǎo ba,   kuài pǎo ba,
快 跑 吧，快 跑 吧，
fast | **run** | [aux.] | fast | **run** | [aux.]
Let's run quickly, let's run quickly,

wǒmen jiù yào chídào le.
我们就要迟到了。
I | [plural] | at once | want | **tardy** | **arrive** | [aux.]
we are about to be late.

Kuài zuò fàn ba,   kuài zuò fàn ba,
快 做饭吧，快 做饭吧，
fast | make | meal | [aux.] | fast | make | meal | [aux.]
Let's cook soon, let's cook soon,

wǒmen dōu yào èsǐ le.
我们 都 要 饿死了。
I | [plural] | all | want | **hungry** | **die** | [aux.]
we are all so hungry that we are about to die.

Kuài xiūxi ba,   kuài xiūxi ba,
快 休 息 吧， 快 休 息 吧，
fast | rest | breath | [aux.] | fast | rest | breath | [aux.]
Let's rest soon, let's rest soon,

wǒmen dōu yào lèisǐ le.
我 们 都 要 累 死 了。
I | [plural] | all | want | **tired** | **die** | [aux.]
we are all so tired that we are about to die.

二　看与说　Read and Speak

Now, listen to the recording while looking at the following sentences. Then read it out aloud. Finally, recite it by heart to yourself and then to your classmates or instructor.

快走吧，快走吧，
电影就要开始了。
快跑吧，快跑吧，
我们就要迟到了。

快做饭吧，快做饭吧，
我们都要饿死了。
快休息吧，快休息吧，
我们都要累死了。

三 理解 Understand

In this lesson, we see that 了 *le* is placed at the end of sentences again. It appears that each of these sentences with 了 *le* attached to the end states an event that has occurred before the moment of the speech; however, we can also see that before each action word, there is the auxiliary verb 要 *yào*, which implies desire or will if not used with 了 *le*. With 了 *le* at the end of a sentence, 要 *yào* used before the verb in the sentence indicates imminence (i.e., the immediate future). The degree of imminence can be enhanced by having the adverb 就 *jiù* (at once) before 要 *yào*. For example,

> *Hànyǔkè jiù yào kāishǐ le.*
> 汉语课就要开始了。
> The Chinese class is about to start.

> *Tā jiù yào qù Zhōngguó le.*
> 他就要去中国了。
> He will soon go to China.

To ask a question about whether an event will soon take place, we either put the question word 吗 *ma* at the end of the 要 *yào* sth. 了 *le* statement or just place 是不是 *shì bu shì* before 要 *yào* or 就要 *jiù yào* in the sentence. If the answer to the question is positive, we can say: 是 *shì* (yes) or 对 *duì* (correct). If the answer is negative, then we often say: 没有 *méiyou* (no). To soften the tone, we can add the adverb 还 *hái* (still) before 没有 *méiyou*. 还没有 *hái méiyou* (still not yet). It is a mild negation which recognizes the fact that an event will take place but not as soon as the 要 *yào* sth. 了 *le* statement implies. For example,

> *Hànyǔkè jiù yào kāishǐ le ma?*
> 汉语课就要开始了吗?
> Is the Chinese class about to start?

> *Méiyou.*
> 没有。
> No.

> *Hànyǔkè shì bu shì jiù yào kāishǐ le?*
> 汉语课是不是就要开始了？
> Is the Chinese class about to start?

> *Hái méiyou.*
> 还没有。
> Still not yet.

快 *kuài* means "fast" or "quick". It can be used before an action word to urge people to hurry up with the action. For example,

快看	*kuài kàn*	look quickly
快吃	*kuài chī*	eat quickly
快走	*kuài zǒu*	walk quickly

死 *sǐ* means "die" or "death". If someone died, we can say 他死了 *tā sǐ le* in Chinese. In colloquial Chinese, putting 死了 *sǐ le* as a consequence after a verb or an adjective creates an exaggerated expression, meaning "extremely" just like the English expression "to death", For example,

> *Wǒ mángsǐ le.*
> 我忙死了。
> I am busy to death.

> *Wǒ yào mángsǐ le.*
> 我要忙死了。
> I am so busy that I am about to die.

四　实践　Practice

1. 对话 Conversation

A: 电影是几点的？
B: 五点半的。
A: 现在都快五点十分了。

B: 我们快走吧。
A: 我去一下儿厕所。
B: 快点儿，快点儿！
A: 好了。走吧。
B: 我们迟到了。快跑吧！

(At home right after the movie)

A: 快做饭吧。我都要饿死了。
B: 我正在做呢。
A: 什么时候能吃啊?
B: 一会儿就好了。

(After dinner)

A: 快来看电视！乐死我了。
B: 我都要累死了。不看，不看。
A: 那你快去睡吧。

2. 交际 Communication

Task 1 On a hot summer day, your classroom is pretty stuffy. When a classmate of yours asks you to go to the snack bar to buy a bottle of water with him/her, say that it is almost class time and suggest not going.

Task 2 When a Chinese friend calls to ask you to eat dinner in a restaurant off campus, say that it is going to rain (下雨 xià yǔ) soon and suggest eating at the school cafeteria instead of at an off-campus restaurant.

Task 3 One day, you have a long chat with your Chinese roommate. Suggest ending your chat by saying: "It is almost 1:00. I am extremely tired. Let's sleep now."

3. 书写 Writing

shǐ begin *Piědiǎn, piě, héng; piězhé, diǎn, shù, héngzhé, héng.*

始									

pǎo run *Shù, héngzhé, héng, shù, héng, shù, tí; piě, héngzhégōu, héngzhé, héng, shùwāngōu.*

跑									

chí tardy *Héngzhé, héng, piě, diǎn; diǎn, héngzhézhépiě, píngnà.*

迟									

dào arrive *Héng, piězhé, diǎn, héng, shù, tí; shù, shùgōu.*

到									

è hungry *Piě, hénggōu, shùtí; piě, héng, shùgōu, tí, xiégōu, piě, diǎn.*

饿									

sǐ die *héng, piě, héngpiě, diǎn, piě, shùwāngōu.*

死									

lèi tired *Shù, héngzhé, héng, shù, héng, piězhé, piězhé, diǎn, shùgōu, diǎn, diǎn.*

累									

Dì–sānshíwǔ   kè   Nǐ   shuìle   duō cháng shíjiān?

第三十五课　　你睡了多长时间？
Lesson 35　　　　How long did you sleep?

一　听与看　Listen and Read

Listen to the recording of the following sentences as many times as possible until you can say it along with the recording. You should also look at the following transcription while listening and try to imitate.

Zuótiān,   zuótiān,   zuótiān,

昨天，昨天，昨天，

past | day | past | day | past | day

Yesterday, yesterday, yesterday,

nǐ   shuìle duō cháng shíjiān?

你睡了多　长　时间？

you | sleep | [aux.] | much | **long** | time | **space**

how long did you sleep?

Bā xiǎoshí,   bā xiǎoshí,

八小时，八小时，

eight | small | time | eight | small | time

Eight hours, eight hours,

wǒ shuìle bā xiǎoshí.

我睡了八小时。

I | sleep | [aux.] | eight | small | time

I slept for eight hours.

Zuò yè ,   zuò yè ,   zuò yè ,

作业，作业，作业，

labor | **doings** | labor | **doings** | labor | **doings**

Homework, homework, homework,

nǐ   zuòle duō cháng shíjiān?

你做了多　长　时间？

you | do | [aux.] | much | **long** | time | **space**

how long did you do it?

Liǎng xiǎoshí,   liǎng xiǎoshí,
两 小时, 两 小时,
two | small | time | two | small | time
Two hours, two hours,

wǒ   zuòle liǎng xiǎoshí.
我 做了 两 小时。
I | do | [aux.] | two | small | time
I did it for two hours.

Wǎnfàn,   wǎnfàn,   wǎnfàn,
晚饭, 晚饭, 晚饭,
late | meal | late | meal | late | meal
Dinner, dinner, dinner,

nǐ   chīle duō cháng shíjiān?
你 吃了 多 长 时间?
you | eat | [aux.] | much | **long** | time | **space**
how long did you eat?

Bàn xiǎoshí,   bàn xiǎoshí,
半 小时, 半 小时,
half | small | time | half | small | time
Half an hour, half an hour,

wǒ   chīle bàn xiǎoshí.
我 吃了 半 小时。
I | eat | [aux.] | half | small | time
I ate for half an hour.

二 看与说 Read and Speak

Now, listen to the recording while looking at the following sentences. Then read it out aloud. Finally, recite it by heart to yourself and then to your classmates or instructor.

昨天, 昨天, 昨天,

你睡了多长时间?

八小时，八小时，
我睡了八小时。

作业，作业，作业，
你做了多长时间？
两小时，两小时，
我做了两小时。

晚饭，晚饭，晚饭，
你吃了多长时间？
半小时，半小时，
我吃了半小时。

三　理解　Understand

When we ask about the time, it is a point of time we want to know. When we ask how long it takes someone to do something, it is a period of time we would like to find out. It is important to make this distinction. Look at the following table.

	Points of Time When? 什么时候?	Periods of Time How long? 多长时间?
Minute	*yì diǎn líng wǔ fēn* [一点 零] 五分 (1:05)	*yì fēnzhōng* 一 分钟 (one minute) *liǎng fēnzhōng* 两 分钟 (two minutes)
Quarter	*[yì diǎn] yí kè* [一点] 一刻 (1:15) *[yì diǎn] sān kè* [一点] 三刻 (1:45)	*yí kè zhōng* 一刻 钟 (one quarter of an hour) *sān kè zhōng* 三 刻 钟 (three quarters of an hour)
Hour	*yì diǎn (zhōng)* 一点 (钟) (1:00) *yì diǎn bàn* 一点 半 (1:30) *liǎng diǎn (zhōng)* 两 点 (钟) (2:00)	*yì xiǎoshí* 一 小时 (one hour) *liǎng xiǎoshí* 两 小时 (two hours) *bàn xiǎoshí* 半 小时 (half an hour) *yí ge bàn xiǎoshí* 一个 半 小时 (an hour and a half)
Day	*zuótiān* 昨天 (yesterday) *jīntiān* 今天 (today) *míngtiān* 明天 (tomorrow) 2008 *nián* 5 *yuè* 1 *rì* 2008 年 5 月 1 日 (May 1st, 2008) *dì-yī tiān* 第一天 (the first day) *dì-èr tiān* 第二天 (the second day)	*yì tiān* 一天 (one day) *yì tiān bàn* 一天 半 (one day and a half) *liǎng tiān* 两 天 (two days)

Week	*Xīngqīyī* 星期一 (Monday) *Xīngqī'èr* 星期二 (Tuesday), … *shàng xīngqī shàng zhōu* 上　星期 / 上　　周 (last week) *zhèi xīngqī zhèi zhōu* 这　星期 / 这　　周 (this week) *xià xīngqī xià zhōu* 下　星期 / 下　周 (next week) *dì-yī zhōu* 第一　周 (the first week) *dì-èr zhōu* 第二　周 (the second week)	*yí ge xīngqī* 一个　星期 (one week) *liǎng ge xīngqī* 两　个　星期 (two weeks) *yì zhōu* 一　周 (one week) *liǎng zhōu* 两　周 (two weeks)
Month	*Yīyuè* 一月 (January), *Èryuè* 二月 (February), … *shàng ge yuè* 上　个月 (last month) *zhèi ge yuè* 这个月 (this month) *xià ge yuè* 下个月 (next month)	*yí ge yuè* 一个月 (one month) *yí ge bàn yuè* 一个 半 月 (one month and a half) *liǎng ge yuè* 两　个月 (two months)
Year	*qùnián* 去年 (last year) *jīnnián* 今年 (this year) *míngnián* 明年 (next year) 2008 *nián* 2008 年 (2008), 2009 *nián* 2009 年 (2009), …	*bàn nián* 半　年 (half a year) *yì nián* 一　年 (one year) *yì nián bàn* 一　年　半 (one year and a half) *liǎng nián* 两　年 (two years)

It is important to distinguish points of time from periods of time because in Chinese, a word or expression for a point of time is placed before the verb in a sentence to denote when the action takes place, whereas an expression for a period of time is usually placed after the verb as a time-measure complement to denote the duration of the action. For example,

> *Tā měi tiān **xiàwǔ liù diǎn** xiūxi.*
> 他每天**下午六点**休息。
> Every day he takes a rest **at 6 o'clock in the afternoon**.

> *Tā měi tiān xiūxi **yì xiǎoshí**.*
> 他每天休息**一小时**。
> Every day he takes a rest **for one hour**.

The two example sentences are about habitual actions, so there is no need to use 了 *le*. However, if we want to say that he rested for two hours yesterday afternoon (i.e., the action of resting was realized for two hours yesterday afternoon), we can say,

> *Tā zuótiān xiàwǔ xiūxi le liǎng xiǎoshí.*
> 他昨天下午休息了两小时。
> He rested for two hours yesterday afternoon.

If we want to know how long he rested yesterday afternoon, then 多长时间 *duō cháng shí jiān* (how long) should be used:

> *Tā zuótiān xiàwǔ xiūxi le duō cháng shíjiān?*
> 他昨天下午休息了多长时间？
> How long did he rest yesterday afternoon?

Periods of time are placed after the action of a sentence to inform how long the action lasts. 休息 *xiūxi* is a two-syllable verb that does not take any recipient. If the action in a sentence has a recipient, then we usually need to reduplicate the action and attach the period of time to the action. For example,

> *Tā zuótiān xiàwǔ kàn shū kàn le duō cháng shíjiān*
> 他昨天下午看书看了多长时间？
> How long did he read a book yesterday afternoon?

> *Tā zuótiān xiàwǔ kàn shū kànle sān xiǎoshí.*
> 他昨天下午看书看了三小时。
> He read a book for three hours yesterday afternoon.

A commonly used variation of this sentence structure with a reduplicated verb is to move the recipient after the expression for the period of time and use 的 *de* in between. See the example below,

> *Tā zuótiān xiàwǔ   kànle sān xiǎoshí de shū.*
> 他昨天下午看了三小时**的**书。
> He read a book for three hours yesterday afternoon.

If the recipient of the action is definite (e.g., a definite book), then the recipient becomes the topic of the sentence and is often moved to the very beginning of the sentence, and the rest of the sentence serves as the comment on the topic. After the move, there is no need to reduplicate the verb because the expression for a period of time will be right after the verb. See the example below,

> *Zhè bèn shū tā zuótiān xiàwǔ   kànle sān xiǎoshí.*
> 这本书他昨天下午看了三小时。
> He read **this book** for three hours yesterday afternoon.

Now, we know and we should keep this in mind: In Chinese, if the recipient of an action appears at the beginning of a sentence, it is definite; and if the recipient of an action is definite, it can be moved to the very beginning of the sentence.

四 实践 Practice

1. 对话 *Conversation*

A: 你怎么还没做作业?
B: 我睡了一觉。
A: 你睡了多长时间?

B: 睡了两个多小时。

A: 快做吧！ 昨天的作业你也没做。

B: 昨天我不是跟朋友去吃晚饭了吗？

A: 你们吃什么晚饭吃了三小时？

B: 中国饭！ 特好吃！

2. 交际 Communication

Task 1 When you are chatting with your host family at their apartment, the topic of foreign language learning is brought up. Tell them that when you were in your home country, you studied French for three years and studied Chinese for one year.

Task 2 You are studying with your Chinese friend at the library. Your friend notices you keep on yawning and asks you why you are so tired. Tell him/her that you only slept for 5 hours last night. When you are asked why you slept so little, say that you spent 3 hours doing your homework.

Task 3 Soon after your return to your dorm at 11 p.m., your phone rings. It is your dad who calls. Your dad says he called three times and asks why you come back so late. Tell him that you went out to eat dinner with a few Chinese friends. When your dad asks how long you ate, say that you ate for one hour but talked for three hours.

3. 书写 Writing

cháng   long   *Piě, héng, shùtí, nà.*

长									

jiān   space   *Diǎn, shù, héngzhégōu; shù, héngzhé, héng, héng.*

间									

yè   doings; course of study   *Shù, shù, diǎn, piě, héng.*

业									

Dì–sānshíliù   kè   Nǐ xuéle   jǐ nián le?

第三十六课　你学了几年了？
Lesson 36   How many years have you been learning?

一　听与看　Listen and Read

Listen to the recording of the following sentences as many times as possible until you can say it along with the recording. You should also look at the following transcription while listening and try to imitate.

Zài Měiguó,   zài Měiguó,

在美国，在美国，

at | beautiful | country | at | beautiful | country

In the U.S., in the U.S.,

nǐ   zhùle   jǐ nián le?

你 住了几年了？

you | live | [aux.] | how many | **year** | [aux.]

how many years have you been living here?

Hěn duō nián le,   hěn duō nián le,

很 多 年 了，很 多 年 了，

very | many | **year** | [aux.] | very | many | **year** | [aux.]

Many years, many years,

wǒ   zhùle hěn duō nián le.

我 住了很 多 年 了。

I | live | [aux.] | very | many | **year** | [aux.]

I have been living here for many years.

Zhèi běn shū, zhèi běn shū,

这 本书，这 本书，

this | [meas.] | book | this | [meas.] | book

This book, this book,

nǐ   kànle   jǐ tiān le?

你 看了几天了？

you | look | [aux.] | how may | day | [aux.]

how many days have you been reading it?

Liǎng tiān le,　　liǎng tiān le.
两　天了，两　天了，
two | day | [aux.] | two | day | [aux.]
Two days, two days,

wǒ　kànle liǎng tiān le.
我 看了两　天了。
I | look | [aux.] | two | day | [aux.]
I have been reading it for two days.

Zhōngwén,　　Zhōngwén　Zhōngwén
中　文，　中　文，　中　文，
middle | **language** | middle | **language** | middle | **language**
Chinese language, Chinese language, Chinese language,

nǐ　xuéle　jǐ nián le?
你学了几年了？
you | learn | [aux.] | how many | **year** | [aux.]
how many years have you been learning it?

Yì nián le,　　yì nián le,
一年了，一年了，
one | **year** | [aux.] | one | **year** | [aux.]
One year, one year,

wǒ　xuéle　yì nián le.
我学了一年了。
I | learn | [aux.] | one | **year** | [aux.]
I have been learning it for one year.

二　看与说　Read and Speak

Now, listen to the recording while looking at the following sentences. Then read it out aloud. Finally, recite it by heart to yourself and then to your classmates or instructor.

在美国，在美国，
你住了几年了？

很多年了，很多年了，

我住了很多年了。

这本书，这本书，

你看了几天了？

两天了，两天了，

我看了两天了。

中文，中文，中文，

你学了几年了？

一年了，一年了，

我学了一年了。

三 理解 Understand

In the previous lesson, we have learned that in Chinese, a period of time for an action is usually placed after the action. If the action has already taken place and has lasted for a period of time, then 了 *le* is added right after the action word and before the period of time. However, in this lesson, we see another 了 *le* placed at the end of a sentence, which is also the end of an expression for a period of time. With one 了 *le* after the verb and another 了 *le* at the end of the sentence, the expression for a period of time is sandwiched. In a sentence like this, it means that the action has lasted for the period of time up to the moment of the speech and will continue. It is the same as the "perfect continuous" aspect in English. Look at the following examples,

Wǒmen hē chá hēle liǎng ge xiǎoshí le.	*Wǒmen hēle liǎng ge xiǎoshí de chá le.*
我们喝茶喝了两个小时了。	or 我们喝了两个小时的茶了。

We **have been drinking** tea for two hours.

Tā shuì jiào shuìle yì tiān le.	*Tā shuìle yì tiān de jiào le.*
他睡觉睡了一天了。	or 他睡了一天的觉了。

He **has been sleeping** for one day.

Although we have learned the rule to put expressions for durations of time after actions, there is one situation where expressions for durations of time are not placed after but before actions. Whenever we want to express the idea that we have not done something for a period of time, we put the period of time before the negated action. For example,

Wǒmen liǎng tiān méi hē chá le.
我们**两天没**喝茶了。
We have not drunk tea **for two days**.

Wǒ hěn cháng shíjiān méi shuō Zhōngwén le.
我很长时间没说中文了。
I have not spoken Chinese **for a long time**.

中文 *Zhōngwén* and 汉语 *Hànyǔ* both refer to "the Chinese language." However, 中文 *Zhōngwén* also contains Chinese literature, whereas 汉语 *Hànyǔ* does not. If we say 我爱学汉语 *wǒ ài xué Hànyǔ*, native Chinese speakers will know that we love to learn the Chinese language, and no one will think that we love to learn Chinese literature as well.

四　实践　Practice

1. 对话 Conversation

A: 你在美国住了几年了？
B: 住了很多年了。
A: 你看的这本书是中文的吧？

B: 是。我已经看了两天了。

A: 好吗?

B: 很有意思! 你也应该看看。

A: 你常看中文书吗?

B: 上学期没时间, 这学期每天都看。

A: 你的朋友也能看中文书吗?

B: 他会说一点儿汉语, 认识的汉字太少。

A: 他学汉语学了几年了?

B: 学了两年了。

2. 交际 Communication

Task 1 When you chat with your host family, ask them how long they have lived in the city they are living in and ask whether they enjoy living here.

Task 2 When you are eating at your school cafeteria, a Chinese student initiates a talk with you in pretty good English. Give compliment for his/her English proficiency and ask how long he/she has been learning English.

Task 3 When your Chinese friend sees that you are close to the last page of a pretty sophisticated Chinese story book and shows astonishment, tell him/her that you love the book and you read it with a dictionary and you have been reading it for two months.

✐ 3. 书写 Writing

nián   year   *Piě, héng, héng, shù, héng, shù.*

年									

wén   language; writing   *Diǎn, héng, piě, nà.*

文									

第三十七课　你去过吗？

Lesson 37 　　Have you ever been there?

一　听与看　**Listen and Read**

Listen to the recording of the following sentences as many times as possible until you can say it along with the recording. You should also look at the following transcription while listening and try to imitate.

Zhōngguó, Zhōngguó, Zhōngguó,

中国，中国，中国，

middle | country | middle | country | middle | country

China, China, China,

nǐ   qùguo   ma?   Nǐ   qùguo   ma?

你去过吗？你去过吗？

you | go | [aux.] | [ques.] | you | go | [aux.] | [ques.]

have you ever been there? Have you ever been there?

Qùguo,   qùguo,   qùguo.

去过，去过，去过。

go | [aux.] | go | [aux.] | go | [aux.]

Yes, yes, yes.

Qùguo jǐ cì?   Qùguo jǐ cì?

去过几次？去过几次？

go | [aux.] | how many | **occurrence** | go | [aux.] | how many | **occurrence**

How many times? How many times?

Yí cì,   liǎng cì,   sān cì,

一次，两次，三次，

one | **occurrence** | two | **occurrence** | three | **occurrence**

Once, twice, three times,

wǒ   qùguo hěn duō cì.

我去过很多次。

I | go | [aux.] | very | many | **occurrence**.

I have been there many times.

Zhōngguófàn, Zhōngguófàn,

中国饭，中国饭，

middle | country | meal | middle | country | meal

Chinese food, Chinese food,

nǐ chīguo ma?   Nǐ chīguo ma?

你吃过吗？你吃过吗？

you | eat | [aux.] | [ques.] | you | eat | [aux.] | [ques.]

have you ever had it? Have you ever had it?

Chīguo,   chīguo,   chīguo.

吃过，吃过，吃过。

eat | [aux.] | eat | [aux.] | eat | [aux.]

Yes, yes, yes.

Chīguo jǐ cì?   Chīguo jǐ cì?

吃过几次？吃过几次？

eat | [aux.] | how many | occurrence | eat | [aux.] | how many | occurrence

How many times? How many times?

Yí cì,   liǎng cì,   sān cì,

一次，两次，三次，

one | occurrence | two | occurrence | three | occurrence

Once, twice, three times,

wǒ chīguo hěn duō cì.

我吃过很多次。

I | eat | [aux.] | very | many | occurrence

I have had it many times.

Zhèi ge diànyǐng, zhèi ge diànyǐng,

这个电影，这个电影，

this | [meas.] | electric | shadow | this | [meas.] | electric | shadow

This movie, this movie,

nǐ kànguo ma?   Nǐ kànguo ma?

你看过吗？你看过吗？

you | look | [aux.] | [ques.] | you | look | [aux.] | [ques.]

have you ever seen it? Have you ever seen it?

Kànguo,   kànguo,   kànguo.
看过，看过，看过。
look | [aux.] | look | [aux.] | look | [aux.]
Yes, yes, yes.

Kànguo jǐ biàn?   Kànguo jǐ biàn?
看过几遍？看过几遍？
look | [aux.] | how many | time through | look | [aux.] | how many | time through
How many times? How many times?

Yí biàn,   liǎng biàn,   sān biàn,
一遍，两遍，三遍，
one | time through | two | time through | three | time through
Once through, twice through, three times through,

wǒ kànguo   hěn duō biàn.
我看过很多遍。
I | look | [aux.] | very | many | time through
I have seen it many times through.

Nánjí,   Nánjí,   Nánjí,
南极，南极，南极，
south | extreme | south | extreme | south | extreme
South Pole, South Pole, South Pole,

nǐ qùguo ma?   Nǐ qùguo ma?
你去过吗？你去过吗？
you | go | [aux.] | [ques.] | you | go | [aux.] | [ques.]
have you ever been there? Have you ever been there?

Méi qùguo,   méi qùguo,
没去过，没去过，
not | go | [aux.] | not | go | [aux.]
I have never been there, I have never been there,

wǒ yí cì dōu méi qùguo.
我一次都没去过。
I | one | occurrence | all | not | go | [aux.]
I have not been there even once.

Máotáijiǔ,   Máotáijiǔ,

茅台酒，茅台酒，

thatch | platform | alcohol | thatch | platform | alcohol

Maotai Liquor, Maotai Liquor,

nǐ hēguo ma?   Nǐ hēguo ma?

你喝过吗？你喝过吗？

you | drink | [aux.] | [ques.] | you | drink | [aux.] | [ques.]

have you ever drunk it? Have you ever drunk it?

Méi hēguo,   méi hēguo,

没喝过，没喝过，

not | drink | [aux.] | not | drink | [aux.]

I have never drunk it, I have never drunk it,

wǒ yí cì dōu méi hēguo.

我一次都 没喝过。

I | one | occurrence | all | not | drink | [aux.]

I have not drunk it even once.

Zhèige gùshi,   zhèige gùshi,

这个故事，这个故事，

this | [meas.] | former | matter | this | [meas.] | former | matter

This story, this story,

nǐ tīngguo ma?   Nǐ tīngguo ma?

你听过吗？你听过吗？

you | listen | [aux.] | [ques.] | you | listen | [aux.] | [ques.]

have you ever listened to it? Have you ever listened to it?

Méi tīngguo,   méi tīngguo,

没听过，没听过，

not | listen | [aux.] | not | listen | [aux.]

I have never listened to it, I have never listened to it,

wǒ yí biàn dōu méi tīngguo.

我一遍 都没听过。

I | one | time through | all | not | listen | [aux.]

I have not listened to it even once through.

二 看与说　Read and Speak

Now, listen to the recording while looking at the following sentences. Then read it out aloud. Finally, recite it by heart to yourself and then to your classmates or instructor.

中国，中国，中国，

你去过吗？你去过吗？

去过，去过，去过。

去过几次？去过几次？

一次，两次，三次，

我去过很多次。

中国饭，中国饭，

你吃过吗？你吃过吗？

吃过，吃过，吃过。

吃过几次？吃过几次？

一次，两次，三次，

我吃过很多次。

这个电影，这个电影，

你看过吗？你看过吗？

看过，看过，看过。
看过几遍？看过几遍？
一遍，两遍，三遍，
我看过很多遍。

南极，南极，南极，
你去过吗？你去过吗？
没去过，没去过，
我一次都没去过。

茅台酒，茅台酒，
你喝过吗？你喝过吗？
没喝过，没喝过，
我一次都没喝过。

这个故事，这个故事，
你听过吗？你听过吗？
没听过，没听过，
我一遍都没听过。

三　理解　Understand

过 *guo* is an auxiliary word used right after a verb to denote the past experiential nature of the action, meaning "have had the experience of doing something". The negation is formed by adding 没有 *méiyou* or simply 没 *méi* before the verb immediately followed by 过 *guo*. For example,

Nǐ qùguo Zhōngguó ma?
你去过 中国 吗?
Have you ever been to China?

Wǒ qùguo.   Tā méi qùguo.
我去过。他没去过。
Yes, I have. He has not.

To ask whether someone has a certain experience or not, we can also use one of the following forms:

Nǐ qù méi qùguo Zhōngguó ?   méi   guo
你去没去过 中国 ? (verb + 没 verb 过)
Have you ever been to China?

Nǐ qùguo Zhōngguó méiyou?   méiyou
你去过 中国 没有? (attach 没有 at the end of an affirmative statement)
Have you ever been to China?

If we count the number of occurrences an action is carried out, we use a numeral word with an action measure word such as 次 *cì* or 遍 *biàn* to form a numeral-measure phrase and place it right after the verb and before the recipient of the action if there is one. While both 次 *cì* and 遍 *biàn* denote the number of times for an action, 遍 *biàn* is always chosen if the entire process of an action from the beginning to the end needs to be emphasized. For example,

Wǒ qùguo yí cì Zhōngguó.
我去过一次中国。
I have been to China once.

Wǒ kànguo sān biàn zhèige diànyǐng.
我看过三遍 这个电影。
I have seen this movie three times through.

We know that if the recipient of an action is definite, then it can be placed at the beginning of a sentence. So, the above two sentences can also be:

> *Zhōngguó wǒ qùguo yí cì.*
> 中国 我去过一次。
> I have been to China once.

> *Zhèi ge diànyǐng wǒ kànguo sān biàn.*
> 这个电影我看过三遍。
> I have seen this movie three times through.

If we want to express the idea that not even once have we had the experience of doing something in Chinese, then we will need to say:

> *Zhōngguó wǒ yí cì dōu yě méi qùguo.*
> 中国 我一次都（or 也）没去过。
> As for China, I have not been there even once.

> *Zhèi ge diànyǐng wǒ yí cì dōu yě méi kànguo.*
> 这个电影我一次都（or 也）没看过。
> As for this movie, I have seen it even once.

四 实践 Practice

1. 对话 Conversation

A: 我朋友说，你去过中国。
B: 是啊，去过一次。
A: 这个电影你看过吗？
B: 在中国的时候，看过一次。是中文的。
A: 这个是英文的，还想看吗？
B: 想啊。这是个好电影。
A: 我这儿还有一个电影，叫《南极》。
B: 没听说过这个名字。看两个电影，没那么多时间吧？

A: 行，那就看一个。

B: 看完 *wán* (finish) 以后，我请你吃饭。我们去蓝星酒
家。

A: 不好意思，又要让你花钱。

B: 不用客气。他们那儿的菜做得很好。

A: 你常去这个饭馆儿吃吗?

B: 去过很多次。

☞ 2. 交际 Communication

Task 1 You go out to eat dinner with a Chinese friend at a restaurant. When discussing your orders, make your suggestions by pointing at one entry on the menu and say that you have had that dish before and it is extremely good. Point at another entry and say that you have never had that dish before, but its name is very interesting and suggest that as a choice as well.

Task 2 When you ask your Chinese friend about his plan for his vocation week, he says he is going to Beijing since he has never been there before. When he asks you whether you have been to Beijing before, tell him that you have been there twice and think Beijing is a fun place to go to.

Task 3 At a banquet, a friendly Chinese sitting next to you says that the smallest glass in front of you contains the famous Chinese Maotai liquor and asks whether you have drunk it before. Tell him that you have learned the word 茅台酒 *Máotáijiǔ* in your Chinese language class and have seen Chinese people drinking it in movies but you have never had a personal experience drinking it. Say that you will just have a little bit to know whether you like it or not.

3. 书写 Writing

guo; guò [aux. for past experience]; pass   *Héng, shùgōu, diǎn; diǎn, héngzhézhépiě, píngnà.*

过								

cì occurrence   *Diǎn, tí; piě, hénggōu, piě, nà.*

次								

biàn once through   *Diǎn, héngzhé, héng, piě, shù, héngzhégōu, héng, shù, shù; diǎn, héngzhézhépiě, píngnà.*

遍								

nán south   *Héng, shù, shù, héngzhégōu, diǎn, piě, héng, héng, shù.*

南								

jí extreme   *Héng, shù, piě, diǎn; piě, héngzhézhépiě, nà.*

极								

máo thatch grass   *Héng, shù, shù; héngpiě, diǎn, hénggōu, shùgōu, piě.*

茅								

tái platform   *Piězhé, diǎn, shù, héngzhé, héng.*

台								

gù former   *Héng, shù, shù, héngzhé, héng; piě, héng, piě, nà.*

故								

shì   matter   *Héng, shù, héngzhé, héng, héngzhé, héng, héng, shùgōu.*

事									

tīng   listen   *Shù, héngzhé, héng; piě, piě, héng, shù.*

听									

Dì-sānshíbā   kè   Zánmen bié qù   le.

第三十八课　咱们别去了。
Lesson 38
Let's not go any more.

一　听与看　Listen and Read

Listen to the recording of the following sentences as many times as possible until you can say it along with the recording. You should also look at the following transcription while listening and try to imitate.

Zhēn hǎo,   zhēn hǎo!

真 好，真 好！

really | good | really | good

Really good , really good!

Jīntiān   tiānqì zhēn hǎo.

今 天 天 气 真 好。

present | day | sky | air | really | good

Today's weather is really good.

Zánmen qù gōngyuánr ba.

咱 们 去 公 园 儿 吧。

I | [plural] | go | public | garden | [suffix] | [aux.]

Let's go to a park.

Zāogāo,   zāogāo!

糟 糕，糟 糕！

rotten | cake | rotten | cake

Too bad, too bad!

Guā fēng le,   xià yǔ le.

刮 风 了，下 雨 了。

blow | wind | [aux.] | down | rain | [aux.]

It's windy now, and it is raining now.

Zánmen bié qù gōngyuánr le.

咱 们 别 去 公 园 儿 了。

I | [plural] | don't | go | public | garden | [suffix] | [aux.]

Let's not go to the park any more.

Zhēn hǎo,　zhēn hǎo!
真 好，真 好！
really | good | really | good
Really good, really good!

Chūntiān tiānqì zhēn hǎo.
春 天天气真 好。
spring | sky | sky | air | really | good
The spring weather is really good.

Zánmen qù zhàoxiàng ba.
咱们去 照相 吧。
I | [plural] | go | shine | appearance | [aux.]
Let's go to take pictures.

Nǐ kàn,　nǐ kàn,
你看，你看，
you | look | you | look
Look, look,

huā kāi le,　shù lǜ le.
花开了，树绿了。
flower | open | [aux.] | tree | green | [aux.]
flowers have come into bloom, and trees have turned green.

Zánmen bié wàngle zhàoxiàng le.
咱们 别 忘 了 照相 了。
I | [plural] | don't | forget | [aux.] | shine | appearance | [aux.]
Let's not forget to take pictures. (Let's stop forgetting to take pictures.)

Jǐ diǎn le? Jǐ diǎn le?
几点了？几点了？
how many | o'clock | [aux.] | how many | o'clock | [aux.]
What time is it now? What time is it now?

Xiànzài yǐjīng shí diǎn le.
现在已经十点了。
present | at | already | undergo | ten | o'clock | [aux.]
It's already 10 o'clock now.

Tài wǎn le,   tài wǎn le,

太 晚 了，太 晚 了，

too | late | [aux.] | too | late | [aux.]

Too late now, too late now,

wǒmen dōu bù xiǎng qù le.

我们 都 不 想 去 了。

I | [plural] | all | not | think | go | [aux.]

none of us would like to go any more.

Duōshao qián?   Duōshao qián?

多少 钱？多少 钱？

much | little | money | much | little | money

How much is it? How much is it?

Xiànzài zhǐ yào yì bǎi le.

现在 只要一百了。

present | at | **only** | want | one | **hundred** | [aux.]

It is only one hundred now.

Tài guì le,   tài guì le,

太 贵 了，太 贵 了，

too | expensive | [aux.] | too | expensive | [aux.]

Too expensive, too expensive,

wǒmen dōu bù xiǎng mǎi le.

我们 都 不 想 买 了。

I | [plural] | all | not | think | buy | [aux.]

none of us would like to buy it any more.

二 看与说 Read and Speak

Now, listen to the recording while looking at the following sentences. Then read it out aloud. Finally, recite it by heart to yourself and then to your classmates or instructor.

真好，真好！

今天天气真好。

咱们去公园儿吧。
糟糕，糟糕！
刮风了，下雨了。
咱们别去公园儿了。

真好，真好！
春天天气真好。
咱们去照相吧。
你看，你看，
花开了，树绿了。
咱们别忘了照相了。

几点了？几点了？
现在已经十点了。
太晚了，太晚了，
我们都不想去了。

多少钱？多少钱？
现在只要一百了。

太贵了，太贵了，
我们都不想买了。

三　理解　Understand

If a sentence contains no expression for a period of time and has a 了 *le* at its end, then this 了 *le* indicates that the event stated in the sentence has occurred, implying a change in situation. How do we understand the sentences with 了 *le* in this lesson? Look at the following discussion.

In English, sentences that describe natural phenomena often use "it" as the subject, but in Chinese, no subject is used. When 了 *le* is put at the end of these sentences, it means that it was not then, it is now. For example,

Guā fēng le.
刮风了。 (了 *le* implied that the old situation of being not windy has been changed.)
It is windy now.

Xià yǔ le.
下雨了。 (了 *le* implied that the old situation of having no rain has been changed.)
It is raining now.

Xià xuě le.
下雪了。 (了 *le* implied that the old situation of having no snow has been changed.)
It is snowing now.

When asking what time it is, we can say 现在几点 *xiànzài jǐ diǎn* without using 了 *le*. However, if we have lost the track of time and wonder what time it has become now, we use 了 *le* to imply that we knew what time it was, but we want to know what time it is now as there has been a change in time: 现在几点了 *xiànzài jǐ diǎn le*? As it is obvious that the new time we want to know is the current time, 现在 *xiànzài* can be omitted:

> *Jǐ diǎn le?*
> 几点了？
> What time is it now? (What time has it become now?)

> *Shíyī diǎn le.*
> 十一点了。
> It's 11 o'clock now. (It has become 11 o'clock now.)

已经 *yǐjīng* means "already". It is often used in a sentence to stress that the action or the event stated in the sentence has occurred by the moment of the speech. Therefore, it is often used with 了 *le* at the end of a sentence. 已经 *yǐjīng* sth. 了 *le* is also used in a sentence that has an action attached with the experiential maker 过 *guo* to emphasize the past experience.

> *Yǐjīng   shíyī diǎn le.*
> 已经十一点了。
> It's already 11 o'clock now. (It has already become 11 o'clock now.)

> *Wǒ yǐjīng   qùguo Zhōngguó le.*
> 我已经去过中国了。
> I have already been to China.

太 *tài* means "too" or "excessively". When it is used with a descriptive word, it implies that it is more than acceptable. However, 太 *tài* can also mean "extremely" when used with positive words like 美 *měi* (beautiful), 好 *hǎo* (good, nice), including the words formed with 好 *hǎo*, such as 好吃 *hǎochī* (delicious), 好喝 *hǎohē* (tasty to drink), and 好玩儿 *hǎowánr* (fun), as they can never be excessive for people. It does not matter whether 太 *tài* means "too" or "extremely", it is often used with 了 *le*, probably indicating that it is not what our mind set is ready for, and therefore, it is a new circumstance for us.

> *Tài zǎo le.*   *Tài cháng le.*   *Tài hǎo le.*
> 太早了。   太长了。   太好了。
> Too early.   Too long.   Wonderful.

If 了 *le* is used in a sentence that has 不 *bù* to negate an action or a state, then it indicates that the situation which was going on earlier has now ceased. For example,

Jīntiān wǒ bú qù kàn diànyǐng le.
今天我不去看电影了。
I am not going to see a movie today. (I was going to, but I have changed my mind.)

Tā bù xué Zhōngwén le.
他不学中文了。
He does not learn Chinese any more. (He used to, but he has stopped now.)

When 别 *bié* (don't) is used without 了 *le* in a sentence, it just means "don't do something". However, when 别 *bié* (don't) is used in a sentence with 了 *le* in the end, the meaning conveyed now is "stop doing something". For example,

Bié dǎ diànhuà.
别打电话。
Don't make phone calls.

Bié dǎ diànhuà le.
别打电话了。
Don't make phone calls **any more**. (**Stop** making phone calls.)

忘 *wàng* means "to forget". If we forget something, we will not say 我忘 *wǒ wàng*; instead, we say 我忘了 *wǒ wàng le*. The verb 忘 *wàng* must have 了 *le* after it to indicate the realization stage of the action. When we say "don't forget" in English, what it means is to avoid the result of "having forgotten" rather than to stop the process of "forgetting". Therefore, the Chinese equivalent for "don't forget" is 别忘了 *bié wàng le*. In fact, 忘 *wàng* is almost always used with 了 *le*. So, "don't forget to take pictures" in Chinese is 别忘了照相 *bié wàngle zhàoxiàng*. If someone has or is viewed to have the tendency to forget to take pictures, then to remind him or her to avoid the result of having forgotten to take pictures, we will say 别忘了照相了*bié wàngle zhàoxiàng le* (stop forgetting to take pictures).

咱们 *zánmen* is always used to include both the speaker and the listener(s). On the other hand, 我们 *wǒmen* may be used to denote the same meaning as 咱们 *zánmen*, it may also be used to refer to the speaker only. Whether 我们 *wǒmen* includes or excludes the listener(s), we can usually tell from the context. For example,

Bàba,　**zánmen** qù kàn　diànyǐng ba.
爸爸，**咱们去看** 电影吧。(including the listener)
Dad, **let's** go to see a movie.

Bàba,　**wǒmen** qù kàn　diànyǐng ba.
爸爸，**我们去看** 电影吧。(including the listener)
Dad, **let's** go to see a movie.

Bàba,　**wǒmen** xiǎng　kàn diànyǐng.
爸爸，**我们** 想 看电影。(excluding the listener)
Dad, **we** want to see a movie.

四 实践 Practice

1. 对话 Conversation

A: 啊，昨天这一觉睡得太好了！

B: 你看，今天天气真好。咱们去公园吧。

A: 好啊。树都绿了，花也开了，太美了。

B: 别忘了照相了。

A: 不会忘的。

B: 吃点儿饭，咱们就走。

A: 我去做饭。你想吃什么？

B: 都行。

A: 糟糕，刮风了！哎呀，又下雨了！

B: 咱们别去了。

A: 行。那就不去了。

B: 现在几点了？

A: 十二点四十了。

B: 咱们去商店吧。你不是想买个大电视吗？

A: 可是太贵了。我又不想买了。

👋 2. 交际 Communication

Task 1 You are on a weekend tour with your school group. At the end
of your trip, you return to the parking lot to get on your bus.
Since you are one of the earliest students there, you decide to
look at the items at the stand nearby. Bargain for a low price.
When you are not satisfied with the offer of the seller, say that
you are not buying it any more since the price is higher than
your expectation and that your bus is leaving any minute.

Task 2 You told your friends earlier that you would join them for an
outing day at a local park to take photos of the beautiful spring
flowers. When they call you to talk about the leaving time,
apologize and say that you don't feel like going any more since
you are extremely tired and would like to get some extra sleep
on Sunday, so that on Monday during class time you will not
feel tired.

Task 3 One summer night, you are studying in your dorm with your
Chinese roommate. After about two hours, your roommate starts
to feel hungry and ask whether you would like to go out to eat
a snack. Respond by saying that it is too late and suggest not go
out to eat but to eat some instant noodle at the dorm.

✏️ 3. 书写 Writing

zán I *Shù, héngzhé, héng; piě, shù, héngzhé, héng, héng, héng.*

咱									

zāo rotten *Diǎn, piě, héng, shù, piě, diǎn; héng, shù, héngzhé, héng, shù, shù, héng, shù, héngzhé, héng, héng.*

糟									

gāo   cake   Diǎn, piě, héng, shù, piě, diǎn; diǎn, piě, héng, héng, shù, héng, diǎn, diǎn, diǎn, diǎn.

糕

guā   blow; shave   Piě, héng, shù, shù, héngzhé, héng; shù, shùgōu.

刮

fēng   wind   Piě, héngzhéxiégōu, piě, diǎn.

风

chūn   spring   Héng, héng, héng, piě, nà, shù, héngzhé, héng, héng.

春

shù   tree   Héng, shù, piě, diǎn; héngpiě, diǎn; héng, shùgōu, diǎn.

树

wàng   forget   Diǎn, héng, shùzhé; diǎn, wògōu, diǎn, diǎn.

忘

zhào   shine   Shù, héngzhé, héng, héng; héngzhégōu, piě, shù, héngzhé, héng; diǎn, diǎn, diǎn, diǎn.

照

xiàng   appearance   Héng, shù, piě, diǎn; shù, héngzhé, héng, héng, héng.

相

yǐ   already   Héngzhé, héng, shùwāngōu.

已

jīng   undergo   *Piězhé, piězhé, tí; héngpiě, diǎn, héng, shù, héng.*

经

tài   too   *Héng, piě, nà, diǎn.*

太

zhǐ   only   *Shù, héngzhé, héng, piě, diǎn.*

只

bǎi   hundred   *Héng, piě, shù, héngzhé, héng, héng.*

百

第三十九课   桌 上 放着什么？
Lesson 39   What is placed on the table?

一 听与看 Listen and Read

Listen to the recording of the following sentences as many times as possible until you can say it along with the recording. You should also look at the following transcription while listening and try to imitate.

Zhuō shàng fàngzhe   shénme?

桌 上 放着 什么？
table | up | place | [aux.] | what | [suffix]
What is placed on the table?

Zhuō shàng fàngzhe shū.

桌 上 放着书。
table | up | place | [aux.] | book
Books are placed on the table.

Shū shàng xiězhe shénme?

书 上 写着什么？
book | up | write | [aux.] | what | [suffix]
What is written on the book?

Shū shàng xiězhe zì.

书 上 写着字。
book | up | write | [aux.] | character
Characters are written on the book.

Qiáng shàng guàzhe   shénme?

墙 上 挂着 什么？
wall | up | hang | [aux.] | what | [suffix]
What is hung up on the wall?

Qiáng shàng guàzhe huàr.

墙 上 挂着画儿。
wall | up | hang | [aux.] | picture | [suffix]
A painting is hung up on the wall.

Huàr shàng huàzhe　shénme?

画儿 上 画着 什么？
picture | [suffix] | up | paint | [aux.] | what | [suffix]
What is painted on the painting?

Huàr shàng huàzhe huār.

画儿 上 画着花儿。
picture | [suffix] | up | paint | [aux.] | flower | [suffix]
Flowers are painted on the painting.

Fáng qián tíngzhe　shénme?

房 前 停着 什么？
house | front | stop | [aux.] | what | [suffix]
What is parked in front of the house?

Fáng qián tíngzhe　chē.

房 前 停着 车。
house | front | stop | [aux.] | vehicle
A vehicle is parked in front of the house.

Chē shàng xiězhe　shénme?

车 上 写着 什么？
vehicle | up | write | [aux.] | what | [suffix]
What is written on the vehicle?

Chē shàng xiězhe　"mài".

车 上 写着 "卖"。
vehicle | up | write | [aux.] | sell
"For sale" is written on the vehicle.

二　看与说　Read and Speak

Now, listen to the recording while looking at the following sentences. Then read it out aloud. Finally, recite it by heart to yourself and then to your classmates or instructor.

桌上放着什么？

桌上放着书。

书上写着什么？

书上写着字。

墙上挂着什么？

墙上挂着画儿。

画儿上画着什么？

画儿上画着花儿。

房前停着什么？

房前停着车。

车上写着什么？

车上写着"卖"。

三　理解　Understand

In Lesson 26, we have learned the sentence pattern "position word/phrase + 是 *shì* + sth.," which is used to identify what it is at a particular location. For examples, 前边是书店 *qiánbian shì shūdiàn* (in the front is a bookstore). In Lesson 27, we have learned a similar sentence pattern with 有 *yǒu*: position word/phrase + 有 *yǒu* + sth. It is used to report what a particular location physically has in existence. If we see a big cup on a particular table, we can report by saying 桌上有一个大杯子 *zhuō shàng yǒu yí ge dà bēizi* (there is a big cup on the table).

If we want to be more descriptive, we can include more information by reporting that the big cup was placed rather than thrown by somebody on the table by using the verb 放 *fàng* (to place, to put) to replace 有 *yǒu* (to have, to possess) in the sentence. However, unlike 有 *yǒu*, the verb 放 *fàng* is an active action, so 着 *zhe* is used right after it to indicate the continuous stage or state of the action. For example,

> *Zhuō shàng fàngzhe yí ge dà bēizi.*
> 桌   上 放着一个大杯子。
> There is a big cup placed on the table.

The auxiliary word 着 *zhe* used after verbs allows us to be more descriptive in telling other people about what we see how something or somebody is situated as a result of an action in a particular place or at a particular location.

> *Qiáng shàng guàzhe huàr,   huàr shàng huàzhe huār.*
> 墙   上 挂着画儿，画儿上 画着花儿。
> There is a painting hung up on the wall, and there are flowers painted in the painting.

四 实践 Practice

1. 对话 Conversation

A: 你看，这是我爷爷的爷爷住过的房子。

B: 这房子有两百多年了吧。

A: 有了。

B: 那个桌子上放着什么？

A: 一本书。

B: 书上写着什么？ 你认识吗?

A: 这是很老的字，我不认识。

B: 那边墙上，还挂着画呢。

A: 这画儿上画着的花儿，美吧?

B: 真美! 你们家房前停着什么?

A: 那是马车。

B: 马车? 去看看。

A: 这马车上写着"大明车行"。

B: "大明车行"是什么意思?

A: 是我爷爷的爷爷开的店的店名，意思是Big Bright Cart Firm。

2. 交际 Communication

Task 1 You are at a museum in China. Express to your guide your exclamation for the stunning beauty of the flower painting. Ask about what characters are written on the left side of the painting and what their meanings are.

Task 2 On your way to dinner at the school cafeteria, you see about five buses parked near the main school gate. Your language instructor happens to be there on his way to buy dinner at the school cafeteria. Ask him why so many buses are parked here and ask what characters are written on the signs posted in front of the bus window. Your instructor tells you that the Chinese students are going home for their summer vacation and the characters on the signs are the names of the destination each bus is heading for.

Task 3 You are on a bike tour with a friend in a Beijing Hutong (胡同 hútòng) inner city lanes area. When you see a beautiful courtyard house, you get off your bike to appreciate the intricate carpenter and paintwork of the fancy gate. Ask your friend since you wonder what kind of important people live here. Your friend checks the tour book and says in the book it says this courtyard house was the home of the famous writer, 老舍 Lǎoshě.

3. 书写 Writing

fàng　place　*Diǎn, héng, héngzhégōu, piě; piě, héng, piě, nà.*

放									

zhe　[auxiliary word]　*Diǎn, piě, héng, héng, héng, piě, shù, héngzhé, héng, héng, héng.*

着									

qiáng　wall　*Héng, shù, tí; héng, shù, diǎn, piě, héng, shù, héngzhé, shù, héngzhé, héng, héng.*

墙									

guà　hang　*Héng, shùgōu, tí; héng, shù, héng, héng, shù, héng.*

挂									

huà　paint; picture　*Héng, shù, héngzhé, héng, shù, héng, shùzhé, shù.*

画									

tíng　stop; park　*Piě, shù; diǎn, héng, shù, héngzhé, héng, diǎn, hénggōu, héng, shùgōu.*

停									

mài　sell　*Héng, shù, hénggōu, diǎn, diǎn, héng, piě, diǎn.*

卖									

Dì-sìshí kè   *Nǐ zěnme chī fàn?*

第四十课   你怎么吃饭?

Lesson 40   **How do you eat meals?**

一   听与看   **Listen and Read**

Listen to the recording of the following sentences as many times as possible until you can say it along with the recording. You should also look at the following transcription while listening and try to imitate.

Nǐ zěnme chī fàn?

你怎么吃饭?

you | how | [suffix] | eat | meal

How do you eat meals?

Wǒ zuòzhe chī fàn.

我坐着吃饭。

I | sit | [aux.] | eat | meal

I sit down when I eat meals.

Nǐ zěnme chàng gē?

你怎么 唱 歌?

you | how | [suffix] | sing | song

How do you sing songs?

Wǒ zhànzhe chàng gē.

我 站着 唱 歌。

I | **stand** | [aux.] | sing | song

I stand when I sing.

Nǐ zěnme shuō huà?

你怎么说话?

you | how | [suffix] | speak | words

How do you talk?

Wǒ xiàozhe shuō huà.

我 笑着 说话。

I | **laugh** | [aux.] | speak | words

I laugh when I talk.

Nǐ zěnme kàn shū?

你怎么看书?

you | how | [suffix] | look | book

How do you read books?

Wǒ tǎngzhe kàn shū.

我 躺 着 看 书。

I | recline | [aux.] | look | book.

I lie down when I read.

二　看与说　Read and Speak

Now, listen to the recording while looking at the following sentences. Then read it out aloud. Finally, recite it by heart to yourself and then to your classmates or instructor.

你怎么吃饭?

我坐着吃饭。

你怎么唱歌?

我站着唱歌。

你怎么说话?

我笑着说话。

你怎么看书?

我躺着看书。

三　理解　Understand

着 *zhe* is used after a verb to indicate the continuous aspect of the action. More importantly, it is used to indicate the static aspect of the action. 在 *zài* is used before a verb to indicate that the action is in progress. Seemingly, both 着 *zhe* and 在 *zài* are the markers of the continuation of an action. In fact, 在 *zài* is used to express the dynamic nature of the action, whereas 着 *zhe* is used to depict the static mode of the action. Compare the following two sentences:

> *Tā zài chuān yí jiàn lán yīfu.*
> 他在穿一件蓝衣服。
> He is putting on a blue coat.

> *Tā chuānzhe yí jiàn lán yīfu.*
> 他穿着一件蓝衣服。
> He is wearing a blue coat.

The first sentence tells us that "he" is in the process of getting dressed, and the second sentence informs us what "he" has on. When we want an action to keep going, we also use 着 *zhe*. For example,

> *Kànzhe.*   *Děngzhe wǒ.*
> 看着。   等着我。
> Keep watching.   Continue to wait for me.

When there are two actions in a situation with one action to be the manner in which the other action is carried out, the manner action uses 着 *zhe* as the marker at its end, and the manner action is placed before the major action. For example, 唱歌 *chàng gē* (sing songs) and 开车 *kāi chē* (drive a car) are two actions. If 唱歌 *chàng gē* (sing songs) is the manner in which开车 *kāi chē* (drive a car) is carried out by us, then we say:

> *Tā chàngzhe gē kāi chē.*
> 他唱着歌开车。
> He drives a car while singing songs.

However, if 唱歌 *chàng gē* (sing songs) is not the main action and 开车 *kāi chē* (drive a car) is the manner in which 唱歌 *chàng gē* (sing songs) is executed, then the sentence will be:

> *Tā kāizhe chē chàng gē.*
> 他开着车唱歌。
> He sings songs while driving a car.

When we ask for in what manner an action is carried out, we use the question word 怎么 *zěnme* (how). For example,

---

Nǐ zěnme zuò zuòyè?
你怎么做作业?
How do you do your homework?

Wǒ hēzhe chá zuò zuòyè.
我喝着茶做作业。
I do my homework while drinking tea.

四 实践 Practice

1. 对话 Conversation

A: 你是哪个大学的?

B: 北京大学 (Peking University) 的。

A: 在那儿上了几年了?

B: 上了两年了。

A: 在那儿好吗?

B: 学习还行, 身体不太好。

A: 怎么了?

B: 吃饭吃得不多, 看书看一会儿就累。

A: 你怎么吃饭? 怎么看书?

B: 我站着吃饭, 躺着看书。

A: 是吗? 那你怎么能身体好?

B: 怎么了?

A: 我听大夫说, 应该坐着吃饭, 坐着看书。

B: 真的吗?

A: 他还说, 看书以后, 应该站着唱唱歌, 就不会忘
了看过的书。

B: 真的?

A: 还有，笑着说话会让人快乐，会有很多朋友。

B: 这是哪个大夫说的?

2. 交际 Communication

Task 1 You are visiting a middle school in China. When you see that Chinese students stand up straight when they ask or answer a question, tell your guide that you are impressed by the fact that they are so disciplined (学生们做得很好 *xuéshengmen zuò de hěn hǎo*，很听老师的话 *hěn tīng lǎoshī de huà*). When the guide asks you how students in your country answer the teacher's questions, say that middle school students do that in a sitting position instead of standing.

Task 2 You are at a doctor's office in China stating your symptoms as the following. When you stand or sit, your head hurts, and when you are in a lying position, it does not hurt as much.

Task 3 Your Chinese roommate comes back from dinner outside and plans to do his/her homework. When he/she notices that the TV is on and that you are writing characters on your homework sheet, he/she asks whether you intend to continue to watch TV, implying it is time to turn off the TV set. Walk over to turn off the TV and say that you are not really watching and that you just have the bad habit of doing your homework while having the TV on.

3. 书写 Writing

zhàn   stand   *Diǎn, héng, diǎn, piě, tí; shù, héng, shù, héngzhé, héng.*

站									

xiào　laugh　*Piě, héng, diǎn, piě, héng, diǎn; piě, héng, piě, nà.*

笑									

tǎng　recline　*Piě, shù, héngzhégōu, héng, héng, héng, piě; shù, diǎn, piě, shù, héngzhégōu, shù, héngzhé, héng.*

躺									

Dì-sìshíyī   kè   Yáo Míng bǐ   wǒ   gāo.

第四十一课　姚明比我高。
Lesson 41　Yao Ming is taller than I.

一　听与看　Listen and Read

Listen to the recording of the following sentences as many times as possible until you can say it along with the recording. You should also look at the following transcription while listening and try to imitate.

Yáo Míng, Yáo Míng, tā hěn gāo

姚明，姚明，他很高！

[a surname] | bright | [a surname] | bright | he | very | tall

Yao Ming, Yao Ming, he is very tall!

Bǐ wǒ gāo,

比我高，

than | I | tall

Taller than I,

yě bǐ nǐ gāo.

也比你高。

also | than | you | tall

also taller than you.

Wǒmen dōu méi tā nàme gāo.

我们都没他那么高。

I | [plural] | all | not | he | that | [suffix] | tall

None of us is as that tall as he.

Yáo Míng, Yáo Míng, hěn yǒumíng!

姚明，姚明，很有名！

[a surname] | bright | [a surname] | bright | very | have | name

Yao Ming, Yao Ming, very famous!

Bǐ wǒ yǒumíng,

比我有名，

than | I | have | name

More famous than I,

yě bǐ nǐ yǒumíng.

也比你有名。

also | than | you | have | name

also more famous than you.

Wǒmen dōu méi tā yǒumíng.

我们都没他有名。

I | [plural] | all | not | he | have | name

None of us is famous than he.

Yáo Míng Zhōngwén shuō de fēicháng hǎo!

姚明 中文 说得非常好！

[a surname] | bright | middle | language | speak | [aux.] | un- | common | well

Yao Ming speaks Chinese very well.

Bǐ wǒ shuō de hǎo,

比我说得好，

than | I | speak | [aux.] | well

Better than I,

yě bǐ nǐ shuō de hǎo.

也比你说得好。

also | than | you | speak | [aux.] | well

also better than you.

Wǒmen dōu méi tā shuō de hǎo.

我们都没他说得好。

I | [plural] | all | not | he | speak | [aux.] | well

None of us speaks as well as he does.

Yáo Míng lánqiú dǎ de fēi cháng hǎo!

姚明 篮球打得非常 好！

[a surname] | bright | basket | ball | play | [aux.] | un- | common | well

Yao Ming plays the basketball very well!

Bǐ wǒ dǎ de hǎo,

比我打得好，

than | I | play | [aux.] | well

Better than I,

yě bǐ   nǐ dǎ de hǎo.

也比你打得好。

also | than | you | play | [aux.] | well

also better than you.

Wǒmen dōu méi tā dǎ de hǎo.

我们 都 没他打得好。

I | [plural] | all | not | he | play | [aux.] | well

None of us plays as well as he does.

二　看与说　Read and Speak

Now, listen to the recording while looking at the following sentences. Then read it out aloud. Finally, recite it by heart to yourself and then to your classmates or instructor.

姚明，姚明，他很高！

比我高，

也比你高。

我们都没他那么高。

姚明，姚明，很有名！

比我有名，

也比你有名。

我们都没他有名。

姚明中文说得非常好！

比我说得好,

也比你说得好。

我们都没他说得好。

姚明篮球打得非常好!

比我打得好,

也比你打得好。

我们都没他打得好。

三　理解　Understand

那么 *nàme* means "to that extent" and can be used before an adjective. If we are surprised at someone's unusual height and wonder how someone can be that tall, we can say 他怎么那么高 *tā zěnme nàme gāo* (how come he is that tall).

When we make a comparison, two entities to be compared will be involved. In Chinese, we use 比 *bǐ* to set two entities up and compare. If we use A and B to represnet the two entities, the sentence pattern for comparison in Chinese is "A 比 *bǐ* B + adjective". For example,

> *Wǒ* **bǐ** *tā máng.*
> 我**比**他忙。
> I am busier than he.

> *Wǒ de shū* **bǐ** *tā de shū guì.*
> 我的书**比**他的书贵。
> My book is more expensive than his.

If I am busier than he is, then he is not as busy as I am. If my book is more expensive than his, then his book is not as expensive as mine. How do we say "he is not as busy as I am" and "his book is not as expensive as mine" in Chinese? Simply use 没 *méi* to replace 比 *bǐ* and switch A and B: B 没 *méi* A + adjective.

> *Tā méi wǒ máng.*
> 他没我忙。
> He is not as busy as I am.

> *Tā de shū méi wǒ de shū guì.*
> 他的书没我的书贵。
> His book is not as expensive as mine.

If we need to compare two entities for their performances of an action, then we use sentences with a complement of degree. The sentence pattern to be used is "A 比 *bǐ* B + verb 得 *de* adjective" or "B 没 *méi* A + verb 得 *de* adjective". For example,

> *Wǒ bǐ tā chī de duō.*
> 我比他吃得多。
> I eat more than he does.

> *Tā méi wǒ chī de duō.*
> 他没我吃得多。
> He does eat as much as I do.

> *Tā bǐ wǒ shuō de hǎo.*
> 他比我说得好。
> He speaks better than I do.

> *Wǒ méi tā shuō de hǎo.*
> 我没他说得好。
> I do not speak as well as he does.

If we need to specify the recipient of the action, that is, to state an object for the verb, then the verb will need to be reduplicated:

A 比 *bǐ* B (+ verb + object) + reduplicated verb 得 *de* adjective

B 没 *méi* A (+ verb + object) + reduplicated verb 得 *de* adjective

> *Wǒ bǐ tā (chī fàn) chī de duō.*
> 我比他(吃饭)吃得多。
> I eat more (food) than he does.

> *Tā méi wǒ (chī fàn) chī de duō.*
> 他没我(吃饭)吃得多。
> He does eat as much (food) as I do.

> *Tā bǐ wǒ (shuō Zhōngwén) shuō de hǎo.*
> 他比我(说中文)说得好。
> He speaks (Chinese) better than I do.

> *Wǒ méi tā (shuō Zhōngwén) shuō de hǎo.*
> 我没他(说中文)说得好。
> I do not speak (Chinese) as well as he does.

However, if the recipient of the action is turned into the topic of the sentence, then the verb does not need to be reduplicated:

> A 比 *bǐ* B (+ object) + verb 得 *de* adjective
>
> B 没 *méi* A (+ object) + verb 得 *de* adjective

---

*Tā **méi** wǒ (fàn) chī de duō.*

他没我(饭)吃得多。

(As for food,) I eat more than he does.

---

*Wǒ **bǐ** tā (fàn) chī de duō.*

我比他(饭)吃得多。

(As for food,) he does not eat as much as I do.

---

*Wǒ **méi** tā (Zhōngwén) shuō de hǎo.*

我没他(中文)说得好。

(As for Chinese,) he speaks better than I do.

---

*Tā **bǐ** wǒ (Zhōngwén) shuō de hǎo.*

他比我(中文)说得好。

(As for Chinese,) I do not speak as well as he does.

In a comparative sentence that has a complement of degree, "比 *bǐ* B" does not have to be placed right after "A". "没 *méi* A" does not have to be placed right after "B" either.

A) It is possible to place them inside the complement in between 得 *de* and the adjective:

> A (+ verb + object) + reduplicated verb 得 *de* 比 *bǐ* B adjective
>
> B (+ verb + object) + reduplicated verb 得 *de* 没 *méi* A adjective

---

*Wǒ (chī fàn) chī de **bǐ** tā duō.*

我(吃饭)吃得比他多。

I eat more (food) than he does.

---

*Tā (chī fàn) chī de **méi** wǒ duō.*

他(吃饭)吃得没我多。

He does not eat as much as (food) I do.

---

*Tā (shuō Zhōngwén) shuō de **bǐ** wǒ hǎo.*

他(说 中文)说得比我好。

He speaks (Chinese) better than I do.

Wǒ (shuō Zhōngwén) shuō de **méi tā hǎo.**
我(说 中文) 说得**没他好**。
I do not speak (Chinese) as well as he does.

B) It is also possible to place them before the reduplicated verb

A (+ verb + object) + 比 *bǐ* B reduplicated verb 得 *de* adjective

B (+ verb + object) + 没 *méi* A reduplicated verb 得 *de* adjective

Wǒ (chī fàn) **bǐ tā** chī de duō.
我(吃饭)**比他**吃得多。
I eat more (food) than he does.

Tā (chī fàn) **méi wǒ** chī de duō.
他(吃饭)**没我**吃得多。
He does not eat as much as (food) I do.

Tā (shuō Zhōngwén) **bǐ wǒ** shuō de hǎo.
他(说 中文)**比我**说得好。
He speaks (Chinese) better than I do.

Wǒ (shuō Zhōngwén) **méi tā** shuō de hǎo.
我(说 中文)**没他**说得好。
I do not speak (Chinese) as well as he does.

C) It is also possible to place them before the verb if the object is the topic of the sentence:

A (+ object) + 比 *bǐ* B verb 得 *de* adjective

B (+ object) + 没 *méi* A verb 得 *de* adjective

Wǒ (fàn) **bǐ tā** chī de duō.
我(饭)**比他**吃得多。
(As for food,) I eat more than he does.

Tā (fàn) **méi wǒ** chī de duō.
他(饭)**没我**吃得多。
(As for food,) he does not eat as much as I do.

Tā (Zhōngwén) **bǐ wǒ** shuō de hǎo.
他(中文)**比我**说得好。
(As for Chinese,) he speaks better than I do.

> Wǒ (Zhōngwén) méi tā shuō de hǎo.
> 我(中文) 没他说得好。
> (As for Chinese,) I do not speak as well as he does.

四 实践 Practice

1. 对话 Conversation

A: 我听说，美国人都会打篮球。

B: 不能说人人都会。喜欢打的人非常多。

A: 你打得怎么样？

B: 我打得不行。我有个朋友，是篮球队的。

A: 是吗？那他篮球一定打得特好。

B: 比我好得多。

A: 他比姚明高吗？

B: 没姚明高，也没姚明那么有名。

A: 他会不会说中文？

B: 会一点儿。他现在正跟我学中文呢。

A: 啊，他是不是想去中国打球？

B: 对。他还想去中国教英文。

2. 交际 Communication

Task 1 On day, you are at your host family's apartment. When the topic in on basketball, they ask you whether Yao Ming (姚明 *Yáo Míng*) is more famous than Michael Jordan (乔丹 *Qiáodān*) in the United States or the other way round. Respond by saying that Yao Ming is more famous than Jordan in Houston and Yao Ming is taller than Jordan, but he is not as famous as Jordan in the whole United States.

Task 2 | After dinner, you decide to join a group of Chinese young men at the campus basketball court playing basketball. When one young man compliments you on your good basketball skills, respond in a modest Chinese way by saying: "不行，不行，I don't play as well as you do."

Task 3 | You are on your way walking to a downtown mall. A Chinese woman starts to talk with you in English. Respond in Chinese to compliment her on her English proficiency. When she says you speak Chinese very well, answer by saying your Chinese is not as good as her English.

3. 书写 *Writing*

yáo [a surname] *Piědiǎn, piě, héng; piě, diǎn, tí, shùwāngōu, piě, diǎn.*

bǐ than; compare *Héng, shùtí, piě, shùwāngōu.*

gāo tall; high *Diǎn, héng, shù, héngzhé, héng, shù, héngzhégōu, shù, héngzhé, héng.*

lán basket *Piě, héng, diǎn, piě, héng, diǎn; shù, shù, piě, héng, diǎn, shù, héngzhé, shù, shù, héng*

qiú ball *Héng, héng, shù, tí; héng, shùgōu, diǎn, tí, piě, nà, diǎn.*

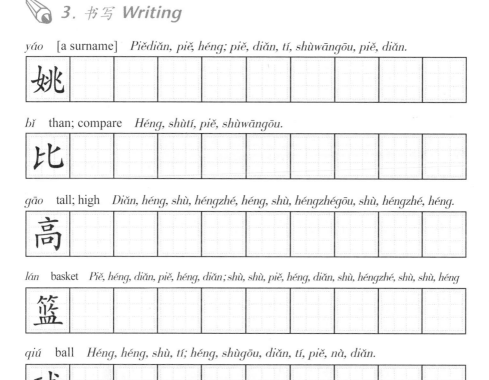

Dì-sìshí'èr   kè

第四十二课

Lesson 42

Wǒmen gēn tā yíyàng máng.

我们跟他一样忙。

We are as busy as he is.

一 听与看 Listen and Read

Listen to the recording of the following sentences as many times as possible until you can say it along with the recording. You should also look at the following transcription while listening and try to imitate.

Yáo Míng, Yáo Míng, tā hěn máng!

姚 明， 姚 明， 他 很 忙！

[a surname] | bright | [a surname] | bright | he | very | busy

Yao Ming, Yao Ming, he is busy!

Wǒ yě hěn máng, nǐ yě hěn máng.

我 也 很 忙， 你 也 很 忙。

I | also | very | busy | you | also | very | busy

I am also busy, and you are also busy.

Wǒmen gēn tā yíyàng máng.

我们 跟他 一样 忙。

I | [plural] | with | he | one | shape | busy

We and he are equally busy.

Wǒmen dàjiā dōu hěn máng.

我们 大家 都 很 忙。

I | [plural] | big | family | all | very | busy

Every one of us is busy.

Yáo Míng, Yáo Míng, tā hěn shuài!

姚 明， 姚 明， 他 很 帅！

[a surname] | bright | [a surname] | bright | he | very | handsome

Yao Ming, Yao Ming, he is handsome!

Wǒ yě hěn shuài, nǐ yě hěn shuài.

我 也 很 帅， 你 也 很 帅。

I | also | very | handsome | you | also | very | handsome

I am also handsome, and you are also handsome.

Wǒmen gēn tā yíyàng shuài.

我们 跟他一样 帅。

I | [plural] | with | he | one | shape | handsome

We and he are equally handsome.

Wǒmen dàjiā dōu hěn shuài.

我们大家都很 帅。

I | [plural] | big | family | all | very | handsome

Every one of us is handsome.

Yáo Míng, Yáo Míng, tā hěn gāo!

姚明，姚明，他很高！

[a surname] | bright | [a surname] | bright | he | very | tall

Yao Ming, Yao Ming, he is tall!

Tā hěn gāo, wǒ bú tài gāo.

他很高，我不太高。

he | very | tall | I | not | too | tall

He is tall, but I am not very tall.

Wǒ gēn tā bù yíyàng gāo.

我 跟他不一样高。

I | with | he | not | one | shape | tall

He and I are not of the same height.

Wǒmen liǎ bù yíyàng gāo.

我们 俩不一样高。

I | [plural] | two | not | one | shape | tall

We two are not of the same height.

Yáo Míng, Yáo Míng, tā hěn kuài!

姚明，姚明，他很快！

[a surname] | bright | [a surname] | bright | he | very | quick

Yao Ming, Yao Ming, he is quick!

Tā hěn kuài, wǒ bú tài kuài.

他很快，我不太快。

he | very | quick | I | not | too | quick

He is quick, but I am not very quick.

Wǒ gēn tā bù yíyàng kuài.

我 跟 他 不 一 样 快。

I | with | he | not | one | shape | quick

He and I are not equally quick.

Wǒmen liǎ bù yíyàng kuài.

我 们 俩 不 一 样 快。

I | [plural] | two | not | one | shape | quick

We two are not equally quick.

二　看与说　Read and Speak

Now, listen to the recording while looking at the following sentences. Then read it out aloud. Finally, recite it by heart to yourself and then to your classmates or instructor.

姚明，姚明，他很忙！

我也很忙，你也很忙。

我们跟他一样忙。

我们大家都很忙。

姚明，姚明，他很帅！

我也很帅，你也很帅。

我们跟他一样帅。

我们大家都很帅。

姚明，姚明，他很高！

他很高，我不太高。

我跟他不一样高。

我们俩不一样高。

姚明，姚明，他很快！

他很快，我不太快。

我跟他不一样快。

我们俩不一样快。

三　理解　Understand

To express the concept that A and B are the same, we use the sentence structure: A 跟 *gēn* B 一样 *yíyàng*. To clarify that A and B are the same in some way, we can add a descriptive word at the end of the sentence structure. The negation is to put 不 *bù* before 一样 *yíyàng*: A 跟 *gēn* B (不 *bù*) 一样 *yíyàng* + adjective. For example,

> *Wǒ gēn tā (bù) yíyàng gāo.*
> 我 跟 他(不)一样 高。
> He and I are (not) of the same height.

> *Wǒ de shū gēn tā de shū (bù) yíyàng guì.*
> 我的 书 跟 他 的 书(不)一样 贵。
> My book and his book are (not) equally expensive.

If we want to express the concept that A and B are doing the same thing, then we can use the same sentence structure except that we use a verb-object segment instead of an adjective. However, with a verb-object segment at the end of the sentence pattern, 不 *bù* cannot be added before 一样 *yíyàng* to form a logical negation: A 跟 *gēn* B 一样 *yíyàng* + verb + object. For example,

Wǒ gēn tā yíyàng zài xué shuō Hànyǔ
我跟他一样在学说汉语。
He and I are the same, learning to speak Chinese.

However, 一样 *yíyàng* or 不一样 *bù yíyàng* can be placed before the adjective in a complement of degree, and 跟 *gēn* B, like 比 *bǐ* B, can be placed in three different places:

A 跟 *gēn* B (+ verb + object) + reduplicated verb 得 *de* (不 *bù*) 一样 *yíyàng* adjective

A (+ verb + object) + reduplicated verb 得 *de* 跟 *gēn* B (不 *bù*) 一样 *yíyàng* adjective

A (+ verb + object) 跟 *gēn* B + reduplicated verb 得 *de* (不 *bù*) 一样 *yíyàng* adjective

For example,

Wǒ gēn tā (shuō Hànyǔ) shuō de (bù) yíyàng hǎo.
我跟他 (说汉语)说得(不)一样好。
He and I (speak Chinese) (not) equally well.

Wǒ (shuō Hànyǔ) shuō de gēn tā (bù) yíyàng hǎo.
我(说汉语)说得跟他(不)一样好。

Wǒ (shuō Hànyǔ) gēn tā shuō de (bù) yíyàng hǎo.
我(说汉语)跟他说得(不)一样好。

大家 *dàjiā* literally means "big family", but it really means "each and every one of us". This term refers to a lot more people than two. To say "we two", we use the term 俩 *liǎ* after 我们 *wǒmen*: 我们俩 *wǒmen liǎ*.

太 *tài* means "too" or "excessively"; however, 不太 *bú tài* does not mean "not too" or "not excessively". Instead, it means "not very".

Wǒ Hànyǔ shuō de bú tài hǎo.
我汉语说得不太好。
I don't speak Chinese very well.

Zhèi běn shū *bú tài* guì.
这本书**不太**贵。
This book is not very expensive.

四　实践　Practice

1. 对话 Conversation

A: 有一个人在中国很有名。

B: 你说说他是谁，看看我知道不知道。

A: 他叫刘翔 *Liú Xiáng* (the name of a well-known Chinese athlete)。

B: 我还真不知道这个人。

A: 他人很高，长得特帅。

B: 跟姚明一样吗？

A: 跟姚明一样帅，可是不一样高。

B: 比姚明还高吗？

A: 没有，没有。没姚明那么高。

B: 打篮球打得比姚明好吗？

A: 他没姚明打得好，可是比姚明跑得快。

B: 他跟姚明一样有名吗？

A: 对，他们都是名人。

B: 那他应该跟姚明一样忙。

A: 你说得对。他们都很忙。他还跟姚明一样都是上海 *Shànghǎi* (Shanghai) 人。

🤝 2. 交际 Communication

Task 1 During your first long chat with a Chinese friend, she is amazed by your height and asks whether Americans are all so tall. Say that the U.S. is the same as China in having some tall people and some not-so-tall people. Add the fact that your younger sister is taller than you and that your mother is only this tall with a gesture showing the height at your shoulder.

Task 2 After dinner at your host family's apartment, your talk is on the topic of work of parents. Tell them that your dad works at a university as a staff member instead of a faculty member and that your mother does not have a job. However since your family has four children, your mother is just as busy as your father, sometimes even busier.

Task 3 On the bus to a local tourist spot, you start to chat with a Chinese college student accompanying your group on the trip. You talk about siblings and hobbies. Tell him/her that you and your elder brother are of the same height and run at about the same speed. However, your elder brother is more handsome than you and likes to sing while you like to play basketball and you play better than your elder brother.

 *3. 书写 Writing*

gēn with; follow *Shù, héngzhé, héng, shù, héng, shù, tí; héngzhé, héng, héng, shùgtí, piě, nà.*

跟								

yàng shape; appearance *Héng, shù, piě, diǎn; diǎn, piě, héng, héng, héng, shù.*

样					·			

shuài handsome *Shù, piě; shù, héngzhégōu, shù.*

帅								

liǎ two *Piě, shù; héng, shù, héngzhégōu, piě, diǎn, piě, diǎn.*

俩								

Dì–sìshísān   kè   Tā   bǐ   wǒmen duō zhèng jǐbǎi   wàn.

第四十三课   他比我们多挣几百万。
Lesson 43
He earns several millions more than we do.

一　听与看　Listen and Read

Listen to the recording of the following sentences as many times as possible until you can say it along with the recording. You should also look at the following transcription while listening and try to imitate.

Dàpéng,   Dàpéng,   qián zhèng de duō!

大朋，大朋，钱 挣 得多！

big | friend | big | friend | money | **earn** | [aux.] | much

Dapeng, Dapeng earns a lot of money!

Bǐ   wǒ zhèng de duō,   yě bǐ nǐ zhèng de duō.

比我 挣 得多，也比你 挣 得多。

than | I | **earn** | [aux.] | much | also | than | you | **earn** | [aux.] | much

He earns more than I, also more than you.

Bǐ wǒmen duō zhèng jǐbǎi   wàn,

比我们 多 挣 几百万，

than | I [plural] | much | **earn** | several | hundred | **ten thousand**

He earns several millions more than we,

bǐ wǒmen zhèng de duō de duō.

比我们 挣 得多得多。

than | I | [plural] | **earn** | [aux.] | much | [aux.] | much

he earns a lot more money than we do.

Dà péng,   Dà péng,   shū kàn de shǎo!

大朋，大朋，书看得少！

big | friend | big | friend | book | look | [aux.] | few

Dapeng, Dapeng reads few books!

Bǐ wǒ kàn de shǎo,   yě bǐ nǐ kàn de shǎo,

比我看得少，也比你看得少，

than | I | look | [aux.] | few | also | than | you | look | [aux.] | few

He reads less than I, also less than you,

bǐ wǒmen shǎo kàn jǐshí běn.
比我们 少 看 几十本。
than | I | plural] | little | look | several | ten | [meas.]
he reads several tens of books less than we.

Bǐ wǒmen kàn de shǎo de duō.
比我们 看 得少 得多。
than | I | [plural] | look | [aux.] | little | [aux.] | much
He reads a lot less than we do.

二 看与说 Read and Speak

Now, listen to the recording while looking at the following sentences. Then read it out aloud. Finally, recite it by heart to yourself and then to your classmates or instructor.

大朋，大朋，钱挣得多！

比我挣得多，也比你挣得多。

比我们多挣几百万，

比我们挣得多得多。

大朋，大朋，书看得少！

比我看得少，也比你看得少，

比我们少看几十本。

比我们看得少得多。

三 理解 Understand

When making a comparison, the difference between two entities being compared can be specified in the sentence. If the difference cannot be measured precisely, then it can be expressed in rough estimation terms, such as 一点儿 *yìdiǎnr* or 一些 *yìxiē* (a little bit more) and 得多 *de duō* or 多了 *duō le* (a lot more). These terms are placed right after the adjective at the end of the comparison sentence:

A 比 B + adjective + 一点儿/一些/得多/多了

A 比 B (verb + object) + reduplicated verb 得 + adjective + 一点儿/一些/得多/多了

For example,

> *Tā bǐ nǐ gāo yìdiǎnr,   bǐ wǒ gāo de duō.*
> 他比你高一点儿，比我高得多。
> He is **a bit taller** than you, but **a lot taller** than I.

> *Tā de shū bǐ wǒ de guì yìxiē,   bǐ nǐ de guì duō le.*
> 他的书比我的贵一些，比你的贵多了。
> His book is a bit more expensive than mine, but a lot more expensive than yours.

> *Tā xué Hànyǔ xué de bǐ wǒ zǎo yìdiǎnr,   bǐ nǐ zǎo de duō.*
> 他学汉语学得比我早一点儿，比你早得多。
> He studied Chinese a little earlier than I, but a lot earlier than you.

> *Tā zuò zuòyè zuò de bǐ wǒ shǎo yìxiē,   bǐ nǐ shǎo duō le.*
> 他做作业做得比我少一些，比你少多了。
> He did a little less homework than I, but a lot less than you.

If the difference can be measured in precise quantities, then appropriate numeral-measure phrases are used. For the sentence structure A 比 B + adjective, the numeral-measure phrases can still be placed right after the adjective: A 比 B + adjective + precise quantity. For example,

> *Tā bǐ wǒ gāo yì límǐ,   bǐ nǐ gāo shí límǐ.*
> 他比我高一厘米，比你高十厘米。
> He is one centimeter taller than I, but ten centimeters taller than you.

> *Tā de shū bǐ wǒ de guì yí kuài,　bǐ nǐ de guì èrshí kuài.*
> 他的书比我的贵一块，比你的贵二十块。
> His book is 1 dollar more expensive than mine, but 20 dollars more expensive than yours.

However, for the sentences with a complement of degree, the numeral-measure phrases cannot be placed after the adjective for the complement of degree. When 多 *duō*, 少 *shǎo*, 早 *zǎo*, and 晚 *wǎn* are used in a comparison sentence with a precise quantity, a different sentence structure has to be used. 多 *duō*, 少 *shǎo*, 早 *zǎo*, and 晚 *wǎn* are used as adverbs and placed before the verb, and numeral-measure phrases specifiying precise quantities are placed after the verb at the end of the sentence: A 比 B (verb + object) + 早/晚/多/少 + verb + precise quantity. A variation of this sentence structure is: A 比 B 早/晚/多/少 + verb + precise quantity (的+ object). For example,

> *Tā bǐ wǒ (xué Hànyǔ) zǎo xué bàn nián,　bǐ nǐ zǎo xué sān nián.*
> 他比我(学汉语)早学半年，比你早学三年。
> He studied Chinese half a year earlier than I, but three years earlier than you.

> *Tā bǐ wǒ zǎo xué bàn nián (de Hànyǔ).　bǐ nǐ zǎo xué sān nián (de Hànyǔ).*
> 他比我早学半年(的汉语)，比你早学三年(的汉语)。
> He studied Chinese half a year earlier than I, but three years earlier than you.

> *Tā bǐ wǒ (zuò zuòyè) shǎo zuò yì tiān,　bǐ nǐ shǎo zuò yí ge xīngqī.*
> 他比我(做作业)少做一天，比你少做一个星期。
> He did the homework one day less than I, but one week less than you.

> *Tā bǐ wǒ shǎo zuò yì tiān (de zuòyè),　bǐ nǐ shǎo zuò yí ge xīngqī (de zuòyè).*
> 他比我少做一天(的作业)，比你少做一个星期(的作业)。
> He did the homework one day less than I, but one week less than you.

几 *jǐ* is a question word, meaning "how many," but it can also be used to stand for a numeral and mean "several": 几个人 *jǐ ge rén* (several people), 几十 *jǐshí* (several tens), 几百 *jǐbǎi* (several hundred), 几千 *jǐqiān* (several thousand), and 几百万 *jǐbǎi wàn* (several million).

四 实践 Practice

1. 对话 Conversation

A: 要这三本。

B: 好的。一共六十五块。

A: 给你一百。

B: 找 zhǎo (give change) 你三十五。

(A leaves and returns with C.)

A: 你找我的钱不对。

B: 怎么不对？

A: 你少找我十块。

B: 怎么少找了？

A: 你找了我两张十块的，一张五块的，还差十块呢。

B: 是吗？我找你钱的时候，你怎么不说呢？

A: 你怎么能这样？

C: 算 suàn 了 (forget it)，算了。别跟他说了。

A: 他不对，我能不说吗？

C: 说了也没用。以后我给你多挣点儿钱。

A: 这不是十块钱的事儿。

C: 你比他看书看得多得多，别理 lǐ (pay attention to)
　　他了。

A: 现在的书比前几年贵多了，他还少找我十块。

C: 以后我给你挣一百万。

A: 你去哪儿挣啊？

2. 交际 Communication

Task 1 After turning in your homework, you realize that you have missed doing one of the exercises. Explain the situation to your instructor, apologize and ask him/her if you can do it on a different piece of paper and give it to him/her in the afternoon.

Task 2 Call your best Chinese friend to share the good news that you have a new job now and each month you make 1,000 *kuài* more than before. Treat your friend to a dinner at an American style restaurant.

Task 3 A new international student asks you about your experience of improving Chinese language proficiency, say that the best method is to make many Chinese friends, do not speak English with your Chinese friends, read Chinese books in the library, and do not often call home.

3. 书写 Writing

zhèng　earn　*Héng, shùgōu, tí; piě, héngpiě, héngzhé, héng, héng, shùgōu.*

挣

wàn　ten thousand　*Héng, héngzhégōu, piě.*

万

第四十四课 你听懂了吗?

Lesson 44 **Have you understood by listening?**

一 听与看 Listen and Read

Listen to the recording of the following sentences as many times as possible until you can say it along with the recording. You should also look at the following transcription while listening and try to imitate.

Tīng, tīng, tīng!

听、听、听!

listen | listen | listen

Listen, listen, listen!

Wǒ zài tīng kèwén.

我在听课文。

I | at | listen | lesson | language

I am listening to the text.

kèwén, kèwén, kèwén,

课文、课文、课文,

lesson | language | lesson | language | lesson | language

Text, text, text,

nǐ tīngdǒng le ma?

你听懂了吗?

you | listen | **understand** | [aux.] | [ques.]

have you understood by listening?

Wǒ yǐjīng tīngdǒng le.

我已经听懂了。

I | already | undergo | listen | **understand** | [aux.]

I have already understood by listening.

Wǒ hái méi tīngdǒng ne.

我还没听懂呢。

I | still | not | listen | **understand** | [aux.]

I have not yet understood by listening.

Nà nǐ jìxù tīng.

那你继续听。

that | you | **follow** | **connect** | listen

Then, you continue to listen.

Xiě, xiě, xiě!
写、写、写！
write | write | write
Write, write, write!

Wǒ zài xiě Hànzì.
我在写汉字。
I | at | write | Han ethnic group | character
I am writing Chinese characters.

Hànzì, Hànzì, Hànzì,
汉字、汉字、汉字，
Han ethnic group | character | Han ethnic group | character | Han ethnic group | character
Chinese characters, Chinese characters, Chinese characters,

nǐ xiěwán le ma?
你写完了吗？
you | write | finish | [aux.] | [ques.]
have you finished writing?

Wǒ yǐjīng xiěwán le.
我已经写完了。
I | already | undergo | write | finish | [aux.]
I have already finished writing.

Wǒ hái méi xiěwán ne.
我还没写完呢。
I | still | not | write | finish | [aux.]
I have not finished writing yet.

Nà nǐ jìxù xiě.
那你继续写。
that | you | follow | connect | write
Then, you continue to write.

Xué, xué, xué!
学、学、学！
learn | learn | learn
Learn, learn, learn!

Wǒ zài xué huá xuě.
我在学滑雪。
I | at | learn | slide | snow
I am learning to ski.

Huá xuě, huá xuě, huá xuě,
滑雪、滑雪、滑雪，
slide | snow | slide | snow | slide | snow
Ski, ski, ski,

nǐ xuéhuì le ma?
你学会了吗?
you | learn | know how | [aux.] | [question]
have you learned it?

Wǒ yǐjīng xuéhuì le.
我已经学会了。
I | already | undergo | learn | know | how | [aux.]
I have already learned it.

Wǒ hái méi xuéhuì ne.
我还没学会呢。
I | still | not | learn | know how | [aux.]
I have not yet learned to ski.

Nà nǐ jìxù xué.
那你继续学。
then | you | follow | connect | learn
Then, you continue to learn.

二 看与说 Read and Speak

Now, listen to the recording while looking at the following sentences. Then read it out aloud. Finally, recite it by heart to yourself and then to your classmates or instructor.

听、听、听!

我在听课文。

课文、课文、课文,

你听懂了吗?

我已经听懂了。

(我还没听懂呢。

那你继续听。)

写、写、写！
我在写汉字。
汉字、汉字、汉字，
你写完了吗？
我已经写完了。
（我还没写完呢。
那你继续写。）

学、学、学！
我在学滑雪。
滑雪、滑雪、滑雪，
你学会了吗？
我已经学会了。
（我还没学会呢。
那你继续学。）

三 理解 Understand

In English, when we say "listen", we intend it to denote a sensory action to use ears to gain awareness of something, and the verb "listen" itself does not tell about the successful result in perception. However, the verb "hear" represents both the sensory action and the perception result. In Chinese, most verbs are like "listen" in English, and they do not tell us the results. We, therefore, often add another word to state the result. The word representing the result is placed right after the action verb. For example,

Action		Result		
tīng 听 listen	+	*jiàn* 见 perceive	→	*tīngjiàn* 听见 hear
kàn 看 look	+	*jiàn* 见 perceive	→	*kànjiàn* 看见 see
tīng 听 listen	+	*dǒng* 懂 understand	→	*tīngdǒng* 听懂 understand through listening
xiě 写 write	+	*wán* 完 finish	→	*xiěwán* 写完 finish writing
xué 学 learn	+	*huì* 会 know how	→	*xuéhuì* 学会 know how to through learning

The combination of the action word and the result word is a compound word that functions as one verbal unit. 了 *le* is not used in between; instead, it is placed after the entire unit. For example,

> *Wǒ tīngdǒng le.*   *Wǒ tīngdǒng tā shuō de huà le.*
> 我听懂了。我听懂他说的话了。
> I have understood by listening. I have understood his words by listening.

> *Wǒ xuéhuì le.*   *Wǒ xuéhuì huá xuě le.*
> 我学会了。我学会滑雪了。
> I have learned it. I have learned to ski.

We use 没 *méi*, rather than 不 *bù*, for the negation of an action-result verbal unit. In a negated sentence with 没 *méi*, 了 *le* is not needed. If 还 *hái* is used before negation word 没 *méi* and 呢 *ne* is attached at the end of a negated sentence, then it means "still not yet." For example,

> Wǒ méi xuéhuì. Wǒ méi xuéhuì huá xuě.
> 我没学会。 我没学会滑雪。
> I have not learned it. I have not learned to ski.

If 还 *hái* is used before negation word 没 *méi* and 呢 *ne* is attached at the end of a negated sentence, then it means "still not yet." For example,

> Wǒ hái méi xuéhuì huá xuě ne.
> 我还没学会滑雪呢。
> I still have not learned how to ski yet.

To ask a question, we can also add 吗 *ma* at the end of a statement. We can also use the affirmative-negative form as a question. For example,

> Nǐ xiěwán le ma? Nǐ xiěwán Hànzì le ma?
> 你写完了吗? 你写完汉字了吗?
> Have you finished writing? Have you finished writing Chinese characters?

> Nǐ xiěwán méi xiěwán? Nǐ xiěwán méi xiěwán Hànzì?
> 你写完没写完? 你写完没写完汉字?
> Have you finished writing? Have you finished writing Chinese characters?

四 实践 Practice

1. 对话 Conversation

A: 我听李贵说，你开始学滑雪了。

B: 对，学了两次了。

A: 已经学会了吗?

B: 差不多会了。

A: 那下午咱们去滑雪吧!

B: 我特想去，可是不行啊。我还没做完作业呢。

A: 什么作业呀?

B: 听课文，写汉字。

A: 两个都没做完吗?

B: 汉字已经写好了。

A: 课文呢?

B: 课文我听了三遍。

A: 三遍差不多了。

B: 可是还没听懂。

A: 那你继续听。我们星期六再去。

B: 好! 太好了! 谢谢你。

2. 交际 Communication

Task 1 Shortly after you are in China, you are excited to be exposed to the natural language environment out on a busy street walking to the nearby bookstore. When you politely ask a Chinese person where Xinhua Bookstore (新华书店 *Xīnhuá Shūdiàn*) is, the Chinese person says quite a few sentences instead of saying "there" while pointing in the direction of the bookstore. Tell him/her that you did not understand everything he/she has said and ask him/her to say it again.

Task 2 Your Chinese speaking partner has helped you tremendously with your Chinese speaking skills. To thank him/her, you offer to teach your Chinese speaking partner how to ski at a Beijing resort. Tell him/her that skiing is not that hard. It takes just a couple of days to learn it.

Task 3 It is around dinner time. Your next-door neighbor knocks on your door to ask if you want to go to eat beef noodle in the nearby restaurant. Say yes but ask your neighbor whether you can finish doing your homework and then go together. Tell him/her that it takes about 10 minutes for you to finish.

314   实用节奏汉语

3. 书写 Writing

dǒng   understand   *Diǎn, diǎn, shù; héng, shù, shù, piě, héng, shù, héngzhé, héng, héng, héng, shù, héng.*

懂

jì   follow   *Piězhé, piězhé, tí; diǎn, piě, héng, shù, piě, diǎn, shùzhé.*

继

xù   connect   *Piězhé, piězhé, tí; héng, shù, hénggōu, diǎn, diǎn, héng, piě, diǎn.*

续

wán   finish   *Diǎn, diǎn, hénggōu; héng, héng, piě, shùwāngōu.*

完

huá   slide; slippery   *Diǎn, diǎn, tí; shù, héngzhé, héngzhé, diǎn, hénggōu, shù, héngzhégōu, héng, héng.*

滑

Dì-sìshíwǔ kè

第四十五课　你找到了没有?

Nǐ zhǎodào le méiyou?

Lesson 45　Have you found it?

一　听与看　**Listen and Read**

Listen to the recording of the following sentences as many times as possible until you can say it along with the recording. You should also look at the following transcription while listening and try to imitate.

Xué, xué, xué!

学，学，学!

learn | learn | learn

Learn, learn, learn!

Wǒ zài xué Hànyǔ.

我 在 学 汉语。

I | at | learn | Han ethnic group | language

I am learning Chinese.

Hànyǔ, Hànyǔ, Hànyǔ,

汉语, 汉语, 汉语,

Han ethnic group | language | Han ethnic group | language | Han ethnic group | language

Chinese, Chinese, Chinese,

nǐ yào xuédào jǐ diǎn?

你要 学到 几点?

you | want | learn | arrive | how many | o'clock

till what time do you want to keep learning?

Wǒ yào xuédào sān diǎn.

我 要 学到 三点。

I | want | learn | arrive | three | o'clock

I want to keep learning till 3 o'clock.

Zhǎo, zhǎo, zhǎo!

找，找，找!

seek | seek | seek

Seek, seek, seek!

Wǒ zài zhǎo yīfu.
我在找衣服。
I | at | seek | garment | attire
I am seeking my clothes.

Yīfu,　　yīfu,　　yīfu,
衣服，衣服，衣服，
garment | attire | garment | attire | garment | attire
Clothes, clothes, clothes,

nǐ zhǎodào le méiyou?
你找到了没有？
you | seek | arrive | [aux.] | not | have
have you found it?

Wǒ hái méi zhǎodào.
我还没找到。
I | still | not | seek | arrive
I still have not found it.

Xiě,　xiě,　xiě!
写，写，写！
write | write | write
Write, write, write!

Wǒ zài xiě Hànzì.
我在写汉字。
I | at | write | Han | characters
I am writing Chinese characters.

Hànzì,　　Hànzì,　　Hànzì,
汉字，汉字，汉字，
Han ethnic group | characters | Han ethnic group | characters | Han ethnic group | characters
Chinese characters, Chinese characters, Chinese characters,

nǐ xiězài nǎr le?
你写在哪儿了？
you | write | at | which | [suffix] | [aux.]
where did you write them?

Wǒ xiězài zhǐ shàng le.
我写在纸 上 了。
I | write | at | **paper** | up | [aux.]
I wrote them on paper.

Jì,   jì,   jì!
记，记，记!
remember | remember | remember
Remember, remember, remember!

Wǒ zài jì shēngcí.
我在记生词。
I | at | **remember** | unfamiliar | word.
I am trying to remember new words.

Shēngcí, shēngcí, shēngcí,
生词，生词，生词，
unfamiliar | word | unfamiliar | word | unfamiliar | word
New words, new words, new words,

nǐ   jìzhù   le méiyou?
你记住了没有?
you | **remember** | stay | [aux.] | not | have?
have you remembered them?

Wǒ hái méi jìzhù.
我还没记住。
I | still | not | **remember** | stay.
I still have not.

二 看与说 Read and Speak

Now, listen to the recording while looking at the following sentences. Then read it out aloud. Finally, recite it by heart to yourself and then to your classmates or instructor.

学，学，学!
我在学汉语。

汉语，汉语，汉语，
你要学到几点？
我要学到三点。

找，找，找！
我在找衣服。
衣服，衣服，衣服，
你找到了没有？
我还没找到。

写，写，写！
我在写汉字。
汉字，汉字，汉字，
你写在哪儿了？
我写在纸上了。

记，记，记！
我在记生词。
生词，生词，生词，
你记住了没有？
我还没记住。

三　理解　Understand

In this lesson, 到 *dào* (arrive), 在 *zài* (to be at), and 住 *zhù* (to live), three of the words we have learned in the past are used after actions to indicate result.

到 *dào* means "arrive". When it is used after an action, it may denote the arrival at a point in place or in time as result of the action. For example,

> *Tā zuótiān zǒudào le shūdiàn.*
> 他昨天走到了书店。(arrival at a place as a result of 走 *zǒu*)
> Yesterday he walked to the bookstore.

> *Wǒmen xuédào dì 45 kè le.*
> 我们学到第45课了。(arrival at a point in place as a result of 学 *xué*)
> We have learned up to Lesson 45.

> *Tā měi tiān kàn shū kàndào wǎnshang 11 diǎn.*
> 他每天看书看到晚上11点。(arrival at a point in time as a result of 看 *kàn*)
> Everyday he reads books till 11 o'clock in the evening.

However, when used as a resultative complement, 到 *dào* may also indicate the successful conclusion of an action. For example,

> *Tā zhǎole yí ge xiǎoshí de cídiǎn.　tā zhǎodào le.*
> 他找了一个小时的词典，他找到了。
> He looked for the dictionary for a hour, and he found it.

> *Wǒ qù mǎi diànzǐ Hànyǔ cídiǎn,　kěshì méi mǎidào.*
> 我去买电子汉语词典，可是没买到。
> I went to buy an electronic Chinese dictionary, but without success.

在 *zài* is always followed by a place to denote a location. We have learned that locative expressions with 在 *zài* usually appear before an action in a sentence as the Chinese language tends to provide background information before an action. However, if a location does not function as background information but as result of an action, then it will be placed right after the action. For example,

Wǒ zài zhǐ shàng xiě wǒ de míngzi ne.
我在纸上写我的名字呢。(location as background
information for 写 *xiě*)
I am writing my name on the paper.

Wǒ de míngzi wǒ xiě zài zhǐ shàng le.
我的名字我写在纸上了。(location as a result of 写 *xiě*)
I wrote down my name on the paper.

Tā zài wǒ de chuáng shàng zuòzhe.
他在我的床上坐着。(location as background information
for 坐 *zuò*)
He is sitting on my bed.

Tā zuòzài wǒ de chuáng shàng le.
他坐在我的床上了。(location as a result of 坐 *zuò*)
He sat down on my bed.

住 *zhù* means "live" or "stay." When used after an action, it implies that
something stays fixed at a place as a result of the action. It is used with a
relatively small number of actions. For example,

Zhànzhù!
站住！(stay still wherever it is as a result of 站 *zhàn*)
Stand still! (Freeze!)

Wǒ yīnggāi jìzhù tā de míngzi.
我应该记住他的名字。(keep in mind as a result of 记 *jì*)
I should remember his name.

In this lesson, for the first time, we have encountered a question formed
with 没有 *méiyou* (not) with 了 *le*. In fact, this is another common way of
forming an affirmative-negative question. Any statement that is ended in 了 *le*
can have 没有 *méiyou* to form a question. For example,

Tā qù Zhōngguó le.　　　　　*Tā qù Zhōngguó le méiyou?*
他去中国了。　→　他去中国了没有？
He went to China.　　　　　Did he go to China?

Tāmen zuòwán zuòyè le.　　　*Tāmen zuòwán zuòyè le méiyou?*
他们做完作业了。　→　他们做完作业了没有？
They have finished doing the homework.　Have they finished doing the homework?

By the way, statements with 过 *guo* (the past experiential marker) or 着 *zhe* (the continuous state marker) right after an action can also be turned into questions by attaching 没有 *méiyou* in the end. For example,

Tā qùguo Nánjí. 他去过南极。	*Tā qùguo Nánjí méiyou?* 他去过南极没有?
He has been to the South Pole.	Has he been to the South Pole?

Tā zài qiánbian zhànzhe. 他在前边站着。	*Tā zài qiánbian zhànzhe méiyou?* 他在前边站着没有?
He is standing in the front.	Is he standing in the front?

生 *shēng* means "person" as we see it for the first time in Lesson 26. However, it is used to mean "unfamiliar" in this lesson when formed with 词 *cí* (word). 生词 *shēngcí* means "unfamiliar word" or "new word".

四 实践 Practice

1. 对话 Conversation

A: 喂，李美。我是张三。

B: 你好，张三。什么事儿?

A: 我要去买衣服，你想去吗?

B: 我还没做完作业呢?

A: 你要做到几点啊?

B: 两点吧。

A: 那好，我两点去你宿舍找你。

B: 行。

......

A: 我妈让我给她买件衣服。

B: 咱们去这个店看看。

A: 好。

B: 我找到一件。你看行吗？

A: 真不错！

B: 你妈穿几号的？

A: 她跟我说过好几次，我都没记住。

B: 那怎么办 bàn (do, handle)？

A: 对了，我写在一张纸上了。

B: 快看看。

A: 八号。

B: 这件就是八号的。

2. 交际 Communication

Task 1 When your Chinese friend sees you yawning, tell him/her that you went to bed very late last night. When you are asked why you went to bed so late, say that you did your homework until midnight.

Task 2 When your Chinese instructor asks for the telephone number of a student in your class, say that you have his phone number since that student wrote his phone number on a piece of paper for you when you were at his dorm.

Task 3 This morning when you were eating breakfast in your dorm, you found yesterday's homework. Obviously, it was placed on the table and then fell down (掉到 diàodào) under the table. Explain the situation to your instructor and ask if it is still OK for you to turn in yesterday's homework today.

3. 书写 Writing

zhǎo   look for; seek   *Héng, shùgōu, tí, héng, xiégōu, piě, diǎn.*

找								

zhǐ   paper   *Piězhé, piězhé, tí; piě, shùtí, héng, xiégōu.*

纸								

jì   memorize; record   *Diǎn, héngzhétí; héngzhé, héng, shùwāngōu.*

记								

Dì–sìshíliù   kè   Nǐmen dào   nǎr   qù?

第四十六课　你们到哪儿去？

Lesson 46　**Where are you going?**

一　听与看　Listen and Read

Listen to the recording of the following sentences as many times as possible until you can say it along with the recording. You should also look at the following transcription while listening and try to imitate.

Dào nǎr qù? Dào nǎr   qù?

到哪儿去？ 到哪儿去？

arrive | which | [suffix] | go | arrive | which | [suffix] | go

Where to go? Where to go?

Nǐmen dào nǎr   qù?

你们 到哪儿去？

you | [plural] | arrive | which | [suffix] | go

Where are you going?

Dào gōngyuán qù,   dào gōngyuán qù,

到 公园 去，到 公园 去，

arrive | public | garden | go | arrive | public | garden | go

Go to the park, go to the park,

wǒmen dào gōngyuán qù.

我们到 公园 去。

I | [plural] | arrive | public | garden | go

we are going to the park.

Jìnqu ba   jìnqu ba,

进去吧，进去吧，

enter | go | [aux.] | enter | go | [aux.]

Get in, get in,

wǒmen jìnqu ba.

我们 进去吧。

I | [plural] | enter | go | [aux.]

let's get in.

Jìn gōngyuán qu,   jìn gōngyuán qu,
进 公园 去, 进 公园 去,
enter | public | garden | go | enter | public | garden | go
Get into the park, get into the part,

wǒmen jìn gōngyuán qu.
我们进 公园 去。
I | [plural] | enter | public | garden | go
we are getting into the park.

Shàngqu ba,   shàngqu ba,
上去 吧, 上去 吧,
ascend | go | [aux.] | ascend | go | [aux.]
Go up, go up,

wǒmen shàngqu ba.
我们 上去 吧。
I | [plural] | ascend | go | [aux.]
let's go up.

Shàng shān qu,   shàng shān qu,
上 山去, 上 山去,
ascend | mountain | go | ascend | mountain | go
Go up the mountain, go up the mountain,

wǒmen shàng shān qu.
我们 上 山去。
I | [plural] | ascend | mountain | go
we are going up the mountain.

Xiàqu ba,   xiàqu ba,
下去吧, 下去吧,
descend | go | [aux.] | descend | go | [aux.]
Go down, go down,

wǒmen xiàqu ba.
我们下去吧。
I | [plural] | descend | go | [aux.]
let's go down.

Xià shān qu,   xià shān qu,

下 山 去， 下 山 去，

descend | mountain | go | descend | mountain | go

Go down the mountain, go down the mountain,

wǒmen xià shān qu.

我们 下 山 去。

I | [plural] | descend | mountain | go

we are going down the mountain.

Huíqu ba,   huíqu ba,

回去 吧， 回去 吧，

return | go | [aux.] | return | go | [aux.]

Go back, go back,

wǒmen huíqu ba.

我们 回去 吧。

I | [plural] | return | go | [aux.]

let's go back.

Huí jiā qu,   huí jiā qu,

回家去， 回家去，

return | home | go | return | home | go

Go back home, go back home,

wǒmen huí jiā qu.

我们 回家去。

I | [plural] | return | home | go

we are going back home.

(With 了 *le* to indicate a past occurrence)

Dào nǎr qù le? Dào nǎr qù le?

到哪儿去了？ 到哪儿去了？

arrive | which | [suffix] | go | [aux.] | arrive | which | [suffix] | go | [aux.]

Where did you go? Where did you go?

Nǐmen dào nǎr qù le?

你们 到哪儿去了？

you | [plural] | arrive | which | [suffix] | go | [aux.]

Where did you go?

Dào gōngyuán qù le,　　dào gōngyuán qù le,
到 公园 去了，到 公园 去了，
arrive | public | garden | go | [aux.] | arrive | public | garden | go | [aux.]
Went to the park, went to the park,

wǒmen dào gōngyuán qù le.
我们 到 公园 去了。
I | [plural] | arrive | public | garden | go | [aux.]
we went to the park.

Jìnqu le ma?　　Jìnqu le ma?
进去了吗? 进去了吗?
enter | go | [aux.] | [ques.] | enter | go | [aux.] | [ques.]
Did you get in? Did you get in?

Nǐmen jìnqu le ma?
你们 进去了吗?
you | [plural] | enter | go | [aux.] | [ques.]
Did you get in?

Jìnqu le,　　jìnqu le,
进去了，进去了，
enter | go | [aux.] | enter | go | [aux.]
We got in, we got in,

wǒmen jìn gōngyuán qu le.
我们 进 公园 去了。
I | [plural] | enter | public | garden | go | [aux.]
we got into the park.

Shàngqu le ma?　Shàngqu le ma?
上去了吗? 上去了吗?
ascend | go | [aux.] | [ques.] | ascend | go | [aux.] | [ques.]
Did you go up? Did you go up?

Nǐmen shàngqu le ma?
你们 上去了吗?
you | [plural] | ascend | go | [aux.] | [ques.]
Did you go up?

Shàngqu le,   shàngqu le,
上去了，上去了，
ascend | go | [aux.] | ascend | go | [aux.]
We went up, we went up,

wǒmen shàng shān qu le.
我们 上 山 去了。
I | [plural] | ascend | mountain | go | [aux.]
we went up the mountain.

Xiàqu le ma?   Xiàqu le ma?
下去了吗？下去了吗？
descend | go | [aux.] | [ques.] descend go [aux.] | [ques.]
Did you go down? Did you go down?

Nǐmen xiàqu le ma?
你们下去了吗？
you | [plural] | descend | go [aux.] | [ques.]
Did you go down?

Xiàqu le,   xiàqu le,
下去了，下去了，
descend | go | [aux.] | descend | go | [aux.]
We went down, we went down,

wǒmen xià shān qu le.
我们 下 山 去了。
I | [plural] | ascend | mountain | go | [aux.]
we went down the mountain.

Huíqu le ma?   Huíqu le ma?
回去了吗？回去了吗？
return | go | [aux.] | [ques.] | return | go | [aux.] | [ques.]
Did you go back? Did you go back?

Nǐmen huíqu le ma?
你们 回去了吗？
you | [plural] | return | go | [aux.] | [ques.]
Did you go back?

Huíqu le,   huíqu le,
回去了，回去了，
return | go | [aux.] | return go [aux.]
We went back, we went back,

wǒmen huí jiā qu le.
我们回家去了。
I | [plural] | return | home | go | [aux.]
we went back home.

二　看与说　Read and Speak

Now, listen to the recording while looking at the following sentences. Then read it out aloud. Finally, recite it by heart to yourself and then to your classmates or instructor.

到哪儿去？到哪儿去？

你们到哪儿去？

到公园去，到公园去，

我们到公园去。

进去吧，进去吧，

我们进去吧。

进公园去，进公园去，

我们进公园去。

上去吧，上去吧，

我们上去吧。

上山去，上山去，

我们上山去。

下去吧，下去吧，

我们下去吧。

下山去，下山去，

我们下山去。

回去吧，回去吧，

我们回去吧。

回家去，回家去，

我们回家去。

(With 了 *le* to indicate a past occurrence)

到哪儿去了？到哪儿去了？

你们到哪儿去了？

到公园去了，到公园去了，

我们到公园去了。

进去了吗？进去了吗？
你们进去了吗？
进去了，进去了，
我们进公园去了。

上去了吗？上去了吗？
你们上去了吗？
上去了，上去了，
我们上山去了。

下去了吗？下去了吗？
你们下去了吗？
下去了，下去了，
我们下山去了。

回去了吗？回去了吗？
你们回去了吗？
回去了，回去了，
我们回家去了。

三 理解 Understand

In Chinese, 你去哪儿 *nǐ qù nǎr* is the expression that can be used to ask where someone is going. If the destination is 图书馆 *túshūguǎn* (library), the answer will be 我去图书馆 *wǒ qù túshūguǎn*. A variation that is commonly used in speech is to use the word 到 *dào* (arrive) to introduce the destination and the word 去 *qù* (go):

> *Nǐ dào nǎr qù?*
> 你到哪儿去?
> Where are you going?

> *Wǒ dào túshūguǎn qù.*
> 我到图书馆去。
> I am going to the library.

The word 去 *qù* (go) indicates the direction away from the speaker and its opposite is 来 *lái* (come), which indicates the direction towards to the speaker. If we are at the library and we try to call a friend to come to the library, we will say,

> *Nǐ dào túshūguǎn lái ba.*
> 你到图书馆来吧。
> Come to the library.

In Chinese, 来 *lái* (come) and 去 *qù* (go) can be used right after an action to indicate its direction towards or away from the speaker. They often appear with the following motion verbs as the directional complement in Chinese:

上 *shàng* (ascend)   →   上来 (come up)   vs.   上去 (go up)
下 *xià* (descend)   →   下来 (come down)   vs.   下去 (go down)
进 *jìn* (enter)   →   进来 (come in)   vs.   进去 (go in)
回 *huí* (return)   →   回来 (come back)   vs.   回去 (go back)

If the destination of a motion verb needs to be specified, then a place word denotes the destination is put after the motion verb and before 来 *lái* or

去 *qù*. Note the place word cannot be placed after 来 *lái* or 去 *qù*.

Motion Verbs		Place		Direction
上 下 进 回	+	[Place]	+	来 or 去

四 实践 Practice

1. 对话 Conversation

A: 你们到哪儿去?

B: 到公园去。你也想去吗?

A: 好啊。

B: 到了。咱们进去吧。

A: 这儿有一座山，谁想跟我上山去?

B: 我去。

A: 走。

B: 已经三点了。我们下山去吧。

A: 行。

B: 李美到哪儿去了?

A: 她妈来了一个电话。她回家去了。

2. 交际 Communication

Task 1 When you arrive at a popular restaurant, the first floor is extremely crowded. Suggest to your Chinese friend you will go upstairs to see whether there is a table available.

Task 2 Over the weekend, you and a few friends enjoy biking to a big park and climb a mountain for fun and for physical exercises. When you notice some dark clouds, tell your friends to go down the mountain since it is going to rain very soon. If not, you will not be able to ride your bike home.

Task 3 You hear a knock at the door. You open the door and find that it is your roommate's Chinese friend. Tell him/her that your roommate is not in since he/she went to the park and is not back yet.

 3. 书写 *Writing*

shān   mountain   *Shù, shùzhé, shù.*

山									

第四十七课　你带什么去？
Lesson 47　　What will you take with you?

一　听与看 Listen and Read

Listen to the recording of the following sentences as many times as possible until you can say it along with the recording. You should also look at the following transcription while listening and try to imitate.

1

Dài shénme qù?   Dài shénme qù?

带 什么 去？带 什么 去？

carry | what | [suffix] | go | carry | what | [suffix] | go

What to take? What to take?

Nǐ dài shénme qù?

你带 什么 去？

you | carry | what | [suffix] | go

What will you take with you?

Dài xiān huā qù,   dài xiān huā qù,

带 鲜花 去，带 鲜花 去，

carry | fresh | flower | go | carry | fresh | flower | go

Take fresh flowers with me, Take fresh flowers with me,

wǒ dài xiān huā qù.

我 带 鲜花 去。

I | carry | fresh | flower | go

I'll take fresh flowers with me.

Gěi shéi dài qù?   Gěi shéi dài qù?

给 谁 带 去？给 谁 带 去？

to | who | carry | go | to | who | carry | go

Whom to carry them to? Whom to carry them to?

Nǐ gěi shéi dàiqù?

你给谁带去？

you | to | who | **carry** | go

Whom will you take them to?

Gěi wǒ péngyou, gěi wǒ péngyou,

给我朋友，给我朋友，

to | I | pal | friend | to | I | pal | friend

To my friend, to my friend,

gěi wǒ péngyou dàiqù.

给我朋友带去。

To | I | pal | friend | **carry** | go

I'll carry them to my friend.

Ná shénme qù? Ná shénme qù?

拿什么去？拿什么去？

hold | what | [suffix] | go | **hold** | what | [suffix] | go

What to take to go? What to take to go?

Nǐ ná shénme qù?

你拿什么去？

you | **hold** | what | [suffix] | go

What will you take to go?

Ná xiàngjī qù, ná xiàngjī qù,

拿相机去，拿相机去，

hold | appearance | machine | go | **hold** | appearance | machine | go

Take a camera to go, take a camera to go,

wǒ ná xiàngjī qù.

我拿相机去。

I | **hold** | appearance | machine | go,

I'll take a camera to go.

Gěi shéi náqù? Gěi shéi náqù?

给谁拿去？给谁拿去？

to | who | **hold** | go | to | who | **hold** | go

Whom to take it to? Whom to take it to?

Nǐ gěi shéi náqù?

你给谁拿去？

you | to | who | hold | go

Whom will you take it to?

Gěi wǒ péngyou,   gěi wǒ péngyou,

给我 朋友， 给我 朋友，

to | I | pal | friend | to | I | pal | friend

To my friend, to my friend,

gěi wǒ péngyou náqù.

给我 朋友 拿去。

to | I | pal | friend | hold | go

I'll take it to my friend.

Jì shénme qù?   Jì shénme qù?

寄 什么去？ 寄 什么去？

mail | what | [suffix] | go | mail | what | [suffix] | go

What to go to mail? What to go to mail?

Nǐ jì shénme qù?

你 寄 什么去？

you | mail | what | [suffix] | go

What will you go to mail?

Jì xìn qù,   jì xìn qù,

寄信去， 寄信去，

mail | letter | go | mail | letter | go

Go to mail a letter, go to mail a letter,

wǒ jì xìn qù.

我 寄信去。

I | mail | letter | go

I'll go to mail a letter.

Gěi shéi jìqù?   Gěi shéi jìqù?

给 谁寄去？ 给 谁寄去？

to | who | mail | go | to | who | mail | go

Mail it to whom? Mail it to whom?

Nǐ gěi shéi jìqù?

你给谁寄去?

you | to | who | **mail** | go

Whom will you mail it to?

Gěi wǒ péngyou　gěi wǒ péngyou

给我朋友，给我朋友，

to | I | pal | friend | to | I | pal | friend

To my friend, to my friend,

gěi wǒ péngyou jìqù.

给我 朋友寄去。

to | I | pal | friend | **mail** | go

I'll mail it to my friend.

2

Tā mǎiláile　yì běn shū;

他买来了一本书;

he | buy | come | [aux.] | one | [meas.] | book

He bought back a book;

tā mǎile　yì běn shū lái.

他买了一本书 来。

he | buy | [aux.] | one | [meas.] | book | come

he bought a book back.

Tā zhǎoláile　yí ge rén;

他 找来了一个人;

he | seek | come | [aux.] | one | [meas.] | person

He found here a person;

tā zhǎole　yí ge rén lá.

他找了一个人来。

he | seek | [aux.] | one | [meas.] | person | come

he found a person here.

Tā náláile　yì bēi chá;

他拿来了一杯茶;

he | **hold** | come | [aux.] | one | [meas.] | tea

He brought here a cup of tea;

tā nále   yi bēi chá lái.

他拿了一杯茶来。

he | hold | [aux.] | one | [meas.] | tea | come

he brought a cup of tea here.

二 看与说 Read and Speak

Now, listen to the recording while looking at the following sentences. Then read it out aloud. Finally, recite it by heart to yourself and then to your classmates or instructor.

1

带什么去？带什么去？

你带什么去？

带鲜花去，带鲜花去，

我带鲜花去。

给谁带去？给谁带去？

你给谁带去？

给我朋友，给我朋友，

给我朋友带去。

拿什么去？拿什么去？

你拿什么去？

拿相机去，拿相机去，

我拿相机去。

给谁拿去？给谁拿去？

你给谁拿去？

给我朋友，给我朋友，

给我朋友拿去。

寄什么去？寄什么去？

你寄什么去？

寄信去，寄信去，

我寄信去。

给谁寄去？给谁寄去？

你给谁寄去？

给我朋友，给我朋友，

给我朋友寄去。

2

他买来了一本书；

他买了一本书来。

他找来了一个人；

他找了一个人来。

他拿来了一杯茶；

他拿了一杯茶来。

三　理解　Understand

  In addition to motion verbs such as 上 *shàng* (ascend), 下 *xià* (descend), 进 *jìn* (enter), and 回 *huí* (return), other types of action verbs such as 带 *dài* (carry with oneself), 拿 *ná* (take by hand), 寄 *jì* (mail), 买 *mǎi* (buy) can also have 来 *lái* (come) or 去 *qù* (go) to follow them to serve as the directional complement, indicating the direction of the action towards or away from the speaker. For example,

  带 *dài* (carry with oneself)
  ⟶ 带来 (carry here = bring)　vs.　带去 (carry there = take)

  拿 *ná* (take by hand)
  ⟶ 拿来 (take here by hand = bring)　vs.　拿去 (take there by hand = take)

  寄 *jì* (mail)
  ⟶ 寄来 (mail in)　vs.　寄去 (mail out)

  买 *mǎi* (buy)
  ⟶ 买来 (buy and bring back)　vs.　买去 (buy and take to)

  When 来 *lái* (come) or 去 *qù* (go) used as the directional complement, unlike a word used as the resultative complement, which has to be attached to the main action verb, it can be placed either right after the verb of the main action or after the object, which is the recipient of the main action. For example,

> *mǎilái yí liàng chē*
> 买来一辆 车
> Verb Direction Object

> *mǎi yí liàng chē lái*
> 买一辆 车 来
> Verb Object Direction

If 了 *le* needs to be used to denote the completive stage of the action with a directional complement, then it is placed after the directional complement that is attached to the action. If the directional complement is separated from the action and is placed after the object of the action, then 了 *le* is attached to the action. For example,

> *Tā mǎiláile   yí liàng chē.*
> 他买来了一辆 车。
> He bought back a car.

> *Tā mǎile yí liàng chē lái.*
> 他买了一辆 车 来。
> He bought a car back.

四　实践　Practice

1. 对话 Conversation

A: 张老师请我们吃饭。

B: 我们带什么去呢?

A: 给她带鲜花吧。

B: 鲜花好。

A: 我回宿舍拿相机去。

B: 对，多照几张相。

A: 李贵今天也来吗?

B: 他在上海呢。他给张老师写来一封信。

......

A: 鲜花买来了。

B: 我去拿一支 *zhī* ([measure word]) 笔来。

A: 对，在纸上写上：我们不会忘记您！

2. 交际 Communication

Task 1 Both you and your roommate are invited to eat dinner at your host family's apartment. When you and your roommate discuss what to bring, say that you think you should bring a bottle of American red wine since your host family parents feel drinking one glass of red wine a day is good for one's health.

Task 2 Call your Chinese speaking partner to say that you brought a few DVDs from the U.S. Ask him/her to find a few Chinese students to come to your dorm to watch a DVD together.

Task 3 One of your Chinese friends has traveled to Beijing for vacation and has sent you a postcard. Since the writing is in Chinese and there are quite a few characters you don't understand, go to another Chinese friend. Explain the situation and ask for help in reading the writing on the postcard.

3. 书写 Writing

dài   strap; carry with oneself   *Héng, shù, shù, shù; diǎn, hénggōu, shù, héngzhégōu, shù.*

带									

xiān   fresh   *Piě, héngpiě, shù, héngzhé, héng, shù, héng, tí; diǎn, piě, héng, héng, héng, shù.*

鲜									

ná   take by hand; hold   *Piě, nà, héng, shù, héngzhé, héng; piě, héng, héng, wāngōu.*

拿									

jì   mail   *Diǎn, diǎn, hénggōu; héng, piě, diǎn, héng, shù, héngzhé, héng, shùgōu.*

寄									

Dì–sìshíbā   kè   Nǐmen kàn de jiàn ma?

第四十八课　　你们看得见吗？
Lesson 48

Are you able to see it?

一　听与看　Listen and Read

Listen to the recording of the following sentences as many times as possible until you can say it along with the recording. You should also look at the following transcription while listening and try to imitate.

Hēibǎn shàng de Hànzì,

黑板 上 的 汉字，

black | **board** | up | [aux.] | Han ethnic group | character

The Chinese characters on the blackboard,

nǐmen kàn de jiàn ma?

你们 看 得 见 吗？

you | [plural] | look | [aux.] | see | [ques.]

are you able to see?

Kàn de jiàn,   kàn de jiàn,

看 得 见，　看 得 见，

look | [aux.] | see | look | [aux.] | see

We are able to, we are able to,

nème dà de Hànzì,

那么 大 的 汉字，

that | [suffix] | big | [aux.] | Han ethnic group | character

such big Chinese characters,

wǒmen kàn de jiàn.

我们 看 得 见。

I | [plural] | look | [aux.] | see

we are able to see.

Lǎoshī jiǎng de yǔfǎ,

老师 讲 的 语法，

old | master | **explain** | [aux.] | language | law

The grammar the teacher explained,

nǐmen tīng de dǒng ma?

你们听得懂吗?

you | [plural] | listen | [aux.] | understand | [ques.]

are you able to understand by listening?

Tīng de dǒng, tīng de dǒng,

听得懂,听得懂,

listen | [aux.] | understand | listen | [aux.] | understand

We are able to, we are able to,

nème róngyì de yǔfǎ,

那么容易的语法,

that | [suffix] | tolerate | change | [aux.] | language | law

such easy grammar,

wǒmen tīng de dǒng.

我们听得懂。

I | [plural] | listen | [aux.] | understand

we are able to understand by listening.

Jīntiān xué de shēngcí,

今天学的生词,

present | day | learn | [aux.] | unfamiliar | word

The new words learned today,

nǐmen jì de zhù ma?

你们记得住吗?

you | [plural] | remember | [aux.] | stay | [ques.]

are you able to remember?

Jì bú zhù, jì bú zhù,

记不住,记不住,

remember | not | stay | remember | not | stay

We are unable to, we are unable to,

nème duō de shēngcí,

那么多的生词,

that | [suffix] | many | [aux.] | unfamiliar | word

so many new words,

wǒmen jì bú zhù.

我们记不住。

I | [plural] | remember | not | stay

we are unable to remember.

Wǒ qí de zìxíngchē,

我骑的自行车，

I | ride | [aux.] | **self** | go | vehicle

The bicycle I ride,

nǐmen xiū de hǎo ma?

你们修得好吗？

you | [plural] | **repair** | [aux.] | well | [ques.]

are you able to fix it?

Xiū de hǎo, xiū de hǎo,

修得好，修得好，

repair | [aux.] | well | **repair** | [aux.] | well

We are able to, we are able to,

nème xiǎo de wèntí,

那么小的问题，

that | [suffix] | small | [aux.] | ask | **topic**

such a small problem,

wǒmen xiū de hǎo.

我们修得好。

I | [plural] | **repair** | [aux.] | well

we are able to fix.

Māma mǎi de dōngxi,

妈妈买的东西，

mom | buy | [aux.] | **east** | west

The stuff mother bought,

nǐmen ná de dòng ma?

你们拿得动吗？

you | [plural] | take | [aux.] | **move** | [ques.]

are you able to carry?

Ná bú dòng,　ná bú dòng,

拿不动，拿不动，

take | not | **move** | take | not | **move**

We are unable to, we are unable to,

nème duō de dōngxi,

那么多的东西，

that | [suffix] | many | [aux.] | **east** | **west**

so much stuff,

wǒmen ná bú dòng.

我们拿不动。

I | [plural] | take | not | **move**

we are unable to carry.

Bàba zuò de mǐfàn,

爸爸做的米饭，

dad | make | [aux.] | **rice** | meal

The rice dad cooked,

nǐmen chī de liǎo ma?

你们吃得了吗？

you | [plural] | eat | [aux.] | complete | [ques.]

are you able to finish eating?

Chī bù liǎo,　chī bù liǎo,

吃不了，吃不了，

eat | not | complete | eat | not | complete

We are unable to, we are unable to,

zhème duō de mǐfàn,

这么多的米饭，

this | [suffix] | much | [aux.] | **rice** | meal

so much rice,

wǒmen chī bù liǎo.

我们吃不了。

I | [plural] | eat | not | complete

we are unable to finish eating.

二 看与说 Read and Speak

Now, listen to the recording while looking at the following sentences. Then read it out aloud. Finally, recite it by heart to yourself and then to your classmates or instructor.

黑板上的汉字，

你们看得见吗？

看得见，看得见，

那么大的汉字，

我们看得见。

老师讲的语法，

你们听得懂吗？

听得懂，听得懂，

那么容易的语法，

我们听得懂。

今天学的生词，

你们记得住吗？

记不住，记不住，

那么多的生词，

我们记不住。

我骑的自行车，
你们修得好吗?
修得好，修得好，
那么小的问题，
我们修得好。

妈妈买的东西，
你们拿得动吗?
拿不动，拿不动，
那么多的东西，
我们拿不动。

爸爸做的米饭，
你们吃得了吗?
吃不了，吃不了，
这么多的米饭，
我们吃不了。

三 理解 Understand

When we estimate whether there is the possibility to achieve a desired result through an action, we use 得 *de* or 不 *bù* after the action and before the result. If our estimate is positive, we use 得 *de*; otherwise, we use 不 *bù*. For example,

Action + (得 or 不) + Result				Action + Potential Complement
kàn 看 look	+ *de* 得 able to	+ *jiàn* 见 see	→	*kàn de jiàn* 看得见 able to see by looking
tīng 听 listen	+ *de* 得 able to	+ *dǒng* 懂 understand	→	*tīng de dǒng* 听得懂 able to understand by listening
kàn 看 look	+ *bú* 不 unable to	+ *jiàn* 见 see	→	*kàn bú jiàn* 看不见 unable to see by looking
tīng 听 listen	+ *bù* 不 unable to	+ *dǒng* 懂 understand	→	*tīng bù dǒng* 听不懂 unable to understand by listening

A question to ask if it is possible for an action to get a desired result can be formed by an affirmative-negative question format:

Nèi ge Hànzì nǐ kàn de jiàn kàn bú jiàn?
那个汉字你看得见看不见？
Are you able to see that Chinese character or not?

When the word 了 *le* is used as a potential complement, it is pronounced as *liǎo* instead of *le*: 得了 *de liǎo* and 不了 *bù liǎo*. Here 了 liǎo may have two meanings: 1) able to finish; 2) possible or able to. The different meanings can be figured out from the contexts in which it is used. For example,

Mǐfàn bú tài duō,   wǒ chī de liǎo.
米饭不太多，我吃得了。
There is not much rice. I am able to finish eating it.

Zhèi běn shū de shēngcí bù duō,   wǒ kàn de liǎo.

这本书的生词不多，我看得了。

There are not many new words, I am able to read it.

Mǐfàn tài duō le,   wǒ chī bù liǎo.

米饭太多了，我吃不了。

There is too much rice, I am unable to finish eating it.

Zhèi běn shū de shēngcí tài duō le,   wǒ kàn bù liǎo.

这本书的生词太多了，我看不了。

There are too many new words, I am unable to read it.

四 实践 Practice

1. 对话 Conversation

T: 黑板上的字，你们看得见吗？

A: 那么大的字，我们看得见。

T: 今天讲的语法，你们听得懂吗？

B: 不太难，听得懂。

T: 今天回去，要记住这些生词。

C: 啊，这么多！我们记不住。

T: 多听多看，就记得住了。

　　……

A: 你买了这么多东西！

B: 是啊。我都快拿不动了。

A: 放我自行车上吧。

B: 怎么不走了？你这自行车出问题了吧？

A: 真的。我们找个修车的师傅 *shīfu* (master) 看看。

　　……

A: 师傅，您看我这自行车修得好吗？

M: 问题不大，修得好。

A: 要多长时间？

M: 一个小时吧。

A: 我们去那儿的饭馆吃点儿饭吧。

B: 好！我请客！

A: 你要这么多的菜，吃得了吗？

B: 吃吧！吃不了，我们带回家去。

2. 交际 Communication

Task 1   You are at a restaurant for dinner with a few Chinese friends. When one friend pours beer into your glass, tell him/her not to give you too much since you will not be able to drink that much.

Task 2   You are at a park in China. When a Chinese person starts to talk with you in the local dialect, tell him/her that you can't understand the local dialect and ask him/her if he/she can speak with you in the standard Chinese (普通话 *pǔtōnghuà*).

Task 3   You go to a dance show with a Chinese friend. When you friend wants to sit at the back, tell him/her that you can't see clearly at the back and ask him/her to sit in the front with you.

3. 书写 Writing

bǎn   board   *Héng, shù, piě, diǎn; piě, piě, héngpiě, nà.*

jiǎng   explain; speak   *Diǎn, héngzhétí; héng, héng, piě, shù.*

讲

fǎ   law   *Diǎn, diǎn, tí; héng, shù, héng, piězhé, diǎn.*

法

róng   tolerate   *Diǎn, diǎn, hénggōu; piě, diǎn, piě, nà, shù, héngzhé, héng.*

容

yì   change   *Shù, héngzhé, héng, héng; piě, héngzhégōu, piě, piě.*

易

zì   self   *Piě, shù, héngzhé, héng, héng, héng.*

自

xiū   repair   *Piě, shù, shù, piě, héngpiě, nà, piě, piě, piě.*

修

tí   topic; subject   *Shù, héngzhé, héng, héng, héng, shù, héng, piě, nà; héng, piě, shù, héngzhé, piě, diǎn.*

题

dōng   east   *Héng, piězhé, shùgōu, diǎn, diǎn.*

东

xī   west   *Héng, shù, héngzhé, piě, shùwān, héng.*

西

dòng   move; act   *Héng, héng, piězhé, diǎn; héngzhégōu, piě.*

动

mǐ   rice   *Diǎn, piě, héng, shù, piě, nà.*

米

第四十九课　谁从楼上走下来了？
Lesson 49　Who came down by walking from upstairs?

一　听与看　Listen and Read

Listen to the recording of the following sentences as many times as possible until you can say it along with the recording. You should also look at the following transcription while listening and try to imitate.

Shéi cóng lóu shàng zǒu xialai le?

谁 从 楼 上 走 下 来 了？
who | from | building | up | walk | down | come | [aux.]
Who came down by walking from upstairs?

Wǒ bà cóng lóu shàng zǒu xialai le.

我 爸 从 楼 上 走 下 来 了。
I | dad | from | building | up | walk | down | come | [aux.]
My dad came down by walking from upstairs.

Shéi cóng lóu xià zǒu shangqu le?

谁 从 楼 下 走 上 去 了？
who | from | building | down | walk | up | go | [aux.]
Who went up by walking from downstairs?

Wǒ mā cóng lóu xià zǒu shangqu le.

我 妈 从 楼 下 走 上 去 了。
I | mom | from | building | down | walk | up | go | [aux.]
My mom went up by walking from downstairs.

Shéi cóng lóu lǐ zǒu chuqu le?

谁 从 楼 里 走 出 去 了？
who | from | building | inside | walk | exit | go | [aux.]
Who went out by walking from the inside of the building?

Wǒ gē cóng lóu lǐ zǒu chuqu le.

我 哥 从 楼 里 走 出 去 了。
I | elder brother | from | building | inside | walk | exit | go | [aux.]
My elder brother went out by walking from the inside of the building.

Shéi cóng lóu wài zǒu jinlai le?

谁 从 楼外 走进来了？

who | from | building | outside | walk | enter | come | [aux.]

Who walked and came in from the outside of the building?

Wǒ mèi cóng lóu wài zǒu jinlai le.

我 妹 从 楼外 走进来了。

I | younger sister | from | building | outside | walk | enter | come | [aux.]

My younger sister came in by walking from the outside of the building.

Qǐng nǐ zǒu guolai, bú yào pǎo guolai.

请 你 走过来，不要 跑过来。

please | you | walk | over | come | not | need | run | over | come

Please walk over here, don't run over here.

Qǐng nǐ dài huilai, bú yào jì huilai.

请 你 带回来，不要 寄 回来。

please | you | carry | return | come | not | need | mail | return | come

Please bring it back here, don't mail it back here.

Qǐng nǐ zuò xialai, bú yào zhàn qilai.

请 你 坐下来，不要 站 起来。

please | you | sit | down | come | not | need | stand | rise | come

Please sit down here, don't stand up.

Qìchē ne? Qìchē ne?

汽车 呢？汽车 呢？

steam | vehicle | [ques.] | steam | vehicle | [ques.]

Where is the car? Where is the car?

Nǐ de qìchē ne?

你的汽车 呢？

you | [aux.] | steam | vehicle | [ques.]

Where is your car?

Kāi guolai, kāi guolai, ràng wǒ zuòzuo.

开 过来，开 过来，让 我 坐坐。

drive | cross | come | drive | cross | come | let | I | sit | sit

Drive it over here, drive it over here, and let me sit in it.

Xiàngjī ne?   Xiàngjī ne?

相机 呢？ 相机 呢？

appearance | machine | [ques.] | appearance | machine | [ques.]

Where is the camera? Where is the camera?

Nǐ de xiàngjī ne?

你的相机 呢？

you | [aux.] | appearance | machine | [ques.]

Where is your camera?

Dài guolai,   dài guolai,   ràng wǒ zhàozhao.

带 过来， 带 过来， 让 我 照照。

carry | over | come, carry | over | come | let | I | shine | shine

Bring it over, bring it over, and let me take pictures with it.

Cídiǎn ne?   Cídiǎn ne?

词典 呢？ 词典 呢？

word | classics | [ques.] | word | classics | [ques.]

Where is the dictionary? Where is the dictionary?

Nǐ de cídiǎn ne?

你的词典 呢？

you | [aux.] | word | classics | [ques.]

Where is your dictionary?

Ná guolai,   ná guolai,   ràng wǒ yòngyong.

拿 过来， 拿 过来， 让 我 用用。

hold | over | come | hold | over | come | let | I | use | use

Hand it over here, hand it over here, and let me use it a bit.

Dàngāo ne?   Dàngāo ne?

蛋糕 呢？ 蛋糕 呢？

egg | cake | [ques.] | egg | cake | [ques.]

Where is the cake? Where is the cake?

Nǐ de dàngāo ne?

你的蛋糕 呢？

you | [aux.] | egg | cake | [ques.]

Where is your cake?

Sòng guolai,　sòng guolai,　ràng wǒ chángchang.

送过来，送过来，让我 尝尝。

send | over | come | send | over | come | let | I | taste

Send it over here, send it over here, and let me taste it a bit.

Wǒ shì bu shì hěn zìsī?

我是不是很自私？

I | be | not | be | very | self | private

I am very selfish, am I not?

二　看与说　Read and Speak

Now, listen to the recording while looking at the following sentences. Then read it out aloud. Finally, recite it by heart to yourself and then to your classmates or instructor.

谁从楼上走下来了？

我爸从楼上走下来了。

谁从楼下走上去了？

我妈从楼下走上去了。

谁从楼里走出去了？

我哥从楼里走出去了。

谁从楼外走进来了？

我妹从楼外走进来了。

请你走过来，不要跑过来。

请你带回来，不要寄回来。

请你坐下来，不要站起来。

汽车呢？汽车呢？

你的汽车呢？

开过来，开过来，让我坐坐。

相机呢？相机呢？

你的相机呢？

带过来，带过来，让我照照。

词典呢？词典呢？

你的词典呢？

拿过来，拿过来，让我用用。

蛋糕呢？蛋糕呢？

你的蛋糕呢？

送过来，送过来，让我尝尝。

我是不是很自私？

三 理解 Understand

In this lesson, we see that many actions take two words for directions: the first one being one of those motion verbs and the second being 来 *lái* or 去 *qù*. These motion verbs are combined with 来 *lái* or 去 *qù* to form complex directional complements for the actions they are attached to. Although the direction of an action expressed by a complex directional complement is no longer simple, it is still simple enough to understand. A motion verb indicates an upward, downward, inward, outward, returning, crossing, or rising movement, and 来 *lái* is still used to indicate the action moving towards the speaker, and 去 *qù*, away from the speaker. The pronunciations for all motion verbs as well as 来 *lái* and 去 *qù* are all neutralized when used in a complex directional complement. For example,

Action	**Direction 1**	**Direction 2**	
Verbs +	**Motion Verbs +**	**来 lái (come)** or	**去 qù (go)**
zǒu 走 walk	*zǒushàng* 走上 walk upward	*zǒu shanglai* 走 上来 walk upward coming	*zǒu shangqu* 走 上去 walk upward going
zǒu 走 walk	*zǒuxià* 走下 walk downward	*zǒu xialai* 走 下来 walk downward coming	*zǒu xiaqu* 走 下去 walk downward going
zǒu 走 walk	*zǒujìn* 走进 walk inward	*zǒu jinlai* 走 进来 walk inward coming	*zǒu jinqu* 走 进去 walk inward going
zǒu 走 walk	*zǒuchū* 走出 walk outward	*zǒu chulai* 走 出来 walk outward coming	*zǒu chuqu* 走 出去 walk outward going
zǒu 走 walk	*zǒuhuí* 走回 walk returning	*zǒu huilai* 走 回来 walk returning coming	*zǒu huiqu* 走 回去 walk returning going
zǒu 走 walk	*zǒuguò* 走过 walk crossing	*zǒu guolai* 走 过来 walk crossing coming	*zǒu guoqu* 走 过去 walk crossing going
zhàn 站 stand	*zhànqǐ* 站起 stand rising	*zhàn qilai* 站 起来 stand rising coming	**(Not applicable)**

起 *qǐ* means "rise" as used in the word 起床 *qǐ chuáng*, meaning "to rise from bed". It is different from the other motion verbs that can be followed by either 来 *lái* or 去 *qù*. 起 *qǐ* is only followed by 来 *lái* and never by 去 *qù*. 起来 *qilai* is mostly used with these action verbs to mean "off and up": 站 *zhàn* "stand", 坐 *zuò* "sit", and 拿 *ná* "take by hand". For example,

> *zhàn qilai*
> 站起来
> stand up

> *zuò qilai*
> 坐起来
> sit up

> *ná qilai*
> 拿起来
> take up by hand

回 *huí* is a motion verb, meaning "returning". It is used to indicate a movement that comes or goes back to the original starting point. If our dorm is the starting place from which we leave for our day of work or study, when we want to return to the dorm and we choose to walk, we say 我们走回去吧 *wǒmen zǒu huiqu ba*.

If we want to specify the place to return to, we will need to put the place in between the motion verb and the directional verb, and never at the end of a complex directional complement. For example,

> *Wǒmen zǒuhui sùshè qu ba.*
> 我们走回宿舍去吧。
> Let's return to the dorm by walking.

从 *cóng* is a preposition, meaning "from". It is used to introduce a starting point in place or in time. Used with 从 *cóng*, 到 *dào*, which means "to", often introduces a destination or an ending point in time.

> *Tā jiù yào cóng Měiguó dào Zhōngguó qù xuéxí Zhōngwén le.*
> 他就要从美国到 中国 去学习 中文了。
> He will soon go from the United States to China to study Chinese.

> *Wǒ měi tiān cóng 12 diǎn dào 1 diǎn chī wǔfàn.*
> 我每天从12点 到1点吃午饭。
> Everyday I have lunch from 12 o'clock to 1 o'clock.

Reduplication of a verb in Chinese softens the tone for the action. It gives the sense of "do it a little bit" or "do it for a short while". For example,

Wǒ kànkan.		*Wǒ kàn yíxiàr.*
我看看。	=	我看一下儿。
I'll **have a look**.		

Wǒ yòngyong.		*Wǒ yòng yíxiàr.*
我 用用。	=	我用一下儿。
I'll **use it for a short while**.		

Wǒ chángchang.		*Wǒ cháng yíxiàr.*
我 尝尝。	=	我尝一下儿。
I'll **taste it a bit**.		

四 实践 Practice

1. 对话 Conversation

M: 你去看看，谁从楼下上来了？

A: 是我哥。

M: 是走上来的吗？

A: 不是，是跑上来的。

M: 你告诉 gàosu (tell) 他，不要跑上跑下，跑来跑去。

A: 哥，妈说不让你跑。

B: 为什么？

M: 楼里的人会生气的。

B: 我也是楼里的人啊。

M: 你站起来，看看，都快跟我一样高了。

B: 一样高怎么了？

M: 应该懂事了。

B: 我怎么不懂事了？

M: 你的作业呢？拿过来让我看看。

🤝 *2. 交际 Communication*

Task 1 | You are at a market in China. When you find something you are interested in, point at that item and ask the stand owner to take it over for you to see closely.

Task 2 | You see your friend at the lobby of a student dormitory building, but your friend comes to see a classmate of yours, not you. When you tell your friend that this classmate of yours is not in, your friend doubts whether what you have said is true. Support yourself by saying that you saw your classmate walking down the stairs with a girl and walking out of this door.

Task 3 | When a Chinese friend comes over to say goodbye to you before you leave for your home country, he/she is surprised to see that you have so much stuff and wonder how you can take everything home. Tell your Chinese friend that you will mail some of your stuff home and take some with you.

✐ *3. 书写 Writing*

cóng   from   *Piě, diǎn; piě, nà.*

从								

lóu   storied building   *Héng, shù, piě, diǎn; diǎn, piě, héng, shù, piě, nà, piědiǎn, piě, héng.*

楼								

wài   outside   *Piě, héngpiě, diǎn; shù, diǎn.*

外								

qì　steam　*Diǎn, diǎn, tí; piě, héng, héng, héngzhéxiégōu.*

汽

sòng　deliver　*Diǎn, piě, héng, héng, piě, diǎn; diǎn, héngzhézhépiě, píngnà.*

送

dàn　egg　*Hénggōu, shù, héng, piě, nà; shù, héngzhé, héng, shù, héng, diǎn.*

蛋

cháng　taste　*Shù, diǎn, piě, diǎn, hénggōu; héng, héng, piězhé, diǎn.*

尝

sī　private　*Piě, héng, shù, piě, diǎn; piězhé, diǎn.*

私

Dì-wǔshí   kè   Tā   shì   shénme   shíhou   qù   de?

第五十课　他是什么时候去的？

Lesson 50   When did he go?

一　听与看　Listen and Read

Listen to the recording of the following sentences as many times as possible until you can say it along with the recording. You should also look at the following transcription while listening and try to imitate.

Tā qùnián gēn tā bà   yìqǐ cóng Qīngdǎo zuò chuán dào Shànghǎi qù lǚyóu le.

他去年跟他爸一起从 青岛 坐 船 到 上海 去旅游了。

he|go|year|with|he|dad|one|rise|from|**blue**|**island**|sit|**boat**|arrive|up|**sea**|go|**travel**|**wander**|[aux.]

Last year he went with his dad by ship from Qingdao to Shanghai to have a tour.

Tā shì shénme shíhou qù de?

他是 什么 时候 去 的？

he|be|what|[suffix]|time|condition|go|[aux.]

When did he go? (when was it that he went?)

Tā shì qùnián qù de.

他是 去年 去 的。

he|be|go|year|go|[aux.]

He went last year. (It was last year that he went.)

Tā shì gēn shéi qù de?

他是 跟 谁 去 的？

he|be|with|who|go|[aux.]

Whom did he go with? (Who was it that he went with?)

Tā shì gēn tā bà qù de.

他是 跟他爸 去 的。

he|be|with|he|father|go|[aux.]

He went with his father. (It was with his father that he went.)

Tā shì cóng nǎr qù de?

他是 从 哪儿 去 的？

he|be|from|which|[suffix]|go|[aux.]

Where did he go from? (Where was it that he went from?)

Tā shì cóng Qīngdǎo qù de.

他是从 青岛去的。

he | be | from | **blue** | **island** | go | [aux.]

He went from Qingdao. (It was from Qingdao that he went.)

Tā shì qù de nǎr?

他是去的哪儿？

he | be | go | [aux.] | [which] | [suffix]

Where did he go? (Where was it that he went?)

Tā shì qù de Shànghǎi.

他是去的 上海。

he | be | go | [aux.] | **up** | **sea**

It was Shanghai that he went to.

Tā shì zěnme qù de?

他是怎么去的？

he | be | how | [suffix] | go | [aux.]

How did he go? (How was it that he went?)

Tā shì zuò chuán qù de.

他是坐 船 去的。

he | be | sit | **boat** | go | [aux.]

He went by ship. (It was by ship that he went.)

Tā shì qù zuò shén me de?

他是去做 什么的？

he | be | go | do | what | [suffix] | [aux.]

What did he go for? (What was it for that he went?)

Tā shì qù lǚyóu de.

他是去旅游的。

he | be | go | **travel** | **wander** | [aux.]

He went to travel. (It was for traveling that he went.)

二 看与说 Read and Speak

Now, listen to the recording while looking at the following sentences. Then read it out aloud. Finally, recite it by heart to yourself and then to your classmates or instructor.

他去年跟他爸一起从青岛坐船到上海去旅游了。

他是什么时候去的?

他是去年去的。

他是跟谁去的?

他是跟他爸去的。

他是从哪儿去的?

他是从青岛去的。

他是去的哪儿?

他是去的上海。

他是怎么去的?

他是坐船去的。

他是去做什么的?

他是去旅游的。

三   理解 Understand

The 是……的 *shì... de* sentence structure is used to provide information about an action or an event that has already occurred. In other words, whenever we are curious about a particular piece of information that is related to a past action or event, such as when, where, why, how, with whom, and for what purpose, we use the 是……的 *shì...de* sentence structure to ask questions and to answer them. Structurally, 是 *shì* is placed before the needed information, and 的 *de* is usually put at the end of the sentence. For example,

> *Nǐ shì shénme shí hou lái de?*
> 你是什么时候来的？
> When did you come? (When was it that you came?)

> *Wǒ shì zuótiān lái de.*
> 我是昨天来的。
> I came yesterday. (It was yesterday that I came.)

> *Nǐ shì zěnme qù shūdiàn de?*
> 你是怎么去书店的？
> How did you go to the bookstore? (How was it that you went to the bookstore?)

> *Wǒ shì zuò chē qù shūdiàn de.*
> 我是坐车去书店的。
> I went the bookstore by bus. (It was by bus that I went to the bookstore.)

In the 是……的 *shì...de* sentence structure, in daily conversations, we often hear that 是 *shì* is omitted, whereas 的 *de* cannot as it has to be kept as the marker of this special sentence structure for past actions or events. However, if the verb in a 是……的 *shì...de* sentence has a recipient or a destination, then 的 *de* does not have to be at the end of the sentence. Instead, it can be moved right after the verb and before the receipt or destination. If we still use the example sentences given above, they will be as follows:

> *Nǐ shénme shíhou lái de?*
> 你什么时候来的？
> When did you come? (When was it that you came?)

Wǒ zuótiān lái de.
我昨天来的。
I came yesterday. (It was yesterday that I came.)

Nǐ zěnme qù de shūdiàn?
你怎么去的书店？
How did you go to the bookstore (How was it that you went to the bookstore?)

Wǒ zuò chē qù de shūdiàn.
我坐车去的书店。
I went to the bookstore by bus. (It was by bus that I went to the bookstore.)

四　实践　Practice

1. 对话 Conversation

A: 暑假你去旅游了吗？

B: 去了。

A: 去哪儿了？

B: 去上海了。

A: 跟谁去的？

B: 跟我爸去的。

A: 哪天去的？

B: 七月二十号。

A: 在那儿呆了几天？

B: 三天。

A: 好玩儿吗？

B: 好玩儿，就是太热了。

A: 是坐飞机去的吗？

B: 不是。从青岛坐船去的。

🖐 2. 交际 Communication

Task 1 | When your Chinese friend learns that you went to Beijing last week, he/she asks whether you went by plane. Tell him/her you went by train, not by plane.

Task 2 | You have got acquainted with a Chinese student from Shanghai. When you call him/her one day, you are told that he/she has returned to his/her hometown. Ask which day he/she left and whether he/she took the airplane or the train.

Task 3 | During the winter recess, you traveled to Xi'an. When your Chinese friend asks whether you went with your classmates, say that you went by yourself, not with your classmates.

✏ 3. 书写 Writing

qīng　blue; green　*Héng, héng, shù, héng, shù, héngzhégōu, héng, héng.*

青									

dǎo　island　*Piě, héngzhégōu, diǎn, shùzhézhégōu, shù, shùzhé, shù.*

岛									

chuán　boat; ship　*Piě, piě, héngzhégōu, diǎn, héng, diǎn; piě, héngzhéwān, shù, héngzhé, héng.*

船									

hǎi　sea　*Diǎn, diǎn, tí; piě, héng, shùzhé, héngzhégōu, diǎn, héng, diǎn.*

海									

lǚ   travel   *Diǎn, héng, héngzhégōu, piě; piě, héng, piě, shùtí, piě, nà.*

旅									

yóu   wander; swim   *Diǎn, diǎn, tí; diǎn, héng, héngzhégōu, piě; piě, héng, héngpiě, wāngōu, héng.*

游									

第五十一课　你把这些生词记住了吗？

Lesson 51　　Have you learned these new words by heart?

一　听与看　Listen and Read

Listen to the recording of the following sentences as many times as possible until you can say it along with the recording. You should also look at the following transcription while listening and try to imitate.

Nǐ bǎ zhèixiē shēngcí jìzhù   le ma?

你把这些生词记住了吗？

you | handle | this | some | unfamiliar | word | memorize | stay | [aux.] | [ques.]

Have you learned these new words by heart?

Jìzhù le.

记住了。

memorize | stay | [aux.]

Yes, I have learned them by heart.

nǐ bǎ zhèixiē Hànzì   xiěduì le ma?

你把这些汉字写对了吗？

you | handle | this | some | Han ethnic group | character | write | correct | [aux.] | [ques.]

Have you written these Chinese characters correctly?

Xiěduì le.

写对了。

write | correct | [aux.]

Yes, I have written them correctly.

Nǐ bǎ zhèi piān kèwén niànhuì le ma?

你把这篇课文念会了吗？

you | handle | this | [meas.] | text | language | read loudly | know how | [aux.] | [ques.]

Have you got to know this text by reading loudly?

Niànhuì le.

念会了。

read loudly | know how | [aux.]

Yes, I got to know it by reading loudly.

Nǐ bǎ zhèige duìhuà liànhǎo le ma?

你把这个对话 练好了吗？

you | handle | this | [meas.] | vis-à-vis | words | practice | good | [aux.] | [ques.]

Have you practiced this dialogue well?

Liànhǎo le.

练好了。

practice | good | [aux.]

Yes, I have practiced it well.

Nǐ bǎ nǐ de zuòyè zuòwán le ma?

你把你的作业做完了吗？

you | handle | you | [aux.] | labor | doings | do | finish | [aux.] | [ques.]

Have you finish doing your homework?

Zuòwán le.

做完了。

do | finish | [aux.]

Yes, I have finished doing it.

Nǐ bǎ dēng kāikai,

你把灯 开开，

you | handle | light | open | open

Turn the light on,

zài bǎ mén guānshàng;

再把门 关上；

again | handle | door | close | up

then close the door;

nǐ bǎ yào chī le,

你把药吃了，

you | handle | medicine | eat | [aux.]

take the medicine,

zài bǎ shuǐ hē le.

再把水喝了。

again | handle | water | drink | [aux.]

then drink the water.

二　看与说　Read and Speak

Now, listen to the recording while looking at the following sentences. Then read it out aloud. Finally, recite it by heart to yourself and then to your classmates or instructor.

你把这些生词记住了吗？

记住了。

你把这些汉字写对了吗？

写对了。

你把这篇课文念会了吗？

念会了。

你把这个对话练好了吗？

练好了。

你把你的作业做完了吗？

做完了。

你把灯开开，

再把门关上；

你把药吃了，

再把水喝了。

三　理解　Understand

In Chinese, the recipient of an action is usually placed after the action. If the recipient of the action is known to both the speaker and the listener, then it can be moved to the beginning of the sentence as the topic of the sentence. The topic of the sentence represents the known or old information, and the rest of the sentence provides new information about what has happened or will happen to the recipient or what has been done or what is to be done to the recipient. For example,

> *Wǒ kànwánle　yì běn shū.*
> 我看完了一本书。
> I have finished reading **a book**.

> *Zhèi běn shū wǒ kànwán le.*
> 这本书我看完了。
> As for **this book**, I have finished reading it.

> *Shū wǒ kànwán le.*
> 书我看完了。
> As for **the book**, I have finished reading it.

> *Wǒmen míngtiān qù kàn yí ge diànyǐng.*
> 我们明天去看一个电影。
> We will see **a movie** tomorrow.

> *Nèige diànyǐng wǒmen míngtiān kàn.*
> 那个电影我们明天看。
> As for **that movie**, we will see it tomorrow.

> *Diànyǐng wǒmen míngtiān kàn.*
> 电影我们明天看。
> As for **the movie**, we will see it tomorrow.

把 *bǎ* means "handle", and it can be used as a preposition to lead the recipient (i.e., the object), which is known to both the speaker and the listener, of an action. It is placed before the verb denoting this action and a complement (excluding the potential complement) or an element that is related to the verb is placed after the verb. Thus, the combination of the verb and the complement or the element related to the verb provides information on how the recipient was, has been, is, or will be handled. Because a verb without anything to follow does not indicate how the recipient, which is definite in reference, was, has been, is, or will be handled, it is ungrammatical to have a simple verb in a 把-sentence. Because what 把 *bǎ* leads is a recipient (i.e., the object) that is definite in reference, it is also ungrammatical to place an indefinite object after the preposition 把 *bǎ*. For example,

> *Wǒ bǎ zhèi běn shū kànwán le.*
> 我把这本书看完了。
> I have finished reading this book.

> **Wǒ bǎ zhèi běn shū kàn.*
> *我把这本书看。(Ungrammatical: bare verb)

> **Wǒ bǎ yì běn shū kànwán le.*
> *我把一本书看完了。(Ungrammatical: indefinite object)

The demonstrative pronouns 这 *zhèi* (this) and 那 *nèi* (that) are often used before a noun to indicate the definiteness of this noun. However, in the 把-sentence, a noun headed by 把 *bǎ* is still definite in reference without having the demonstrative pronoun 这 *zhèi* or 那 *nèi*. For example,

> *Wǒ xiǎng kàn shū.*
> 我想看书。(Indefinite in reference)
> I want to read **a book**.

> *Wǒ xiǎng bǎ shū kànwán.*
> 我想把书看完。(Definite in reference)
> I want to finish reading **the book**.

> *Kāi dēng.*
> 开灯。(Indefinite in reference)
> Turn on a **light**.

> *Bǎ dēng kāikai.*
> 把灯开开。(Definite in reference)
> Turn on **the light**.

> *Hē shuǐ.*
> 喝水。(Indefinite in reference)
> Drink **water**.

> *Bǎ shuǐ hē le.*
> 把水喝了。(Definite in reference)
> Drink **the water**.

In daily life, native Chinese speakers tend to use the 把-sentence, rather than a plain who-does-what sentence without 把 *bǎ*, whenever they want to report how something or somebody known both to the speaker and the listener was, has been, is, or will be handled. For example, both of the following sentences are good, but the second one is preferred and more commonly used if what happened to 这本书 *zhèi běn shū* is the focus of a conversation.

> *Wǒ kànwánle zhèi běn shū.*
> 我看完了这本书。
> I have finished reading this book.

> *Wǒ bǎ zhèi běn shū kànwán le.*
> 我把这本书看完了。
> I have finished reading this book.

四　实践　Practice

1. 对话 Conversation

A: 小明，我去开会，晚上九点回来。

B: 好。爸爸回来，我跟他说。

A: 吃完晚饭以后，别忘了做中文作业。

B: 忘不了。

A: 那你把该做的事说一遍

B: 吃完晚饭以后，做中文作业。

A: 做什么中文作业？

B: 把课文念一遍，把汉字写好，把生词记住。

A: 好。我走了，你把门关好。

B: 好，再见。

A: 还有，你爸回来，让他先把饭吃了，再把药吃了。

B: 行。

2. 交际 Communication

Task 1 Your Chinese friend calls to tell you that he/she bought a new movie on a DVD and invites to go to his/her dorm room to watch it together. Ask your friend to wait until you finish doing your homework.

Task 2 You bought some cough medicine from a local drug store near your Chinese university. When a classmate of yours asks whether the medicine you bought is effective, say that you will tell him/her after you finish all the medicine.

Task 3 When a new international student asks you about your experience of learning the Chinese language effectively, say that you first memorize the new vocabulary, listen to the text several times, and then finish doing the homework.

3. 书写 Writing

bǎ   handle   *Héng, shùgōu, tí; héngzhé, shù, héng, shùwāngōu.*

把								

xiē   some   *Shù, héng, shù, tí, piě, shùwāngōu; héng, héng.*

些								

piān [measure word for writings] *Piě, héng, diǎn, piě, héng, diǎn; diǎn, héngzhé, héng, piě, shù, héngzhégōu, héng, shù, shù.*

篇

niàn read loudly; think of *Piě, nà, diǎn, héngpiě; diǎn, wògōu, diǎn, diǎn.*

念

liàn practice *Piězhé, piězhé, tí; héng, piězhé, héngzhégōu, diǎn, diǎn.*

练

dēng light *Diǎn, piě, piě, diǎn; héng, shùgōu.*

灯

mén door *Diǎn, shù, héngzhégōu.*

门

guān close *Diǎn, piě, héng, héng, piě, nà.*

关

yào medicine *Héng, shù, shù; piězhé, piězhé, tí, piě, héngzhégōu, diǎn.*

药

第五十二课   你把什么忘在家里了？
Lesson 52   What have you forgotten at home?

一 听与看 Listen and Read

Listen to the recording of the following sentences as many times as possible until you can say it along with the recording. You should also look at the following transcription while listening and try to imitate.

Nǐ bǎ shénme fàngzài zhuō shàng le?
你把什么 放在 桌 上 了？
you | handle | what | [suffix] | place | at | table | up | [aux.]
What have you placed on the table?

Wǒ bǎ cídiǎn fàngzài zhuō shàng le.
我把词典放在 桌 上 了。
I | handle | word | classic | place | at | table | up | [aux.]
I have placed the dictionary on the table.

Nǐ bǎ shénme guàzài qiáng shàng le?
你把什么 挂在 墙 上 了？
you | handle | what | [suffix] | hang | at | wall | up | [aux.]
What have you hung up on the wall?

Wǒ bǎ zhàopiàn guàzài qiáng shàng le.
我把 照片 挂在 墙 上 了。
I | handle | shine | piece | hang | at | wall | up | [aux.]
I have hung up the photo on the wall.

Nǐ bǎ shénme fānchéng Yīngwén le?
你把什么 翻成 英文了？
you | handle | what | [suffix] | turn | become | English | language | [aux.]
What have you translated into English?

Wǒ bǎ zhèigè jùzǐ fānchéng Yīngwén le.
我把这个句子 翻成 英文了。
I | handle | this | [meas.] | sentence | [suffix] | turn | become | English | language | [aux.]
I have translated this sentence into English.

Nǐ bǎ shénme xiěchéng xiǎoshuō le?

你把什么 写成 小说了？

you | handle | what | [suffix] | write | **become** | small | speak | [aux.]

What have you written into a novel?

Wǒ bǎ zhèige gùshi xiěchéng xiǎoshuō le.

我把这个故事 写成 小说了。

I | handle | this | [meas.] | former | matter | write | **become** | small | speak | [aux.]

I have written this story into a novel.

Nǐ bǎ shénme jiāogěi lǎoshī le?

你把什么交给老师了？

you | handle | what | [suffix] | **submit** | to | old | mater | [aux.]

What have you submitted to the teacher?

Wǒ bǎ zuòyè jiāogěi lǎoshī le.

我把作业交给老师了。

I | handle | labor | doings | **submit** | to | old | mater | [aux.]

I have submitted the homework to the teacher.

Nǐ bǎ shénme huángěi péngyou le?

你把什么还给 朋友了？

you | handle | what | [suffix] | return | to | pal | friend | [aux.]

What have you returned to the friend?

Wǒ bǎ zázhì huángěi péngyou le.

我把杂志还给 朋友了。

I | handle | **miscellaneous** | **aspiration** | return | to | pal | friend | [aux.]

I have returned the magazine to the friend.

Nǐ bǎ shéi sòng dào yīyuàn le?

你把谁 送到医院了？

you | handle | who | deliver | arrive | medical | **yard** | [aux.]

Whom have you sent to the hospital?

Wǒ bǎ zhèige bìngrén sòngdào yīyuàn le.

我把这个病人送到 医院了。

I | handle | this | [meas.] | **sick** | person | deliver | arrive | medical | **yard** | [aux.]

I have sent this patient to the hospital.

Nǐ bǎ shéi jiēdào fàndiàn le?

你把谁接到饭店了？

you | handle | who | receive | arrive | meal | store | [aux.]

Whom have you picked up and sent to the hotel?

Wǒ bǎ zhèige kèren jiēdào fàndiàn le.

我把这个客人接到饭店了。

I | handle | this | [meas.] | guest | person | receive | arrive | meal | store | [aux.]

I have picked up this guest and sent him to the hotel.

Nǐ bǎ shénme làzài chē lǐ le?

你把什么落在车里了？

you | handle | what | [suffix] | miss | at | vehicle | inside | [aux.]

What have you left behind in the car?

Wǒ bǎ shūbāo làzài chē lǐ le.

我把书包落在车里了。

I | handle | book | bag | miss | at | vehicle | inside | [aux.]

I have left the schoolbag in the car.

Nǐ bǎ shénme wàngzài jiā lǐ le?

你把什么忘在家里了？

you | handle | what | [suffix] | forget | at | home | inside | [aux.]

What have you forgotten at home?

Wǒ bǎ yàoshi wàngzài jiā lǐ le.

我把钥匙忘在家里了。

I | handle | door-bar | key | forget | at | home | inside | [aux.]

I have forgotten the key at home.

二　看与说　Read and Speak

Now, listen to the recording while looking at the following sentences. Then read it out aloud. Finally, recite it by heart to yourself and then to your classmates or instructor.

你把什么放在桌上了？

我把词典放在桌上了。

你把什么挂在墙上了？

我把照片挂在墙上了。

你把什么翻成英文了？

我把这个句子翻成英文了。

你把什么写成小说了？

我把这个故事写成小说了。

你把什么交给老师了？

我把作业交给老师了。

你把什么还给朋友了？

我把杂志还给朋友了。

你把谁送到医院了？

我把这个病人送到医院了。

你把谁接到饭店了？

我把这个客人接到饭店了。

你把什么落在车里了？

我把书包落在车里了。

你把什么忘在家里了？

我把钥匙忘在家里了。

三　理解　Understand

In this lesson, all sentences have used 把 *bǎ* because they have all met the two major conditions for using the 把 *bǎ* sentence: first, the recipient is definite; second, the action has a complement expression after it. In fact, the use of 把 *bǎ* in these sentences is compulsory.

1) In Chinese, to indicate placement or relocation of something or somebody as a result of an action, we place a locative complement, which is formed with 在 *zài* (to be at) or 到 *dào* (to get to) plus a place word, right after the action. To express this concept, the 把-sentence is always used. For example,

Wǒ bǎ cídiǎn fàngzài zhuō shàng le.
我把词典放在桌上了。
I have put the book on the table.

Wǒ bǎ bìngrén sòngdào yīyuàn le.
我把病人送到医院了。
I have sent the patient to the hospital.

2) To describe transformation of something or somebody into something or somebody else as a result of an action, we use the 把-sentence with the word 成 *chéng* (to become) to lead the complement. For example,

Wǒ bǎ jùzi fānchéng Yīngwén le.
我把句子翻成英文了。
I have translated the sentence into English.

Tā bǎ gùshi xiěchéng xiǎoshuō le.
他把故事写成小说了。
He has written the story into a novel.

3) To express the concept of taking, bringing, presenting, submitting or returning something definite in reference to somebody, we use the 把-sentence with one of these actions to be followed by a complement that is headed with 给 *gěi* (to give). For example,

> *Wǒ bǎ huār sònggěi lǎoshī le.*
> 我把花儿送给老师了。
> I have **presented** the flowers to the teacher.

> *Tā bǎ qián huángěi tā péngyou le.*
> 他把钱还给他朋友了。
> He has **returned** the money to his friend.

To negate a 把-sentence, we put a negation word before 把 *bǎ*. For example,

> *Wǒ méi bǎ shūbāo làzài chē lǐ.*
> 我没把书包落在车里。
> I have not left the school bag in the car.

> *Bié bǎ yàoshi wàngzài jiā lǐ.*
> 别把钥匙忘在家里。
> Don't forget the key at home.

四 实践 Practice

1. 对话 Conversation

A: 我的词典呢?

B: 我把你的词典放在桌上了。

A: 词典里的照片呢?

B: 我把照片都挂在墙上了。

A: 我去看看。

B: 别看了。我们应该开始做作业了。

A: 今天的作业是什么?

B: 这个你都忘了!

A: 老师说做什么作业, 我没太听懂。

B: 把这些句子翻译成英文。

A: 这个不难。明天我第一个把作业交给老师。

B: 你先把作业做完了再说吧。

A: 我的书包呢?

B: 你是不是把书包落在教室里了?

2. 交际 Communication

Task 1 When you meet your Chinese host family for a holiday gathering, they tell you about an exciting new book on China. Tell your host family that you hope someone will translate this book into English so that more American people will be able to read it.

Task 2 Tell your instructor that you left your homework at your dorm room. Apologize and say that you will go back to your dorm to get it when the class is over and then hand it in to your instructor.

Task 3 During your trip to Tibet, you took a lot of beautiful photos. Your roommate borrowed your photo album for a look. Now he/she has just returned it to you, but you have found that the photo with your classmate and you in it is missing. Ask him/her where he/she has placed this photo.

3. 书写 Writing

piàn   piece   *Piě, shù, héng, héngzhé.*

片

jiāo   submit   *Diǎn, héng, piě, diǎn, piě, nà.*

交

zá   miscellaneous   *Piě, héngzhéwāngōu; héng, shùgōu, diǎn, diǎn.*

杂

zhì   aspiration; will   *Héng, shù, héng; diǎn, wògōu, diǎn, diǎn.*

志

fān   turn over   *Piě, diǎn, piě, héng, shù, piě, diǎn, shù, héngzhé, héng, shù, héng; héngzhégōu, diǎn, tí, héngzhégōu, diǎn, tí.*

翻

chéng   become   *Héng, piě, héngzhégōu, xiégōu, piě, diǎn.*

成

jù   sentence   *Piě, héngzhégōu, shù, héngzhé, héng.*

句

yuàn   yard   *Héngpiěwāngōu, shù; diǎn, diǎn, hénggōu, héng, héng, piě, shùwāngōu.*

院

bìng   sick   *Diǎn, héng, piě, diǎn, tí; héng, shù, héngzhégōu, piě, diǎn.*

病

jiē   receive; connect   *Héng, shùgōu, tí; diǎn, héng, diǎn, piě, héng, piědiǎn, piě, héng.*

接

là; luò   miss; drop   *Héng, shù, shù; diǎn, diǎn, tí; piě, héngpiě, nà, shù, héngzhé, héng.*

落

bāo   bag   *Piě, héngzhégōu, héngzhé, héng, shùwāngōu.*

包

yào   door-bar   *Piě, héng, héng, héng, shùtí; piě, héngzhégōu, héng, héng.*

钥

shi; chí   key; spoon   *Shù, héngzhé, héng, héng, héng, shù, héng, piě, nà; piě, shùwāngōu.*

匙

Dì-wǔshísān   kè   Fángjiān shōushi hǎo le ma?
第五十三课   房间收拾好了吗？
Lesson 53   Has the room been tidied up?

一 听与看 Listen and Read

Listen to the recording of the following sentences as many times as possible until you can say it along with the recording. You should also look at the following transcription while listening and try to imitate.

Fángjiān,   fángjiān,
房间， 房间，
house | space | house | space
The room, the room,

shōushi hǎo le ma?
收拾 好了吗？
accept | pick | good | [aux.] | [ques.]
has it been **tidied up**?

Shōushi hǎo le.
收拾 好了。
accept | pick | good | [aux.]
Yes, it has been **tidied up**.

Zhuōzi,   zhuōzi,
桌子， 桌子，
table | [suffix] | table | [suffix]
The table, the table,

bǎihǎo le ma?
摆好了吗？
arrange | good | [aux.] | [ques.]
has it been arranged?

Bǎihǎo le.
摆好了。
arrange | good | [aux.]
Yes, it has been arranged.

Lǐwù,　　lǐwù,
礼物，礼物，
ritual | matter | ritual | matter
The present, the present,

mǎilái le ma?
买来了吗？
buy | come | [aux.] | [ques.]
has it been bought back?

Mǎilái le.
买来了。
buy | come | [aux.]
Yes, it has been bought back.

Fàncài,　fàncài,
饭菜，饭菜，
meal | vegetable | meal | vegetable
The meal, the meal,

zuòhǎo le ma?
做好了吗？
do | good | [aux.] | [ques.]
has it been cooked?

Zuòhǎo le.
做好了。
do | good | [aux.]
Yes, it has been cooked.

Péngyou, péngyou,
朋友，朋友，
pal | friend | pal | friend
The friends, the friends,

qǐngdào le ma?
请到了吗？
invite | arrive | [aux.] | [ques.]
have they been invited with success?

Méi qǐngdào.

没 请 到。

not | invite | arrive

No, without success.

Yōu,   zěnme méi qǐngdào wa?

哟，怎么没 请 到 哇？

oh | how | [suffix] | not | invite | arrive | [interjection]

Oh, how come they have been invited without success?

二 看与说   Read and Speak

Now, listen to the recording while looking at the following sentences. Then read it out aloud. Finally, recite it by heart to yourself and then to your classmates or instructor.

房间，房间，

收拾好了吗？

收拾好了。

桌子，桌子，

摆好了吗？

摆好了。

礼物，礼物，

买来了吗？

买来了。

饭菜，饭菜，

做好了吗?

做好了。

朋友，朋友，

请到了吗?

没请到。

哟，怎么没请到哇?

三 理解 Understand

If we are not interested in the doer of the action in a 把-sentence, we can omit the doer of the action and the preposition 把 *bǎ*. The sentence is still grammatically correct. For example,

Nǐ bǎ fángjiān shōushihǎo le ma? 你把房间收拾好了吗? Have you tidied up the room?	*Fángjiān shōushihǎo le ma?* 房间 收拾好了吗? Has the room been tidied up?
Wǒ bǎ fángjiān shōushihǎo le. 我把房间收拾好了。 I have tidied up the room.	*Fángjiān shōushihǎo le.* 房间 收拾好了。 The room has been tidied up.
Nǐ bǎ lǐwù mǎilái le ma? 你把礼物买来了吗? Have you bought back the present?	*Lǐwù mǎilái le ma?* 礼物买来了吗? Has the present been bought back?
Wǒ bǎ lǐwù mǎilái le. 我把礼物买来了。 I have bought back the present.	*Lǐwù mǎilái le.* 礼物买来了。 The present has been bought back.

These sentences on the right side are notionally passive. We know that "the room" cannot tidy up and can only be tidied up and that "the present" cannot purchase but be purchased, so in Chinese. Therefore, in these sentences even though the recipients are placed before the actions, there can be no misunderstanding.

好 *hǎo* can be used to indicate a result of an action, but it conveys two meanings: 1) adequate result, 2) completion of an action with satisfaction. For example,

> *Tā yào bǎ Hànyǔ xuéhǎo.*
> 他要把汉语学好。(adequate result)
> He wants to study Chinese well.

> *Qǐng zuòhǎo,   fēijī   jiù yào qǐfēi   le.*
> 请坐好，飞机就要起飞了。(adequate result)
> Please sit properly, and the airplane will soon take off.

> *Tā bǎ fàn zuòhǎo le.*
> 他把饭做好了。(completion of cooking with satisfaction)
> He finished cooking the meal well.

> *Fēi jī xiūhǎo le.*
> 飞机修好了。(completion of repairing with satisfaction)
> The airplane is repaired.

完 *wán* can also be used to indicate a completive result, but it only refers to the completion of a job without considering the quality of the performance; whereas 好 *hǎo* encompasses both the completion of a job and the quality of the performance. For example,

> *Wǒ bǎ zuòyè zuòwán le.*
> 我把作业做完了。
> I have finished doing the homework.

> *Zuòyè zuòwán le.*
> 作业做完了。
> The homework is finished.

> *Wǒ bǎ zuòyè zuòhǎo le.*
> 我把作业做好了。
> I have finished doing the homework well.

> *Zuòyè zuòhǎo le.*
> 作业做好了。
> The homework is finished well.

哟 *yōu* is an interjection uttered when in a slight surprise. 哇 *wa* is the way the auxiliary word 啊 *a*, which is used at the end of a sentence to soften the tone, is pronounced and written when preceded by a syllable that is ended in such vowel sounds as *u*, *ou*, and *ao*. For example,

> *Nǐ zěnme méi zhǎodào shū (a→) wa.*
> 你怎么没找到书(啊→)哇。
> You did not find the book.

> *Zhèi shì yí ge hěn dà de lóu (a→) wa*
> 这是一个很大的楼(啊→)哇。
> This is a huge building.

> *Wǒmen qù shūdiàn,   hǎo ma?*
> A: 我们去书店，好吗？
>   We'll go to a store, OK?

> *Hǎo (a→) wa.*
> B: 好(啊→)哇。
>   OK.

四 实践 Practice

1. 对话 Conversation

A: 时间快到了。

B: 好。没问题。

A: 房间收拾好了吗？

B: 已经收拾好了。

A: 桌子摆了吗？

B: 也已经摆好了。

A: 给老师的礼物呢？

B: 早就买来了。你看。

A: 很好。

B: 就等你的饭菜了。

A: 饭菜很快就做好了。

B: 电话！我去接。

A: 是谁啊？

B: 李贵。他说老师去外地开会了，没请到。

A: 啊？！

2. 交际 *Communication*

Task 1 You share an apartment with a Chinese student and the two of you decide to take turns to cook. Today is your turn to cook. Tell your friend that the dinner will be done in about five minutes and ask him/her whether the dinner table is set already.

Task 2 You went shopping earlier in the day. When you are back, your roommate asks whether you bought the umbrella for him/her. Say that the kind that your roommate wanted is sold out, but you found a better one and bought it for him/her.

Task 3 At end of the semester, you and your classmates plan to take all your language instructors to a fancy restaurant for a dinner in order to show your appreciation for their hard work. Since you are the coordinator for this event, report to your classmates that three instructors have accepted the invitation, but one can not be found because this instructor has been out of town to attend a meeting.

3. 书写 Writing

shōu   accept; receive   *Shùtí, shù; piě, héng, piě, nà.*

收

shí   pick   *Héng, shùgōu, tí; piě, nà, héng, shù, héngzhé, héng.*

拾

bǎi   arrange   *Héng, shùgōu, tí; shù, héngzhé, shù, shù, héng, héng, shù, héng, piězhé, diǎn.*

摆

lǐ   ritual; ceremony   *Diǎn, héngpiě, shù, diǎn; shùwāngōu.*

礼

wù   matter   *Piě, héng, shù, tí; piě, héngzhégōu, piě, piě.*

物

yōu   oh   *Shù, héngzhé, héng; piězhé, piězhé, tí, piě, héngzhégōu, diǎn.*

哟

wa   wow   *Shù, héngzhé, héng; héng, shù, héng, héng, shù, héng.*

哇

第五十四课   让 谁 借 走 了？
Lesson 54   **Who has borrowed it?**

一 听与看 Listen and Read

Listen to the recording of the following sentences as many times as possible until you can say it along with the recording. You should also look at the following transcription while listening and try to imitate.

Wǒ de Hànyǔshū ne?
我的汉语书呢？
I | [aux.] | Han ethinc group | language | book | [ques.]
Where is my Chinese book?

Ràng shéi jièzǒu le?
让 谁 借走了？
let | who | borrow | walk | [aux.]
Who has borrowed it? (Whom has it been borrowed by?)

Wǒ de zhàoxiàngjī ne?
我的 照相机 呢？
I | [aux.] | shine | appearance | machine | [ques.]
Where is my camera?

Ràng shéi názǒu le?
让 谁 拿走了？
let | who | hold | walk | [aux.]
Who has taken it away? (Whom has it been taken away by?)

Wǒ de zìxíngchē ne?
我的 自行车 呢？
I | [aux.] | self | go | vehicle | [ques.]
Where is my bike?

Jiào shéi qízǒu le?
叫 谁 骑走了？
call | who | ride | walk | [aux.]
Who has ridden it away? (Whom has it been ridden away by?)

Wǒ de Lóngjǐngchá ne?

我的 龙井茶 呢?

I | [aux.] | **dragon** | **well** | tea | [ques.]

Where is my Longjing tea?

Jiào shéi hēwán le?

叫 谁 喝完了?

call | who | drink | finish | [aux.]

Who has drunk it up? (Whom has it been drunk up by?)

Wǒ de hǎo péngyou ne?

我的好 朋友 呢?

I | [aux.] | good | pal | friend | [ques.]

Where is my good friend?

Bèi shéi jiàozǒu le?

被 谁 叫走了?

by | who | call | walk | [aux.]

Who has called him/her away? (Whom has he/she been called away by?)

Wǒ de nǚpéngyou ne?

我的 女朋友 呢?

I | [aux.] | **female** | pal | friend | [ques.]

Where is my girl-friend?

Bèi shéi dàizǒu le?

被 谁 带走了?

by | who | carry | walk | [aux.]

Who has taken her away? (Whom has she been taken away by?)

Ài, wǒ zhēn hútu!

唉，我真 糊涂!

alas | I | really | **paste** | smear

Alas, how foolish of me!

二 看与说 Read and Speak

Now, listen to the recording while looking at the following sentences. Then read it out aloud. Finally, recite it by heart to yourself and then to your classmates or instructor.

我的汉语书呢?

让谁借走了?

我的照相机呢?

让谁拿走了?

我的自行车呢?

叫谁骑走了?

我的龙井茶呢?

叫谁喝完了?

我的好朋友呢?

被谁叫走了?

我的女朋友呢?

被谁带走了?

唉,我真糊涂!

三 理解 Understand

In English, a sentence in the passive voice starts with the recipient of an action and the verb "be" is used to indicate the passive voice of the sentence: The homework is done. We know from the previous lesson that in Chinese, the passive voice can be expressed notionally without using any special word to mark the passiveness: 作业做完了 *zuòyè zuòwán le*. However, if a notional passive sentence may cause misunderstanding, then the word 被 *bèi* is placed after somebody or something and before the action to indicate that somebody or something before 被 *bèi* is the recipient of the action. For example,

> *Tā bèi dǎ le.*
> 他被打了。
> He was hit.

If the doer of the action should be mentioned in the sentence, then 被 *bèi*, 让 *ràng*, or 叫 *jiào* can be used to lead the doer. For example,

> *Tā de zhàoxiàngjī bèi (ràng/jiào) tā bàba názǒu le.*
> 他的照相机被(让／叫)他爸爸拿走了。
> His camera has been taken away by his father.

In comparison with 被 *bèi*, 让 *ràng* and 叫 *jiào* are often used in daily life informally. Another important difference between 被 *bèi* and 让 *ràng* as well as 叫 *jiào* is that 被 *bèi* can be used alone without having the doer after it, whereas 让 *ràng* and 叫 *jiào* must have the doer to follow in order to be grammatically correct. Therefore, even though it is correct to say 他被打了 *tā bèi dǎ le*, it is wrong to simply replace 被 *bèi* with 让 *ràng* or 叫 *jiào*. To make it correct, the doer has to be added: 他让人打了 *tā ràng rén dǎ le* or 他叫人打了 *tā jiào rén dǎ le* (He was hit by someone)。

四 实践 Practice

🗣 1. 对话 Conversation

A: 你昨天去哪儿了？

B: 跟同学出去玩儿了。

A: 你的东西怎么都不见了？

B: 自行车让张三骑走了。

A: 照相机呢？

B: 让李四拿去用了。

A: 书包里的书哪儿去了？

B: 我的书叫一个新同学借走了。

A: 龙井茶呢？那么一大盒，都喝完了？

B: 您那个茶太好了，一下子就被大家喝完了。

A: 你女朋友不是要来吗？她去哪儿了？

B: 她被王五带去买东西了。

A: 你这个人，怎么这么糊涂！

B: 妈，我可不糊涂。同学们说我是最可爱的人。

2. 交际 Communication

Task 1 You bought a good movie on a DVD. When a classmate asks to borrow it, tell him/her that your new DVD was borrowed by your Chinese speaking partner yesterday.

Task 2 You are at a party with a group of young people. When you come back to the table where you placed your half-empty beer bottle, you found that your beer is gone. Ask in a half-joking tone: "Where is my beer? Whom has my beer been drunk by?"

Task 3 You love getting around in Beijing with your bike. When someone notices that you take a bus today to go to the Beijing National Library, he/she is curious about your reason for not riding your bike there. Explain that your bike was taken by your roommate.

3. 书写 Writing

jiè　borrow　*Piě, shù; héng, shù, shù, héng, shù, héngzhé, héng, héng.*

借									

lóng　dragon　*Héng, piě, shùwāngōu, piě, diǎn.*

龙									

jǐng　well　*Héng, héng, piě, shù.*

井									

bèi　by　*Diǎn, héngpiě, shù, piě, diǎn; hénggōu, piě, shù, héngpiě, nà.*

被									

nǚ　female; woman　*Piědiǎn, piě, héng.*

女									

ài　alas　*Shù, héngzhé, héng; piězhé, diǎn, piě, héng, héng, piě, nà.*

唉									

hú　paste　*Diǎn, piě, héng, shù, piě, diǎn; héng, shù, shù, héngzhé, héng; piě, héngzhégōu, héng, héng.*

糊									

tú　smear　*Diǎn, diǎn, tí; piě, nà, héng, héng, shùgōu, diǎn, diǎn.*

涂									

第五十五课

Lesson 55

Tā shénme dōu chī.

他什么都吃。

He eats anything.

一 听与看 Listen and Read

Listen to the recording of the following sentences as many times as possible until you can say it along with the recording. You should also look at the following transcription while listening and try to imitate.

Tā ài chī,   tā ài chī,

他爱吃，他爱吃，

he | love | eat | he | love | eat

He loves to eat, he loves to eat,

tā shénme dōu chī.

他什么都吃。

he | what | [suffix] | all | eat

he eats anything.

Tā ài lǚyóu,   tā ài lǚyóu,

他爱旅游，他爱旅游，

he | love | travel | wander | he | love | travel | wander

He loves to travel, he loves to travel,

tā   nǎr   dōu xiǎng qù.

他哪儿都 想 去。

he | which | [suffix] | all | want | go

he would like to go anywhere.

Tā ài hē chá,   tā ài hē chá,

他爱喝茶，他爱喝茶，

he | love | drink | tea | he | love | drink | tea

He loves to drink tea, he loves to drink tea,

tā něi zhǒng chá dōu hē.

他哪 **种** 茶都喝。

he | which | **kind** | tea | all | drink

he drinks all kinds of tea.

Tā ài liáotiānr,　tā ài liáotiānr,
他爱聊天儿，他爱聊天儿，
he | love | **chat** | sky [suffix] | he | love | **chat** | sky | [suffix]
He loves to chat, he loves to chat,

tā shéi dōu rènshi.
他谁都认识。
he | who | all | recognize | know
he knows everyone.

二　看与说　Read and Speak

Now, listen to the recording while looking at the following sentences. Then read it out aloud. Finally, recite it by heart to yourself and then to your classmates or instructor.

他爱吃，他爱吃，

他什么都吃。

他爱旅游，他爱旅游，

他哪儿都想去。

他爱喝茶，他爱喝茶，

他哪种茶都喝。

他爱聊天儿，他爱聊天儿，

他谁都认识。

三　理解　Understand

In English, the question words, such as who, what, which, when, and where, are used to form questions, but they can form indefinite expressions with "ever". In Chinese, the question words, such as 什么 *shénme* (what), 谁 *shuí/shéi* (who), 哪 *něi* (which), and 哪儿 *nǎr* (where), are used to form questions requesting information. To answer these questions, we can provide very specific information that is requested. However, we can also provide an all-inclusive answer to these questions by adding the adverb 都 *dōu* (all) after the question words. For example,

Question	Specific answer	All-inclusive answer
Shénme hǎochī? 什么 好吃？ What is delicious?	*Jiǎozi hǎochī.* 饺子 好吃。 Dumplings are delicious.	*Shénme dōu hǎochī.* 什么 都 好吃。 Everything is delicious.
Nǎr yǒu shū? 哪儿 有 书？ Which place has books?	*Shūdiàn yǒu shū.* 书店 有 书。 Bookstores have books.	*Nǎr dōu yǒu shū.* 哪儿 都 有 书。 Any place has books.
Něi běn shū bú shì nǐ de? 哪 本 书 不 是 你 的？ Which book is not yours?	*Zhèi běn shū bú shì wǒ de.* 这 本 书 不 是 我 的。 This book is not mine.	*Něi běn shū dōu bú shì wǒ de.* 哪 本 书 都 不 是 我 的。 None of the books is mine.
Shéi shì nǐ de lǎoshī? 谁 是 你 的 老师？ Who is your teacher?	*Tā shì wǒ de lǎoshī.* 她 是 我 的 老师。 She is my teacher.	*Shéi dōu shì wǒ de lǎoshī.* 谁 都 是 我 的 老师。 Everyone is my teacher.

All-inclusive answers formed by question words and 都 *dōu* can also be provided to questions about a recipient of an action. However, the all-inclusive term is placed before the action, rather than after the action. For example,

Question	Specific answer	All-inclusive answer
Nǐ chī shénme? 你吃什么？ What do you eat?	*Wǒ chī jiǎozi.* 我吃饺子。 I eat dumplings.	*Wǒ shénme dōu chī.* 我什么都吃。 Everything is delicious.
Nǐ yào qù nǎr? 你要去哪儿？ Where do you want to go?	*Wǒ yào qù Zhōngguó.* 我要去中国。 I want to go to China.	*Wǒ nǎr dōu yào qù.* 我哪儿都要去。 I want to go everywhere.
Nǐ kàn něi běn shū? 你看哪本书？ Which book will you read?	*Wǒ kàn zhèi běn shū.* 我看这本书。 I will read this book.	*Wǒ něi běn shū dōu kàn.* 我哪本书都看。 I will read any book.
Nǐ rènshi shéi? 你认识谁？ Whom do you know?	*Wǒ rènshi tā.* 我认识她。 I know her.	*Wǒ shéi dōu rènshi.* 我谁都认识。 I know everyone.

聊天儿 *liáotiānr* is a colloquial term. 聊 *liáo* means "to chat." 天 *tiān* means "sky", and it does not mean the topic of the chat is the sky. 天 *tiān* is used for the variety of chatting topics. Chatting topics can be anything under the sky. Local people in Beijing love to add the endearment suffix 儿 *ér* to the end of 天 *tiān* to make it something likeable and enjoyable. Therefore, to chit-chat as a pastime is 聊天儿 *liáotiānr*.

四 实践 Practice

1. 对话 Conversation

A: 别忘了明天到我家吃饭。

B: 是六点半吧？

A: 对。你有什么不吃的东西吗？

B: 没有。我什么都吃。

······

A: 请进！

B: 这是给你们的花儿。

A: 你太客气了。

B: 哪里，哪里。

A: 喝点儿茶吧。

B: 好。

A: 你爱喝花茶还是爱喝绿茶？

B: 哪个都好。

A: 我跟你打听 *dǎting* (ask about) 一个人。

B: 你说吧。我这个人爱聊天，咱们这儿的人，我谁都认识。

2. 交际 Communication

Task 1 You and your Chinese friend plan to see a movie on Saturday. When your friend asks what time's movie you would prefer to see, say that you have no other plan on Saturday and that you can see any time's movie.

Task 2 You are at a Chinese restaurant. When you and your Chinese friend try to decide what to order on the menu, say that you are not familiar with this restaurant and since you love to eat all kinds of Chinese dishes ask your friend to order.

Task 3 You are at the lobby of an international student dormitory building. When someone asks you about an American student, say that you just got here yesterday and do not know anybody yet.

3. 书写 Writing

zhǒng   kind of   *Piě, héng, shù, piě, diǎn; shù, héngzhé, héng, shù.*

种								

liáo   chat   *Héng, shù, shù, héng, héng, tí; piě, shùtí, piě, héngzhégōu, shù.*

聊								

Dì-wǔshíliù   kè   *Wǒmen huì shuō Hànyǔ   le!*

第五十六课   我们会说汉语了！

Lesson 56   We know how to speak Chinese now!

一 听与看 Listen and Read

Listen to the recording of the following sentences as many times as possible until you can say it along with the recording. You should also look at the following transcription while listening and try to imitate.

Yuǎnfāng kāilai yí liàng chē,

远方 开来一 辆 车，

far | side | drive | come | one | [meas.] | vehicle

There comes a car from afar,

chē lǐ   xiàlai yí ge rén,

车里下来一个人，

vehicle | inside | down | come | one | [meas.] | person

from inside of the car a person comes out,

shǒu lǐ   jǔzhe   yí miàn qí,

手里举着一面 旗，

hand | inside | raise | [aux.] | one | [meas.] | flag

raised in his hand is a flag,

qí shàng xiězhe qī gè zì:

旗上 写着七个字：

flag | up | write | [aux.] | seven | [meas.] | character

written on the flag are seven characters:

wǒmen huì shuō Hànyǔ le!

我们会说 汉语了！

I | [plural] | know how | speak | Han ethnic group | language | [aux.]

we know how to speak Chinese now!

二 看与说 Read and Speak

Now, listen to the recording while looking at the following sentences. Then read it out aloud. Finally, recite it by heart to yourself and then to your classmates or instructor.

远方开来一辆车，

车里下来一个人，

手里举着一面旗，

旗上写着七个字：

我们会说汉语了！

三 理解 Understand

In Lesson 39, we have learned that using the auxiliary word 着 *zhe* after an action is more descriptive in telling other people how something or somebody is situated at a particular place or location. For example,

> *Zhuō shàng fàngzhe yì běn shū.*
> 桌 上 放着一本书。
> There is a book placed on the table.

> *Qiáng shàng guàzhe yí ge zhōng.*
> 墙 上 挂着一个钟。
> There is a clock hung on the wall.

We can also use the same sentence structure but with the resultative complement or the directional complement and/or the completive marker 了 after an action to describe appearance or disappearance of something or somebody at a particular place or location. For example,

> *Túshūguǎn lǐ zǒu chulai yí ge xuésheng.*
> 图书馆里走出来一个学生。
> A student walked out of the library.

As a sentence of this type reports vividly what exists, appears, or disappears at a place, it is often used in telling a story or what one witnesses. Keep in mind the following three rules when using a sentence of this type to report or describe: 1) start the sentence with a particular place or location, 2) in addition to the action, a resultative complement or directional complement and/or the completive marker 了 le or continuous state marker 着 *zhe* has to be used, 3) end the sentence with something or somebody indefinite in reference. The rhythmic verse of this lesson provides good examples of this type of descriptive sentences. Recite it, understand it, and enjoy it.

四　实践　Practice

1. 对话 Conversation

> A: 快来看！那边开来一辆车。
>
> B: 真的！这辆车不小。
>
> A: 快看，快看！车里下来一个人。
>
> B: 是谁啊？
>
> A: 是个女的。
>
> B: 她手里拿着什么？
>
> A: 是一面旗子。
>
> B: 上边写着什么？我看不清楚 qīngchu (clear)。
>
> A: "到中国去，学说汉语。"

👐 2. 交际 Communication

Task 1 You spotted a textbook in your classroom. Hand it in to your language instructor and say that you don't know whom this textbook belongs to since the book does not bear the owner's name.

Task 2 You have set up a blind date for your friend. Tell you friend that the person he will meet will be sitting at a table on the left side of the restaurant, wearing a white coat, holding a black bag in the left hand, and holding a Chinese dictionary in the right hand.

Task 3 Two of your friends are coming to visit you but are lost on their way to your home after getting off the bus. They are calling you to ask for directions. Tell them to look for a big building, and 中国书店 *Zhōngguó Shūdiàn* are written on its front side. On the right side of this building, a red car is parked there. You will be standing beside the car to pick them up.

✏️ 3. 书写 Writing

yuǎn　far　*Héng, héng, piě, shùwāngōu; diǎn, héngzhézhépiě, píngnà.*

远

fāng　side　*Diǎn, héng, héngzhégōu, piě.*

方

liàng　[measure word for vehicles]　*Héng, piězhé, shù, tí; héng, shù, héngzhégōu, piě, diǎn, piě, diǎn.*

辆

shǒu   hand   *Piě, héng, héng, wāngōu.*

手								

jǔ   hold up   *Diǎn, diǎn, piě, héng, piě, nà, héng, héng, shù.*

举								

qí   flag   *Diǎn, héng, héngzhégōu, piě; piě, héng, héng, shù, shù, héng, héng, héng, héng, piě, diǎn.*

旗								

汉字索引
Character Index

bié	别		甲	Lessons 8, 23, 38
bìng	病		甲	Lesson 52
bù	不		甲	Lessons 3, 4, 5, 8, 11, 12, 13, 14, 16, 22, 23, 30, 31, 38, 42, 48, 49
cāi	猜		乙	Lesson 28
cài	菜		甲	Lessons 7, 53
cè	厕	廁	乙	Lesson 26
chá	茶		甲	Lessons 8, 22, 47, 54, 55
chà	差		甲	Lesson 17
cháng	长	長	甲	Lesson 35
cháng	尝	嘗	乙	Lesson 49
cháng	常		甲	Lessons 11, 14, 41
chǎng	场	場	甲	Lesson 19
chàng	唱		甲	Lessons 29, 40
chāo	超		乙	Lesson 19
chē	车	車	甲	Lessons 5, 19, 31, 39, 48, 49, 52, 54, 56
chéng	成		甲	Lesson 52
chī	吃		甲	Lessons 8, 20, 21, 23, 25, 29, 32, 35, 37, 40, 48, 51, 55
chí	匙		丙	Lesson 52
chí	迟	遲	甲	Lesson 34
chū	出		甲	Lessons 21, 49
chú	厨	廚	乙	Lesson 26
chuán	船		甲	Lesson 50
chuáng	床		甲	Lessons 20, 21, 30
chūn	春		甲	Lesson 38
cí	词	詞	甲	Lessons 13, 45, 48, 49, 51, 52
cì	次		甲	Lesson 37
cóng	从	從	甲	Lessons 49, 50
cuò	错	錯	甲	Lesson 31
dǎ	打		甲	Lessons 14, 19, 41

dà	大		甲	Lessons 23, 27, 29, 42, 43, 48
dài	带	帶	甲	Lessons 47, 49, 54
dàn	蛋		甲	Lesson 49
dǎo	岛	島	乙	Lesson 50
dào	到		甲	Lessons 34, 45, 46, 50, 52, 53
de	的		甲	Lessons 5, 11, 16, 18, 19, 25, 26, 29, 48, 49, 50, 54
de	得		甲	Lessons 30, 31, 41, 43, 48
dēng	灯	燈	甲	Lesson 51
dì	弟		甲	Lesson 4
dì	第		甲	Lessons 1, 2, 3, 4, 5, 6, 7, 8, 9, 10, 11, 12, 13, 14, 15, 16, 17, 18, 19, 20, 21, 22, 23, 24, 25, 26, 27, 28, 29, 30, 31, 32, 33, 34, 35, 36, 37, 38, 39, 40, 41, 42, 43, 44, 45, 46, 47, 48, 49, 50, 51, 52, 53, 54, 55, 56
diǎn	典		甲	Lessons 13, 49, 52
diǎn	点	點	甲	Lessons 17, 18, 20, 22, 38, 45
diàn	店		甲	Lessons 13, 31, 52
diàn	电	電	甲	Lessons 14, 18, 28, 33, 34, 37
dōng	东	東	甲	Lesson 48
dǒng	懂		甲	Lessons 44, 48
dòng	动	動	甲	Lesson 48
dōu	都		甲	Lessons 9, 34, 37, 38, 41, 42, 55
duàn	锻	鍛	甲	Lesson 21
duì	对	對	甲	Lessons 16, 28, 51
duō	多		甲	Lessons 10, 15, 30, 35, 36, 37, 38, 43, 48
è	饿	餓	甲	Lesson 34
ér	儿	兒	甲	Lessons 10, 11, 12, 18, 19, 21, 22, 25, 31, 32, 33, 38, 39, 45, 46, 50, 55
èr	二		甲	Lessons 2, 12, 15, 20, 21, 22, 23, 24, 25, 26, 27, 28, 29, 32, 42, 52
fǎ	法		甲	Lesson 48

fān	翻		甲	Lesson 52
fàn	饭	飯	甲	Lessons 19, 20, 21, 25, 29, 30, 34, 35, 37, 40, 48, 52, 53
fāng	方		甲	Lessons 56
fáng	房		甲	Lessons 26, 27, 39, 53
fàng	放		甲	Lessons 39, 52
fēi	非		甲	Lessons 11, 41
fēi	啡		甲	Lesson 22
fēn	分		甲	Lesson 17
fēng	风	風	甲	Lesson 38
fū	夫		甲	Lesson 23
fú	服		甲	Lessons 16, 45
gāi	该	該	甲	Lesson 31
gǎn	感		甲	Lesson 11
gàn	干	幹	甲	Lesson 28
gāo	糕		乙	Lessons 38, 49
gāo	高		甲	Lessons 41, 42
gē	哥		甲	Lessons 3, 4, 26, 49
gē	歌		甲	Lessons 29, 40
gè	个	個	甲	Lessons 2, 14, 27, 37, 47, 52, 56
gěi	给	給	甲	Lessons 14, 22, 25, 47, 52
gēn	跟		甲	Lessons 42, 50
gōng	工		甲	Lesson 14
gōng	公		甲	Lessons 19, 38, 46
gù	故		甲	Lessons 37, 52
guā	刮	颳	甲	Lesson 38
guà	挂	掛	甲	Lessons 39, 52
guān	关	關	甲	Lessons 16, 51
guǎn	馆	館	甲	Lessons 19, 33
guì	贵	貴	甲	Lessons 9, 38
guó	国	國	甲	Lessons 6, 31, 36, 37

jiàn	件		甲	Lesson 16
jiàn	见	見	甲	Lessons 18, 48
jiǎng	讲	講	甲	Lesson 48
jiāo	交		甲	Lesson 52
jiǎo	饺	餃	甲	Lesson 7
jiào	叫		甲	Lessons 9, 29, 54
jiē	接		甲	Lesson 52
jiě	姐		甲	Lessons 4, 14
jiè	介		甲	Lesson 12
jiè	借	藉	甲	Lesson 54
jīn	今		甲	Lessons 24, 38, 48
jìn	进	進	甲	Lessons 8, 46, 49
jīng	经	經	甲	Lessons 38, 44
jǐng	井		乙	Lesson 54
jiǔ	九		甲	Lessons 9, 19, 29, 39, 49
jiǔ	酒		甲	Lessons 22, 23, 31, 37
jiù	就		甲	Lessons 31, 34
jǔ	举	舉	甲	Lesson 56
jù	句		甲	Lesson 52
jué	觉	覺	甲	Lessons 20, 29, 30, 32, 33
kā	咖		甲	Lesson 22
kāi	开	開	甲	Lessons 31, 34, 38, 49, 51, 56
kàn	看		甲	Lessons 18, 25, 28, 29, 30, 31, 32, 33, 36, 37, 38, 40, 43, 48
kě	可		甲	Lessons 22, 31
kè	课	課	甲	Lessons 1, 2, 3, 4, 5, 6, 7, 8, 9, 10, 11, 12, 13, 14, 15, 16, 17, 18, 19, 20, 21, 22, 23, 24, 25, 26, 27, 28, 29, 30, 31, 32, 33, 34, 35, 36, 37, 38, 39, 40, 41, 42, 43, 44, 45, 46, 47, 48, 49, 50, 51, 52, 53, 54, 55, 56
kò	客		甲	Lessons 8, 26, 52
kè	刻		甲	Lesson 17

kòng	空		甲	Lesson 18
kuài	块	塊	甲	Lesson 15
kuài	快		甲	Lessons 24, 34, 42
lái	来	來	甲	Lessons 12, 22, 47, 49, 53, 56
lán	蓝	藍	甲	Lesson 16
lán	篮	籃	甲	Lesson 41
lǎo	老		甲	Lessons 6, 48, 52
le	了		甲	Lessons 32, 33, 34, 35, 36, 38, 44, 45, 46, 47, 48, 49, 50, 51, 52, 53, 54, 56
lè	乐	樂	甲	Lessons 22, 24
lèi	累		甲	Lesson 34
lǐ	李		乙	Lesson 9
lǐ	里	裏/裡	甲	Lessons 27, 49, 52, 56
lǐ	礼	禮	甲	Lesson 53
liǎ	俩	倆	甲	Lesson 42
liàn	炼	煉	甲	Lesson 21
liàn	练	練	甲	Lesson 51
liǎng	两	兩	甲	Lessons 15, 17, 35, 36, 37
liàng	辆	輛	甲	Lesson 56
liáo	聊		乙	Lesson 55
liù	六		甲	Lessons 6, 16, 20, 24, 26, 36, 46, 56
lóng	龙	龍	乙	Lesson 54
lóu	楼	樓	甲	Lesson 49
lù	路		甲	Lesson 19
luò	落		乙	Lesson 52
lǚ	旅		甲	Lessons 50, 55
lǜ	绿	綠	甲	Lessons 16, 22, 38
ma	吗	嗎	甲	Lessons 2, 3, 8, 11, 12, 14, 18, 28, 31, 37, 44, 45, 46, 48, 51, 53
mā	妈	媽	甲	Lessons 4, 25, 26, 48, 49
mǎi	买	買	甲	Lessons 13, 15, 16, 25, 38, 45, 47, 48, 53
mài	卖	賣	甲	Lesson 39

máng	忙		甲	Lessons 3, 42
máo	茅		丙	Lesson 37
me	么	麼	甲	Lessons 7, 9, 14, 16, 19, 21, 22, 28, 31, 39, 40, 41, 47, 48, 50, 52, 53, 55
méi	没		甲	Lessons 14, 16, 22, 28, 33, 37, 41, 44, 45, 53
měi	美		乙	Lessons 6, 36
měi	每		甲	Lessons 20, 21
mèi	妹		甲	Lessons 4, 26, 28, 49
men	们	們	甲	Lessons 6, 9, 10, 12, 16, 18, 19, 22, 34, 38, 41, 42, 43, 46, 48, 56
mén	门	門	甲	Lesson 51
mǐ	米		甲	Lesson 48
miǎn	免		乙	Lesson 9
miàn	面	麵	甲	Lessons 32, 56
míng	名		甲	Lessons 9, 41
míng	明		甲	Lessons 18, 41, 42
ná	拿		甲	Lessons 47, 48, 49, 54
nǎ	哪		甲	Lessons 6, 10, 16, 28, 31, 33, 45, 46, 50, 55
nà	那		甲	Lessons 2, 6, 7, 10, 22, 37, 41, 44, 48
ne	呢		甲	Lessons 2, 3, 9, 28, 44, 49, 54
nán	南		甲	Lesson 37
nèi	内		甲	Lesson 31
néng	能		甲	Lesson 31
nǐ	你		甲	Lessons 1, 3, 8, 9, 10, 11, 12, 13, 14, 15, 16, 20, 21, 23, 24, 25, 28, 30, 31, 33, 35, 36, 37, 38, 40, 41, 42, 43, 44, 45, 46, 47, 48, 49, 51, 52
nián	年		甲	Lessons 36, 50
niàn	念		甲	Lesson 51
nín	您		甲	Lessons 9, 22, 28

nǚ	女		甲	Lesson 54
pǎo	跑		甲	Lessons 34, 49
péng	朋		甲	Lessons 12, 25, 43, 47, 52, 53, 54
pí	啤		甲	Lesson 22
piàn	片		甲	Lesson 52
píng	瓶		甲	Lesson 22
qī	七		甲	Lessons 7, 17, 18, 20, 27, 37, 47, 56
qī	期		甲	Lesson 24
qí	骑	騎	甲	Lessons 19, 48, 54
qí	旗		乙	Lesson 56
qǐ	起		甲	Lessons 16, 20, 21, 30, 49, 50
qì	气	氣	甲	Lessons 8, 38
qì	汽		甲	Lesson 49
qián	钱	錢	甲	Lessons 15, 38, 43
qián	前		甲	Lessons 26, 39
qiáng	墙	墻	甲	Lessons 39, 52
qīng	青		甲	Lesson 50
qǐng	请	請	甲	Lessons 8, 9, 23, 49, 53
qiú	球		甲	Lesson 41
qù	去		甲	Lessons 13, 18, 19, 21, 23, 31, 33, 37, 38, 46, 47, 49, 50, 55
ràng	让	讓	甲	Lessons 23, 49, 54
rén	人		甲	Lessons 6, 26, 47, 52, 56
rèn	认	認	甲	Lessons 12, 55
rì	日		甲	Lesson 24
róng	容		甲	Lesson 48
ròu	肉		甲	Lessons 7, 23
sān	三		甲	Lessons 3, 13, 17, 23, 30, 31, 32, 33, 34, 36, 37, 38, 39, 43, 45, 53
sǎn	伞	傘	乙	Lesson 11
shān	山		甲	Lesson 46

shāng	商		甲	Lesson 31
shàng	上		甲	Lessons 18, 20, 21, 27, 29, 32, 33, 39, 45, 46, 48, 49, 50, 51, 52, 56
sháo	勺	杓	乙	Lesson 27
shǎo	少		甲	Lessons 10, 15, 38, 43
shào	绍	紹	甲	Lesson 12
shè	舍	捨	甲	Lesson 10
shén	什	甚	甲	Lessons 7, 9, 14, 16, 21, 22, 28, 31, 39, 47, 50, 52, 55
shēng	生		甲	Lessons 23, 24, 31, 45, 48, 51
shi	匙		丙	Lesson 52
shī	师	師	甲	Lessons 6, 48, 52
shí	十		甲	Lessons 10, 11, 12, 13, 14, 15, 16, 17, 18, 19, 20, 21, 22, 23, 24, 25, 26, 27, 28, 29, 30, 31, 32, 33, 34, 36, 37, 38, 39, 40, 41, 42, 43, 44, 45, 46, 47, 48, 49, 50, 51, 52, 53, 54, 55, 56
shí	识	識	甲	Lessons 12, 55
shí	时	時	甲	Lessons 29, 35, 50
shí	拾		甲	Lesson 53
shǐ	始		甲	Lesson 34
shì	是		甲	Lessons 4, 5, 6, 7, 8, 12, 14, 22, 24, 25, 26, 28, 49, 50
shì	市		甲	Lesson 19
shì	视	視	甲	Lesson 28
shì	室		甲	Lesson 31
shì	事		甲	Lessons 37, 52
shōu	收		甲	Lesson 53
shǒu	手		甲	Lesson 56
shū	书	書	甲	Lessons 5, 13, 15, 26, 29, 30, 32, 33, 36, 39, 40, 43, 47, 52, 54
shù	树	樹	甲	Lesson 38

shuài	帅	帥	丁	Lesson 42
shuí	谁	誰	甲	Lessons 5, 6, 8, 11, 25, 28, 47, 49, 50, 52, 54, 55
shuǐ	水		甲	Lessons 32, 51
shuì	睡		甲	Lessons 20, 29, 30, 32, 33, 35
shuō	说	說	甲	Lessons 13, 40, 41, 52, 56
sī	思		甲	Lesson 22
sī	私		乙	Lesson 49
sǐ	死		甲	Lesson 34
sì	四		甲	Lessons 4, 9, 14, 24, 34, 40, 41, 42, 43, 44, 45, 46, 47, 48, 49, 54
sòng	送		甲	Lessons 49, 52
sù	素		乙	Lesson 7
sù	宿		甲	Lesson 10
suǒ	所		甲	Lesson 26
tā	他		甲	Lessons 3, 4, 6, 13, 14, 23, 29, 41, 42, 43, 47, 50, 55
tā	她		甲	Lessons 6, 14
tái	台	臺	乙	Lesson 37
tài	太		甲	Lessons 38, 42
táng	糖		甲	Lesson 8
tǎng	躺		甲	Lesson 40
tè	特		甲	Lesson 23
tí	题	題	甲	Lesson 48
tiān	天		甲	Lessons 18, 20, 21, 24, 32, 33, 35, 36, 38, 48, 55
tīng	厅	廳	乙	Lesson 26
tīng	听	聽	甲	Lessons 37, 44, 48
tíng	停		甲	Lesson 39
tóng	同		甲	Lesson 12
tú	图	圖	甲	Lesson 33
tú	涂	塗	乙	Lesson 54

wa	哇		乙	Lesson 53
wài	外		甲	Lesson 49
wán	玩		甲	Lesson 21
wán	完		甲	Lessons 44, 51, 54
wǎn	晚		甲	Lessons 18, 30, 33, 35, 38
wǎn	碗		甲	Lesson 32
wàn	万	萬	甲	Lesson 43
wáng	王		乙	Lesson 9
wàng	忘		甲	Lessons 38, 52
wèi	喂		甲	Lesson 28
wèi	位		甲	Lesson 28
wén	文		甲	Lessons 36, 41, 44, 51, 52
wèn	问	問	甲	Lessons 9, 23, 48
wǒ	我		甲	Lessons 3, 4, 5, 6, 8, 9, 10, 11, 12, 14, 15, 16, 18, 19, 20, 21, 22, 23, 24, 25, 26, 27, 28, 30, 32, 33, 34, 35, 36, 37, 38, 40, 41, 42, 43, 44, 45, 46, 47, 48, 49, 52, 54, 56
wū	屋		甲	Lesson 27
wǔ	五		甲	Lessons 5, 9, 15, 17, 25, 45, 50, 51, 52, 53, 54, 55, 56
wǔ	午		甲	Lesson 33
wù	物		甲	Lesson 53
xī	息		甲	Lessons 28, 34
xī	吸		乙	Lesson 31
xī	西		甲	Lesson 48
xí	习	習	甲	Lesson 28
xǐ	洗		甲	Lessons 21, 29
xì	系	係	甲	Lesson 16
xià	下		甲	Lessons 11, 12, 21, 33, 38, 46, 49, 56
xiān	鲜	鮮	乙	Lesson 47
xiàn	现	現	甲	Lessons 3, 11, 17, 31, 38

yì	易		甲	Lesson 48
yín	银	銀	甲	Lesson 14
yīng	英		甲	Lessons 13, 52
yīng	应	應	甲	Lesson 31
yǐng	影		甲	Lessons 18, 33, 34, 37
yōu	哟	喲	丙	Lesson 53
yòng	用		甲	Lessons 11, 49
yóu	游	遊	甲	Lessons 50, 55
yǒu	友		甲	Lessons 12, 25, 47, 52, 53, 54
yǒu	有		甲	Lessons 14, 16, 18, 22, 27, 41, 45
yòu	右		甲	Lesson 26
yòu	又		甲	Lesson 32
yǔ	雨		甲	Lessons 11, 38
yǔ	语	語	甲	Lessons 13, 45, 48, 54, 56
yuán	员	員	甲	Lesson 14
yuán	园	園	甲	Lessons 19, 38, 46
yuǎn	远	遠	甲	Lesson 56
yuàn	院		甲	Lesson 52
yuè	月		甲	Lesson 24
zá	杂	雜	甲	Lesson 52
zài	在		甲	Lessons 3, 10, 11, 14, 17, 28, 31, 36, 38, 44, 45, 52
zài	再		甲	Lessons 18, 51
zán	咱		甲	Lesson 38
zāo	糟		乙	Lesson 38
zǎo	早		甲	Lessons 20, 30, 32
zǎo	澡		甲	Lessons 21, 29
zěn	怎		甲	Lessons 19, 40, 50, 53
zhàn	站		甲	Lessons 40, 49
zhāng	张	張	甲	Lesson 28
zhǎo	找		甲	Lessons 45, 47

zhào	照		甲	Lessons 38, 49, 52, 54
zhe	着	著	甲	Lessons 39, 40, 56
zhè	这	這	甲	Lessons 2, 4, 5, 7, 12, 15, 25, 26, 36, 37, 48, 52
zhēn	真		甲	Lessons 11, 25, 38, 54
zhèng	挣	掙	丙	Lesson 43
zhí	职	職	乙	Lesson 14
zhǐ	只	祇	甲	Lesson 38
zhǐ	纸	紙	甲	Lesson 45
zhì	志		甲	Lesson 52
zhōng	中		甲	Lessons 6, 31, 36, 37, 41
zhǒng	种	種	甲	Lesson 55
zhū	猪		甲	Lesson 7
zhù	住		甲	Lessons 10, 36, 45, 48, 51
zhù	祝		甲	Lesson 24
zhuō	桌		甲	Lessons 27, 39, 52, 53
zǐ	子		甲	Lessons 7, 27, 52, 53
zì	字		甲	Lessons 9, 39, 44, 45, 48, 51, 56
zì	自		甲	Lessons 48, 49, 54
zǒu	走		甲	Lessons 19, 34, 49, 54
zuó	昨		甲	Lessons 32, 33, 35
zuǒ	左		甲	Lesson 26
zuò	做		甲	Lessons 14, 21, 25, 30, 48, 50, 53
zuò	作		甲	Lessons 14, 31, 34, 35, 51, 52
zuò	坐		甲	Lessons 19, 40, 49, 50